Beyond the Abortion Wars

A Way Forward for a New Generation

Charles C. Camosy

WILLIAM B. EERDMANS PUBLISHING COMPANY
GRAND RAPIDS, MICHIGAN / CAMBRIDGE, U.K.

Published 2015 by
Wm. B. Eerdmans Publishing Co.
2140 Oak Industrial Drive N.E., Grand Rapids, Michigan 49505 /
P.O. Box 163, Cambridge CB3 9PU U.K.

Printed in the United States of America

21 20 19 18 17 16 15   7 6 5 4 3 2 1

Library of Congress Cataloging-in-Publication Data

Camosy, Charles Christopher.
Beyond the abortion wars: a way forward for a new generation /
Charles C. Camosy.
pages   cm
Includes bibliographical references and index.
ISBN 978-0-8028-7128-2 (cloth: alk. paper)
1. Abortion — Political aspects. 2. Women's rights.   I. Title.

HQ767.C253   2015
305.42 — dc23

2014041218

www.eerdmans.com

This book is dedicated to the thousands of graduate, undergraduate, and high-school students I've had the privilege to teach. Much of what follows comes from our exchanges and arguments.

Contents

Foreword

After decades of acrimony, gridlock, and fundraising on the abortion issue, there is now quite a lot of discussion about forging a working compromise between those who describe themselves as "pro-life" and those who describe themselves as "pro-choice." So far, unfortunately, that conversation is only happening on the pro-life side; at least, I'm unaware of any pro-choice leader who has said publicly that abortion should be limited in any way at any point in pregnancy.

The right-to-life lobby, however, along with many pro-life politicians, does see the "pain-capable" legislation that would limit abortion after twenty weeks — with exceptions for rape, incest, and the life of the mother — as both acceptable and politically possible, though Republicans would, of course, have to take both the U.S. Senate and White House for that to happen. Pro-choice advocates tend to see this concession as merely strategic: a dangerous step on the slippery, sloped road to a total ban. But the split that the "pain-capable" push has caused within the pro-life ranks argues otherwise. As does strongly pro-life South Carolina Senator Lindsey Graham, who recently told me in an interview that only a minority of pro-lifers would ban all abortions. Polling certainly bears that out.

In this book, Fordham theologian Charles Camosy leans pretty heavily on polling that indicates that the public wants first-term but not even second-term (let alone third-term) abortion to remain legal. He argues that major restrictions are thus inevitable, especially with those in the "Millennial" demographic expressing significantly more pro-life views than do their parents. I would counter that, if lawmakers so neatly took their cues from surveys, significant gun-control legislation would have passed easily after twenty first-graders were shot and killed at Newtown, Connecticut.

But the importance of Camosy's book is in his meticulous construction of the ethical and moral case for early abortion in instances of rape. And his proposed compromise fully answers the leading rap on the pro-life approach: that the true aim is to control women, and that the proof of this motivation is the scant pro-life support for women when they're not weighing whether to end a pregnancy — or for children once they're born. Camosy's proposed compromise would change that: his plan offers so much real support to women and children that it could significantly reduce the number of abortions performed for economic reasons.

As Camosy knows, I can't say that I agree with every aspect of his proposal. On the contrary, his compromise suggestion that, after eight weeks of gestation, rape victims would have to provide evidence in court that they were assaulted to get access to a legal abortion is a deal-breaker for me, even though he is right that women in that situation typically know very early that they're pregnant. He argues persuasively that the law is a moral teacher, yet I tend to think that criminalizing the procedure (even if physicians are punished rather than patients) would teach lessons other than that unborn children deserve our protection.

Yet he makes so many important points that I hope this work will be widely read and seriously debated. I particularly urge readers from across the spectrum on this issue to consider Camosy's arguments

- concerning all that's wrong with our binary, "you're either for it or against it" discussion;
- laying out ethical pro-life arguments apart from the religious ones that those who disagree so often assume must motivate any objection;
- challenging and tracking the history of accepted data;
- explaining the implications of the shift from the "privacy" concerns protected by the *Roe* decision to the "undue burden" banned under *Casey;*
- making the case that those who oppose rape exceptions are party to a broader refusal to take violence against women seriously; and
- spelling out how what he calls pro-life "extremists" effectively give the unborn rights that nobody out walking around in the world has, specifically, to be protected from harm even while threatening someone else's life.

"Finally, what about the hardcore pro-lifers who want to ban all abortions?" he asks. "First, let me say something directly to the Catholics who fall into this group. You may not think that the Mother and Prenatal Child Protection Act perfectly reflects your view of abortion, but you really should support something like it nevertheless. You should support it because the Church explicitly teaches that faithful Catholics may support incremental legislative change if the political realities give you a proportionately serious reason to do so. And if you don't think our current discourse on abortion in the United States gives you such a reason, frankly, you need a dose of political reality."

Camosy goes on to say:

> Though the tide is turning against abortion on demand, it is absolutely *not* turning in the direction of banning all abortion. There is overwhelming support for abortion choice in the cases of rape and the life of the mother. Indeed, over 90 percent of "pro-choicers" support these exceptions, *as do almost 70 percent of "pro-lifers."* The position in favor of banning all abortion is a political nonstarter. Those who have pushed this position aggressively in the public sphere have done tremendous damage to the pro-life cause. As "pro-lifers," we achieve our goals when we help focus the public debate on the overwhelming majority of abortions, most of which the public does not support. But the "ban all abortion" strategy has allowed "pro-choicers" to shift our debate away from the reality of our abortion culture by focusing public attention on the two percent of abortions taking place in the cases of rape and when the mother's life is in danger.

Finally, I have to commend the way Camosy consulted his female colleagues in writing this book. One he quotes anonymously but quite powerfully and provocatively buttresses his important argument about what "choice" women really have in a society that in many regards offers us such limited support:

> Women need to ask themselves if access to abortion really has done more to liberate them. If a woman does decide to parent, is she really free to make that decision if she has no partner, limited 12 weeks unpaid maternity leave, hopelessly expensive childcare, and on and on and on? Abortion has made women free not to have children, but it has arguably made it more difficult for women to choose to have children. What else have women gained? A hook-up culture which breeds sexual violence, increasing numbers of STDs, less-committed

and even childlike male partners who couldn't identify responsibility if it hit them in the face, and a culture that values [women] only when they are young and skinny. Is that freedom?

If you're starting to suspect that this is a book that will completely satisfy no constituency, you're right. Whatever your view, it will be challenged here. And if you're willing, you're highly likely to learn something as a result.

Melinda Henneberger
senior writer for BloombergPolitics.com
former reporter for *The Washington Post*

Preface and Acknowledgments

The process that led to my writing this book has lasted for more than thirty years. And as I now look back on how it unfolded, I've noticed that the key players at every stage have been women. From the school sisters of St. Francis of Assisi, to incredible thinkers such as Cathleen Kaveny, Jean Porter, and my thesis advisor in my doctoral work at Notre Dame, Maura Ryan — women have played the key roles in my formal education on the issues addressed in this book. As a young high-school teacher, I was blessed to have Kathleen Cepelka and Linda Johnson as mentors. And the influence of activists like Peggy Hamill, Kristen Day, and Serrin Foster helped to ground lofty academic ideas in the reality and experience of actual individuals and communities.

I have also benefited from the insights of women who, especially through our disagreements, helpfully challenged and refined my point of view. Frances Kissling of Catholics for Choice, my Fordham colleague Barbara Andolsen, and a reproductive-justice advocate who prefers not to be named all forced me to directly face the reprehensible fact that men have historically coerced and controlled women's bodies. Anyone writing on abortion — but especially male authors — should keep this in the front of their minds.

Helen Alvare and Sidney Callahan, model scholar-activists, have demonstrated that one need not choose between making rigorous arguments and fighting for their implications in the public sphere. I want to draw special attention to the particular debt this book owes to the influence of Sidney Callahan's work. Her groundbreaking pro-life feminism shows that our response to the stubborn vulnerability of women in our consumerist culture need not pit mothers against their own offspring. And the example of public intellectuals such as Kirsten Powers and Melinda Henneberger have shown that Callahan's ideas can have persuasive and influential defenders in the public sphere.

I would be remiss if I did not highlight the influence of my undergraduate, masters, and doctoral students at Fordham. The untold hours we have spent with these issues over the past six years have shaped this book in very important ways. Taylor Jacob has been particularly helpful as a student assistant, especially with her work on the citations, bibliography, and index. The following people also helped me with the project at various points along the way: Nic Austriaco, Justin Menno, Christian Brugger, Bill Murphy, Beth Haile, Meg Clark, Tom Cavanaugh, David Albert Jones, Chris Kaczor, Frank Beckwith, Beth Johnson, Terry Tilley, Jana Bennett, Candida Moss, Lauren Shea Saddy, Peter Ryan, SJ, and the staff of Senator Robert Casey. And the following colleagues deserve special recognition for having read the whole manuscript and giving me invaluable and detailed feedback: John Perry, Rachelle Barina, Jason Eberl, Hilary Hammell, Bill Gould, Steve Lammers, Costanza Ramadi, Liz Tenety, Andrea Useem, Therese Lysaught, Jennifer Beste, David Gushee, Julie Hanlon Rubio, Sarah Spieldenner, Rick Garnett, and Sidney Callahan. Special thanks also goes to Jon Pott and everyone at William B. Eerdmans Publishing Company for their generous support of this project, and also to Melinda Henneberger for taking time out of her ridiculous schedule to write the foreword.

It is difficult to write a good book on abortion. Some readers of drafts of this manuscript thought that I should broaden the discussion to make it a purely "popular" book so as to reach the largest audience possible. One suggestion along these lines was that I leave out the challenging philosophical arguments about personhood and instead focus on the more easily accessible fact that a fetus is a member of the species Homo sapiens. But this would have essentially punted on one of the central disputes of the debate, and thus it was unacceptable to me. Others wanted me to write a book that responded in intense detail to nearly every academic argument related to what I say about abortion. For instance, one reader suggested that I make the full case for the way that I use "nature" in discussing the moral status of the fetus. But doing that would not only have added at least another hundred pages to the book, it would have fundamentally changed the book's tone and excluded many nonspecialists in theology and philosophy. I also hope it goes without saying that a multivolume project somewhere north of two thousand pages (which would have been required to respond to every conceivable major objection) is also something that virtually no one would read.

Abortion is a subject that is so important to our political, social, and personal lives that I felt a deep responsibility to include as many people as I could into the conversation without unduly sacrificing the rigor of the arguments. Some will say that I move too quickly through this or that topic, while others will say that I spend too much time unpacking this or that academic point. But I have received substantial feedback from many different kinds of people, and after making many changes based on this feedback, my hope is that this book can be read with interest by multiple audiences. If at any point you are left wanting more, I urge you to follow the footnotes. They will often include further discussion and information on other sources (which have been written by me and others) where you can find more detail on these matters. You should also feel free to contact me via email (ccamosy@gmail.com) or Twitter (@nohiddenmagenta) if you have further questions.

Introduction: Is There Anything Left to Say?

I just searched for "abortion" in Google books — and got 7,270,000 results. This number does not include the innumerable magazine articles, blog posts, pamphlets, newspaper stories, and editorials that have been written on this subject. Could there *really* be anything else left to say? And besides, isn't abortion just one of those polarizing, intractable issues that is useless to talk about? Most people are stubbornly dug into their positions and will almost certainly not change their minds; so the only thing that is likely to come from engaging in a discussion on the topic is an uncomfortable and unhelpful confrontation. It is the kind of issue that can divide families and strain friendships. In a *Wall Street Journal* editorial that was written just after the 2013 verdict against abortion-provider Kermit Gosnell, Dan Henninger wrote: "No other public policy has divided the people of the United States for so long and so deeply. Abortion is America's second civil war."[1]

To get a taste of the how deep the division and polarization is in some quarters, here are four particularly telling examples that I have selected from the innumerable stories that could have made the same point:

- In March 2013, the student government association at Johns Hopkins University denied a local pro-life student group official club status. They claimed that being pro-life violated their harassment policy, and they directly compared pro-life students to white supremacists.[2]
- In March 2010, pro-life Democrat Congressman Bart Stupak, who had just led the charge to add substantial pro-life provisions to the Affordable Care Act, was mocked as a "baby killer" by his Republican opponents because they believed that the bill covered the use of the "morning-after" pill.[3]

1

- In July 2012, the best-selling author and award-winning journalist Caitlin Moran appeared on *The Cycle* on MSNBC and claimed that her decision to have an abortion was "quite easy," much like decisions she made about coloring her hair.[4]
- In May 2012, Bishop Daniel Jenky of Peoria, Illinois, cited President Obama's "radical pro-abortion agenda" as a reason to compare his path to that of Adolf Hitler and Joseph Stalin.[5]

If this is the pathetic state of the debate — if we refuse to acknowledge complexity and nuance — then what is the point of engaging in it? It seems to be governed, not by careful and open presentations of arguments and evidence, but by out-of-control identity politics. Not to add fuel to an already roaring fire, but don't the arguments also usually divide right along religious and gender lines? Isn't it the case that Christian (and particularly Catholic) men and conservatives are going to be pro-life, while women and (particularly secular) liberals are going to be pro-choice, and there just isn't much anyone can do about it?

Beyond the Conventional Wisdom

Many people hold something like the view I just described. As a result, even those who care deeply about abortion are sometimes fatigued, resigned, and simply don't want to talk about it anymore. I get something like this view from dozens of my students every semester. I get it from members of the media during interviews. I get it from audience members attending my public lectures. I get it from my fellow academics. It is a reasonable view to hold, and I sometimes feel pulled in that direction. But it is not my view.

While it is true that much has been written about abortion, it turns out that only a tiny minority of pieces are actually worth reading. Most authors have already decided what the answer is before engaging the evidence and arguments, and they use empty rhetoric in an attempt to "win" and impose a particular point of view. Very few pieces are even aware of what their opponents are actually arguing, much less engaging it in a fair and careful way. The result is confusion and mischaracterization, which, in turn, leads to caricatures and stereotypes; this, in turn, leads to polarization and disengagement. Pro-choicers are supposedly "pro-abortion" and "anti-life." But most women who have abortions already have chil-

dren, an odd place to be for those who are anti-life. Furthermore, a clear
majority of pro-choice people I know are personally opposed to abortion
(and often very strongly opposed) but struggle to find a workable way
to use government to limit abortion access without imposing huge and
medically dangerous burdens on women. Pro-lifers, on the other hand,
are supposedly "anti-freedom" and "anti-women," but this is complicated
by the fact that women are more likely than men to describe abortion as
morally wrong. Indeed, women often see far more clearly than do men
how the legal choice to have an abortion can push them into situations
where they are anything but truly free. As we will see in chapter 5 of this
book, men are often at the center of the coercion, so it is not difficult to
understand why men support a "woman's right to choose" at higher levels
than do women.

Therefore, one important reason we need a new book about abortion
is because (with a few significant exceptions, several of which are cited
in this book) most of what is being written just isn't very good. But there
is another important reason: especially with the rise of the "Millennials"
and Hispanics in the United States, abortion-related views and laws are
in the process of changing. I'll cite the polls that support this claim in
the next chapter, and they will show that while most Americans want to
keep some abortions legal, a record low number of people describe themselves as pro-choice. Millennials are leading the charge: while trending
in favor of gay marriage, they are also trending pro-life, especially when
compared to Generation X and the Baby Boomers when they were young.
While there seems to be very little support for totally banning abortion,
the overwhelming majority of laws being passed in several states have been
restricting abortion in significant ways. Especially when we project how
things will look given our demographic shifts over the next decade, the
question to ask is not "Will our national public policy on abortion change?"
but "What will the coming change look like?" I wrote this book, in part,
as an attempt to wrestle with this question.

One of this book's central arguments is that confusion and polarization, which feed and build on each other (especially with ratings- and
hits-driven media coverage highlighting extreme views), have created the
illusion that we have a hopeless stalemate in the abortion debate. By attempting to unpack the complexity and confusion, and also taking time
to understand the major positions in the debate, I will try to show that a
majority of Americans actually agree about broad ideas with respect to
abortion morality and law. Though our public debates are often dominated

by the extreme and simplistic positions, the vast majority of Americans have fairly complex and moderate views about abortion. I will propose a new public policy that is not only consistent with the beliefs of this broad majority of Americans, but one that will attract even more support over time as Millennials and Hispanics continue to take their rightful places of power in our culture. Before getting to the policy proposal, however, I will spend some time unpacking the complexity of the abortion issue itself and show that my proposal is supported not only by public opinion but by the best ideas and arguments about abortion.

The Complex Reasons Women Have Abortions

It is no secret that popular media have a real struggle communicating complexity. Thus they struggle not only to accurately describe what Americans think about abortion, but also the complex reasons many women have abortions. People like Caitlin Moran can go on MSNBC and compare the decision to have an abortion with coloring their hair, but the reality for most women is far messier and cannot be captured by a headline or Tweet. Though there are obviously exceptions to the rule, social-science data indicate that women who have abortions are subject to a number of coercive forces, and their stories often pulse with a sense of brokenness and tragedy.

Consider, for instance, the terrible story of a graduate student named Charlotte Coursier.[6] Just getting over a sexual relationship with a university professor, she became pregnant (despite using contraception) with her next boyfriend. This young man then informed Charlotte that he was "not ready to be a father" and would support her decision to terminate her pregnancy. Despite canceling her first appointment, she eventually went through with the abortion. She was depressed for weeks after the procedure, which she described as "murdering her child." The professor with whom she had had the previous relationship then reentered the picture, sending her harassing emails, which caused her boyfriend to end the relationship. Devastated about both her abortion and breakup, Charlotte hanged herself.

This story is tragic on so many levels, but it demonstrates the complexity, brokenness, and tragedy that often accompany a woman's choice to have an abortion. A critic may wonder aloud whether I've cherry-picked a single story to make a point, and it is true that one story all by itself shows virtually nothing. But as you read this book, please take note of the

4

number of times (particularly in the chapter on abortion and women) I cite statistics showing that this story — while on the dramatic end of the spectrum — reveals many important things about why many women have abortions. Furthermore, consider that *New York* magazine ran a 2013 feature in which they told similar stories of women who have had abortions.[7] Here are two representative examples:

Heather, 32
Tennessee, 2011 and 2013
I already had two daughters. Neither was planned, and it never, ever, occurred to me to terminate those pregnancies. I was brought up with a very religious background. Now I've had two abortions, and if my family knew, my relationship with my family would be gone. My first was two years ago. My husband and I were having financial problems and were considering separating. I just had to shut my conscience down. The doctor was grotesque. He whistled show tunes. I could hear the vacuum sucking out the fetus alongside his whistling. When I hear show tunes now, I shudder. Later, he lost his license. A few months ago, I got pregnant again. My in-laws have been helping us out financially, so we have no choice but to involve them in our decisions. They gave us $500 cash to bring to the clinic. I felt very forced. I felt like I was required to have an abortion to provide for my current family. Money help is a manipulation. I'm crazy in love with my daughters — imagine if I did that to them? It's almost too much to open the door of guilt and shame because it'll all overcome me. In the waiting room, there was a dead silence that's hard to describe. Everyone was holding in their emotions to a heartbreaking degree. Truly pro-life people should go light on the judgment, because shame motivates abortions.

Madeline, 18
Minnesota, 2012
I didn't think I was ready for sex, but my boyfriend pushed it. Rape feels too strong, but it wasn't really consensual. I didn't think about the whole condom thing. I was going to a Catholic high school, and in health class we never talked about sex. The scariest part of the whole experience was not having anyone to share it with. I was in AP classes and couldn't concentrate. I'd look around and think, *No one knows.* At night I'd think, *What if I wait too long and then suddenly have this baby?* I tried to plan out telling my parents, but my mom's religious

views scared me. I read on the Internet that minors can get a judicial bypass, but I was nervous it would take a long time — when I lay down and sucked in, there was a little bump on my tummy. Finally, I got up the courage to tell them. Both my parents took me. It's a two-day process. I was at twenty weeks, just a few days away from being too late. During the ultrasound, the technician told me how big the head was — it was the most scaring thing. The next day, the procedure took fifteen minutes. I slept for the rest of the day. I was grateful my parents were there. It cost about $2,000, so I definitely couldn't have done it without them. I feel bad that it was so far along developed. In my government class, we spent a whole week on abortion. It was awful.

Most of our public discussion of abortion focuses on a woman's "choice" or "decision." But any honest and informed attempt to discuss the issue must explore the various ways women are pressured into having abortions. Individuals like boyfriends, parents, and bosses are coercive, to be sure, but the very *social structures* of most of the developed world also push women to have abortions. And our current discussion of abortion needs to be far more aware of this fact.

The Place of Religion and Politics

I'm a Catholic theologian. Many infer from this that I am "conservative" on abortion and uncritically "pro-life." This inference is part of the media-driven polarized discourse I referred to above, but it simply does not reflect reality. American Catholics overall aren't much different on abortion than the rest of the population. They describe themselves as "pro-choice" (and even have abortions themselves) at a rate similar to the rest of the population at large.[8] And anyone who is familiar with academic theology and religious studies at major universities knows that the consensus and energy is actually directed against "pro-lifers." In my experience, a clear majority of (especially senior) academic theologians need little encouragement to voice their skepticism of the pro-life movement and pro-life activism. Furthermore, most nationally prominent academic theologians and scholars of religion are anything but conservative. While a few refuse to use secular political categories, most would not hesitate to identify as somewhere on the "liberal" spectrum. While I do believe that the argument I put forward in this book is consistent with defined Catholic doctrine, I certainly did not arrive at it uncritically, and I do make the argument in this book in the face of significant social and professional pressure to take a position more in line with "pro-choice" academic orthodoxy.

The focus on "religion" in our discussion of abortion is everywhere, and most often in very unhelpful ways. For instance, a significant number of pro-lifers will simply say something about how "the Bible says" abortion is murder, as if this is supposed to count as an argument in our public sphere. For starters, the Bible says no such thing. But even if it did, it is unclear how this will convince non-Christians or impact public policy in a secular country that promotes freedom of religion. On the other side, some pro-choicers wish to reduce the pro-life position merely to someone's private "religious opinion," which has no business being imposed on others. But this fails to account for the many arguments against abortion that are not dependent on explicitly religious claims. This book is one of them. I'm putting forth an argument that is capable (at least in principle) of convincing those of any faith or no faith.

Furthermore, whatever one believes about the central issues in the abortion debate (the nature of the human person, the nature of human rights, the nature of women's reproductive rights, what counts as wrongful killing, the role of the law, etc.), one must always begin with basic principles that are not based on science or other evidence. These foundational principles just "grab" or "claim" you as being true based on what I would call "faith" — but what others might call something like "intuition." If you are a utilitarian, for instance, you have faith in at least two foundational doctrines: (1) "ethical behavior requires producing the best outcomes"; and (2) when measuring these outcomes, "one counts as one and none more than one." If you are an American neoconservative, your faith lies in the fundamental goodness of the ideas present in the founding documents of the United States, and you believe that they should be energetically exported to other parts of the world. If you are a humanist, you have faith in the idea that all human persons have a special dignity, which requires that we treat them equally. Foundational first principles in the abortion debate are hardly limited to those who are explicitly religious. All participants in these debates bring faith claims to the table. As we will see in chapter 4, religious people should not receive special discrimination just because they are explicit and up-front about their faith claims.

Interestingly, when push comes to shove, it seems that the faith claims and intuitions of one's *political party* generally trump those of one's *religion.* According to University of Notre Dame social scientist David

Campbell, "For many but not all Americans, when they're faced with this choice between their politics and religion, they hold fast to their politics and switch religion, or more often switch out of their religion."[9] More often than religion, it is secular politics that drives the abortion debate, even in its views of those who identify as religious people. It is hardly surprising, then, that Catholics have views about abortion that are similar to those of the rest of the population at large. It is often their secular political values — and not those of their religion — that are actually running the show.

But for reasons we will explore in the next chapter, American secular politics is confused and incoherent, particularly when it comes to abortion. Perhaps due to that confusion, the final candidates for the 2012 presidential election did their best to avoid the issue. Mitt Romney, the former pro-choice governor of Massachusetts who ran as a pro-life presidential candidate, said virtually nothing about abortion during the campaign. If anything, he sent pro-choice signals, particularly when he told the *Des Moines Register,* "There's no legislation with regard to abortion that I'm familiar with that would become part of my agenda."[10] Even in victory, and despite huge pro-life legislative gains across the country in recent years, Obama and the Democrats sent few signals that they have any intention of advancing an agenda that involves abortion rights.

Somewhat ironically — given that Republicans are supposedly the pro-life party — the same cannot be said of Republicans. CNN's Republican analyst Alex Castellanos, in a 2012 election postmortem, chided his fellow conservatives for foolishly embracing big government on "social issues."[11] In his own postelection analysis, John McCain said that conservatives should "leave [abortion] alone."[12] In a *Washington Post* op-ed, a former member of the Reagan administration said that, "as for morality, our party should live it, not legislate it."[13] Just as this book was about to go to press, the Nevada state Republican Party explicitly dropped pro-life language from their platform.[14] The sentiment is picking up so much momentum that groups like GOP Choice have new openings. In applying what they understand to be conservative principles to abortion-related issues, they make the following claims:[15]

- Individuals and families have the right to unfettered access to reproductive choices, from education to abstinence, contraception, motherhood, adoption, and safe legal abortion.
- There is nothing more fiscally conservative than the proven cost-savings of preventative health policies and initiatives.

- Choice is not a political issue and the government should not be in the business of legislating private behavior or personal medical decisions.

These arguments must puzzle pro-lifers who have hitched their wagon to the Republican political machine, but it is difficult to deny the consistency of the group's reasoning. It is baffling that Republicans, the party of government staying out of the private lives of individuals, have been so energetically standing for big government regulation of some of the most personal choices that one can imagine.

On the other hand, it is equally mystifying that Democrats, the party that claims to advocate the use of government power in the interest of justice for the most vulnerable, can engage in sloganeering about private "choices" without considering how vulnerable populations on the margins might be hurt by those choices. When it comes to abortion, pro-choice liberals reverse course and become suspicious of government intervention into the private lives and choices of individuals. (For anyone wanting an important and detailed history of how this strange situation came to be, the important work of William Saletan is absolutely essential.[16]) They must have difficult relationships with groups like Democrats for Life, Feminists for Life, Latinos for Life, The Radiance Foundation (one of several African-American pro-life groups), Pro-Life Pagans, and the Pro-Life Alliance of Gays and Lesbians. But much like GOP Choice, it is not difficult to understand their logic. Given that they are interested first in nonviolence and social justice for the vulnerable, they are less likely to use the language of "freedom" and "privacy" and "autonomy" that is typical of the pro-choice movement. Perhaps not surprisingly in light of these tensions, a 2011 Gallup poll found that 27 percent of Democrats describe themselves as pro-life, and even 44 percent claimed that abortion should be legal in "few or no circumstances," this while 28 percent of Republicans describe themselves as pro-choice, and 63 percent claim that abortion should remain legal.[17]

Speaking about Abortion

How we choose to speak about abortion is almost as important as the ideas and arguments we put forward. Certain words are fair, are precise, and they invite honest and open debate, while others are unfair and imprecise, close off serious conversation, and even invite an aggressive and defensive response. I've learned this (sometimes the hard way) in previous attempts to build common ground among those who disagree about abortion. In 2010, for instance, I served as the founding member of an organizing committee for an international conference at Princeton University, which brought some of the best minds in the English-speaking world together to find "new ways to think and speak about abortion."[18] I have also developed an important working relationship — and even friendship — with Peter Singer, perhaps the world's best-known living philosopher and a supporter not only of the choice for abortion but even infanticide. In part because we've taken the time to have careful arguments (for each of the last three fall semesters he has invited me to have an abortion debate in front of three hundred-plus undergraduates in his "Practical Ethics" course at Princeton), we have discovered that our disagreement about abortion — though deep — is actually about only one or two fairly narrow issues.[19]

I have developed a similar relationship with a feminist reproductive-justice activist whom I met through the Princeton conference. Again, in part because we chose our words carefully and respectfully, we discovered huge areas of common ground amidst the issues on which we disagree. In one case, she and I were able to cooperate in bringing together a group of (largely pro-life) theologians to work together with (largely pro-choice) reproductive-justice advocates in filing an amicus brief in a terrible case involving an immigrant woman who was shackled while in labor.[20] The goal of dramatically changing the social structures of our culture so that pregnant women are given the respect and resources necessary to keep their children is one that people on multiple sides of the abortion debates should have in common.

So let's get to the point: How should we speak about abortion? The answer to this question is important not only for our public discourse going forward, but also for the words I will use in this book. Some have objected to my use of the term "prenatal child" in previous books because it implies that the fetus has a high moral value — a value that they reject. They point out that virtually no one uses this term to refer to the "fetus," and that we should use the scientifically accepted term that is without bias. But others object to using the term "fetus" precisely because of its artificial and cold nature. They point out that in virtually no other context do we use the scientific language — even in the doctor's office. When an OB-GYN physician gives a pregnant woman an update, she doesn't say, "Your fetus is doing great." She says, "Your baby is doing great." Similarly, a pregnant woman never says, "Honey, the fetus kicked me!" She says, "Honey, the baby kicked me!" And no one, of course, has ever heard of a "fetus bump." A pregnant woman has a "baby bump."

While we must admit that pro-lifers sometimes use the term "baby" in the abortion debate as a calculated rhetorical strategy to raise awareness about the value of the child, those who are pro-choice sometimes use the word "fetus" with precisely the opposite goal in mind. It is easier to connect to the value of a "child" and more difficult to connect to the value of a "fetus." Perhaps this is why some pro-choice-leaning media use the term "fetus" in very odd situations. For instance, in a case where a woman was discovered to have given birth to a child and put the dead body in a bag, *CBS News* ran the following headline: "Shoplifting Suspect Found with Dead Fetus in Bag."[21] Not long after this story, a baby was found on a conveyor belt at a laundry facility, and the UPI headline was, "Remains of Fetus Found at Illinois Laundry."[22] Bizarre, no doubt, but this is the craziness that comes with the words we use in the abortion debate.

I have asked hundreds of my medical ethics students which word we should use in order to be fair and precise. We've spent hours arguing about it. But in part because we want to do justice to the concerns of all participants, I've yet to have a class that has agreed on a word to use. My compromise solution in class has been to sometimes use the word "fetus" and sometimes use the word "prenatal child," and this will be my practice throughout this book as well.

In speaking about abortion, as in other areas of life that involve complexity, we should avoid simplistic and binary language. Not only is it wildly imprecise and irresponsible to operate as if complex problems have only two possible answers, but it also entrenches opposition to "the other side" into the very framework of the debate. Let's take "pro-life vs. pro-choice" as an obvious binary example given that we have already seen some of the problems with this way of thinking. If I call myself pro-life in the context of the abortion debate, it follows that my pro-choice opponent is *not* pro-life. But, as a matter of fact, this is often not the case. Most pro-choice people favor protecting some prenatal children (especially later in pregnancy); and they often hold pro-choice views, not because they don't respect life, but because they don't think the law can protect the fetus without seriously threatening the rights of the mother. Some advocates for reproductive justice, though they generally favor broad abortion rights, are working to reduce the demand for abortion.

On the other hand, those who call themselves pro-choice are implying that their opponents are against choice. But this is problematic as well. Most pro-lifers favor women having the legal right to choose abortion (especially when it does not aim at the death of the fetus) in several situations, including when their lives are threatened and when they have been raped. Furthermore, as mentioned above, many people are pro-life not because they want to limit women's freedom but because they think legalized abortion has coerced many millions of women into having unwanted abortions. They are suspicious of abortion rights as something that, paradoxically, limit women's freedom.

So while the terms "pro-life" and "pro-choice" sometimes stand for something in our culture, I believe this language overall hides and distorts more than it reveals. Its imprecision leads good people to imagine themselves opposed to others with whom they actually share much common ground. It is thus unsurprising that the Public Religion Research Institute discovered the following in a 2011 poll:

> Seven-in-ten Americans say the term "pro-choice" describes them somewhat or very well, and nearly two-thirds simultaneously say the term "pro-life" describes them somewhat or very well. This overlapping identity is present in virtually every demographic group.[23]

I have used the terms "pro-life" and "pro-choice" several times in this book already, and I will continue to use them, but I will now use quotation marks to indicate the imprecise nature of the terms. Sometimes, at least if we want to avoid awkward ways of speaking and writing, we must use the lazy binaries that we would otherwise reject. But if and when we use them, we should be very aware of their limitations and dangers.

Two other binaries that we need to be careful about when we speak of abortion are "religious/secular" and "liberal/conservative." For starters, we should be careful about our culture's tendencies to lump all three of these binaries into a kind of "super binary." We imagine that on one side of the abortion debate are "pro-life" religious conservatives and on the other side there are "pro-choice" secular liberals. But again, these political binaries set people against each other by their very nature and hide more than they reveal. It causes our culture to miss the fact that many liberals consider themselves broadly against abortion, while many conservatives prefer to see government stay out of the private lives of pregnant women. We also saw above that plenty of religious people are "pro-choice" while many secularists are "pro-life." The issues about which people disagree in the abortion debate are simply too complex to be captured by these kinds of lazy and imprecise binaries. And as we shall see shortly, our political and religious social structures are changing so that even the conventional wisdom will soon become outdated.

Here are a few more quick suggestions for speaking and thinking about abortion. I propose them both for our broader public discussion and as rules to which I will hold myself accountable in making the argument of this book.

- *Humility.* We are finite, flawed beings with a history of making serious mistakes — especially when it comes to complex and emotional subjects like this one. We need to enter into abortion discussions and arguments with this at the very front of our minds, reserving the right to change our mind when confronted with new evidence and ideas.
- *Solidarity with our conversation partners.* This involves active listening, presuming that one has something to learn, and (if possible) getting to know them personally. Never dismiss another's ideas because of their gender, race, class, sexual orientation, or social location. Similarly, never reduce them to what you suspect are their "secret personal motivations." Instead, give your conversation partners the courtesy of carefully responding to the actual idea or argument that they are offering for your consideration, especially if you are calling the idea or argument into question.
- *Avoiding dismissive words and phrases that erect fences.* It might feel good to score rhetorical points and get high fives from those on "your side," but doing so is one of the major contributors to our polarized discussion. Let us simply stop using words and phrases like "radical feminist," "war on women," "abortionist," "anti-woman," "heretic," "anti-science," "anti-life," "anti-choice," "pro-abortion," and so on. Instead, we should use language that engages and draws our conversation partners into a fruitful discussion of ideas.
- *Leading with what we are for instead of what we are against.* Not only is this the best way to make a convincing case for the view we currently hold, but it dramatically lessens the defensiveness of those we are "against." This practice also often reveals that many of us are ultimately after very similar things (such as women being able to choose to keep their baby), and we simply need to be able to talk in an open and coherent way about the best plan for getting there.

This section may have felt like I'm asking people to tiptoe around difficult issues in a politically correct way. Far from it. What I'm doing in this book — and what I'm asking people to do in the abortion discussion generally — is to *go directly after the most difficult issues.* That is the only way forward. But if we do this, it means we need to think and speak about these difficult issues fairly, precisely, and in ways that invite fruitful and honest engagement. The stakes are so high (1.2 million prenatal children aborted each year for "pro-lifers," and a fundamental threat to hard-won women's rights for "pro-choicers") that we must choose our language carefully if we are to have the kind of constructive engagement necessary to move forward.

My Plan for This Book

In the first chapter, I will build the case for many of the points made here in the introduction. I will discuss some of the history of the abortion debate, how it ended up in the strange place it is today in the United States, and the hopeful signs for a more coherent and fruitful way forward. My hope is that this will convince readers that we are on the verge of a new moment in the abortion debate, and that it leaves us more open to rethinking the status quo and to the arguments that come later in the book.

Having shown some of the historical reasons the debate over abortion got so confused, I will spend the next several chapters unpacking the complexity of the debate by pulling each major issue out of the confusing mess and addressing it on its own terms — from the moral status of the fetus, to questions about whether it is ever acceptable to kill (or refuse to aid) the prenatal child, to a specific consideration of abortion rights and women's freedom, and whether anything about the moral questions can or should be reflected in law or other public policy.

Finally, based on both public opinion and moral conclusions, I will propose a new public policy on abortion: the Mother and Prenatal Child Protection Act. This proposal will not only reflect the broad views of a solid majority of Americans (both "pro-life" and "pro-choice"), it will also be consistent with currently defined Catholic doctrine.[24] I will conclude the book by suggesting some values and strategies to help our American culture reimagine the ways we think and speak about abortion — so that we can move forward together.

The path I've laid out is a difficult one. Entrenched political and media/corporate interests will strongly resist this kind of shift. Many are too embedded in the fight to imagine it any other way, and sometimes their very identity is strongly connected to the dysfunctional way we currently think and speak about abortion. If we are honest, we must admit that our most influential political parties, interest groups, and media organizations have something close to a need to see abortion through the old binary and polarized lenses. How else will they frighten their donor base into giving them money and turning out to vote each election cycle? How else will they produce television ratings and website hits?

But in the chapter that follows, I argue that this old way of thinking about abortion is confused, unsustainable, and actually the result of historical accident. And oh yes, it's on the way out.

CHAPTER ONE

Shifting Abortion Politics

"There must be a remedy even for such a crying evil as [abortion]. But where shall it be found, at least where begin, if not in the complete enfranchisement and elevation of women?"

Elizabeth Cady Stanton, feminist activist (1868)

"Abortion is a moral right which should be left to the sole discretion of the woman involved."

Ayn Rand, libertarian philosopher (1968)

"I, for one, respect those who believe with all their hearts and conscience that there are no circumstances under which any abortion should ever be available . . . . [T]he choice guaranteed under our Constitution either does not ever have to be exercised or only in very rare circumstances."

Hillary Clinton, presidential candidate (2005)

Introduction

It is often said that the more things change, the more they stay the same. But that is simply not true of the abortion politics and opinion in the United States. Though there has always been diversity of views, Americans have gone from generally thinking that most abortion is fundamentally evil (even in the viewpoint of serious feminists) to thinking that it is either a constitutional right or something in which government has no business being involved, to our current time, in which we are becoming increasingly uncomfortable with abortion. Alongside our shifting public opinion, we've had some downright bizarre political maneuvering. This has led Democrats and Republicans to take positions on abortion in line with something I call the (George) "Costanza strategy."[1] Abortion is one issue where they respond by *doing the opposite* of their natural political instincts and philosophies.

In this chapter I will attempt to tell a shifting, complex, and strange story. I will begin by asking where we are now when it comes to our abortion practices in the United States. I will then, by tracing the political decisions that led us to the bizarre reality of the Costanza strategy, ask: How did we get here? Finally, I will show not only that Americans firmly reject our abortion practices and politics, but also will ask: Where are we going? And I hope to demonstrate that Americans will almost certainly reject these practices even more firmly in the years to come.

Our Current Abortion Practices

One poll-tested mantra for many "pro-choice" politicians is that abortion should be "safe, legal, and rare." But abortion is hardly rare in the United States. According to Planned Parenthood's research arm, "abortion remains a common experience for women in the U.S.; roughly one-third of women will have an abortion during their reproductive lifetime."[2] This equates to about 1.2 million abortions every year in the United States, which means that over 1 in 5 American pregnancies end in elective abortion.[3] Shockingly, that number is 40 percent in New York City. And in the Bronx, the home of the university I work for, the percentage of pregnancies that end in abortion approaches a stunning *50 percent*.[4]

President Obama, giving his now famous commencement address at the University of Notre Dame in 2009, asked us to acknowledge that "any" abortion is "heart-wrenching" and "not done casually."[5] This is surely the case for *many* women, especially when they are pressured and coerced by boyfriends, husbands, bosses, and parents. But given the numbers just cited above, Obama was obviously incorrect in making such a sweeping claim. Indeed, we have already seen that best-selling author Caitlin Moran thinks of her decision to have an abortion much like decisions about coloring her hair. A new book by Katha Pollitt, *PRO: Reclaiming Abortion Rights,* insists that not only is abortion anything but heart-wrenching, but it is part of normal reproductive medicine and a social good. The "1-in-3 Campaign" works hard to highlight the very high numbers of women having abortions so that it is seen as mere "access to basic medical care."[6] Comedian Sarah Silverman Tweeted fake before-and-after photos of herself, joking that she got a "quicky" abortion in case *Roe v. Wade* was overturned.[7] Actress Emily Letts even filmed what she claimed to be her own abortion and put the video online to show "how positive it is."[8]

Obama's view also conflicts with Planned Parenthood's own statistics, which show that most abortions do not come out of the extreme situations for which most Americans think abortion is acceptable — that is, when serious life and health issues are involved or when a woman has become pregnant as a result of rape. Indeed, though women generally give multiple, complex reasons for having an abortion, 38 percent of those surveyed by Planned Parenthood claimed that "having a child would interfere with their education." Interestingly — and important for thinking about the coercive role many men play in abortion — more than half listed "being a single mother" or "having relationship problems" as a reason.[9]

Furthermore, of those who are diagnosed with Down syndrome as prenatal children, a shocking 90 percent are aborted.[10] (This despite the fact that people with Down syndrome are actually happier than those who are "normal."[11]) Even late-term abortion is increasingly used to abort fetuses with issues as minor as a cleft palate.[12] And as more people engage in very expensive rounds of in vitro fertilization, especially in order to have children later in life, abortion is becomingly increasingly important to make sure there is quality control over the product they are purchasing. In a recent *New York Times Magazine* article, a woman who requested that her pregnancy be "reduced" from twins to a single fetus said the following:

> Things would have been different if we were 15 years younger or if we hadn't had children already or if we were more financially secure. . . . If I had conceived these twins naturally, I wouldn't have reduced this pregnancy, because you feel like if there's a natural order, then you don't want to disturb it. But we created this child in such an artificial manner — in a test tube, choosing an egg donor, having the embryo placed in me — and somehow, making a decision about how many to carry seemed to be just another choice. The pregnancy was all so consumerish to begin with, and this became yet another thing we could control.[13]

Quite understandably, a physician in the story asked, "In a society where women can terminate a single pregnancy for any reason — financial, social, emotional — if we have a way to reduce a twin pregnancy with very little risk, isn't it legitimate to offer that service to women with twins who want to reduce to a singleton?"

Some think of abortion as rare at least within the life experience of a woman, but more than 50 percent of Americans who have abortions have already had (at least) one abortion.[14] In addition, 61 percent of women who have abortions in the United States already have (at least) one child.[15] Some point out that the abortion rate would go down if we gave pregnant mothers the support and structures to raise their children and also to be full members of society. Structural injustice does indeed have something important to do with these very high numbers in the United States, and we could save the lives of many prenatal children if we resisted the structural injustices that women face. This must be a very high priority for anyone who identifies as "pro-life," and it will be an essential part of the Mother and Prenatal Child Protection Act. But as we will see, places like Sweden and the United Kingdom (despite having a large social welfare system for women and children) actually have abortion rates similar to that of the United States.[16]

It is also worth noting that the overwhelming majority of abortions in the United States take place early in pregnancy. It appears that only about 10 percent of abortions take place beyond the first 12-13 weeks; but that still means that a whopping 120,000 abortions take place each year in the United States in the second and third trimesters.[17] In fact, tests that (attempt to) confirm that the fetus has Down syndrome are generally performed in the second trimester.[18] "Pro-lifers" have been arguing for decades that late-term abortion is the equivalent of killing newly born children, and in 2013 the country watched with horror and disgust as the Philadelphia abortion provider Kermit Gosnell was convicted of three counts of infanticide after botched abortions.[19] Since that time — though, as *The Washington Post*'s Melinda Henneberger has pointed out, these stories have not been covered by the national media — we have learned that Gosnell's story is hardly unique.[20] Similar stories have been covered by the local press in Houston, Dallas, New York, Florida, and Maryland.

When I engage someone who is "pro-choice" and explain my own basic position on abortion, I often get two questions: "What if the mother's life is in danger?" and "What if the woman has been raped?" We will address both of these incredibly difficult and sensitive questions at several points in this book, and always with the utmost care and respect. But here is some perspective to those questions: about 1 percent of all abortions take place in situations where the mother was raped,[21] and about 1 percent take place when the mother's life is threatened.[22] Let me be absolutely clear: these are agonizing and horrific circumstances, circumstances about which some public "pro-lifers" speak far too casually. However, respect for abortion rights in these cases is quite different from respect for abortion rights in the other cases just mentioned. Indeed, the overwhelming majority of abortions in the United States seem qualitatively different from the 2 percent represented by rape and the mother's endangered life.

How does our current political culture deal with the realty of abortion in the United States? Unsurprisingly, the two major parties try to use our culture's strong feelings about abortion to their own political advantage, and they do so via the Costanza strategy. The evidence appears to show that Republicans play on the concerns for prenatal children by claiming to stand for a big government that will regulate the intimately private and personal reproductive practices of women. And the evidence also appears to show that Democrats play on the concerns of many for women's rights by claiming to stand for privacy and freedom of the individual over and against the government's interest in protecting the vulnerable. How we got to a place where our political parties "do the opposite" on abortion is the focus of the next part of the chapter.

How Did We Get Here?

There was time before the Costanza strategy. The first feminists — those who fought for the right of women to vote, for instance — were strongly skeptical of abortion, not least because they believed that men (and institutions run by men) coerced most abortions. The groundbreaking group Feminists for Life is one of the few organizations that recognizes and highlights this fact. Here are some quotes they have collected from their "Feminist Foremothers":[23]

Susan B. Anthony
Referred to abortion as "child murder"
The Revolution, 4(1):4, July 8, 1869

"We want prevention, not merely punishment. We must reach the root of the evil. . . . It is practiced by those whose inmost souls revolt from the dreadful deed."
The Revolution, 4(1):4, July 8, 1869

Elizabeth Cady Stanton
Stanton wrote, regarding prostitution and the "murder of children, either before or after birth": "For a quarter of a century sober, thinking women have warned this nation of these thick coming dangers, and pointed to the only remedy, the education and enfranchisement of woman. . . . We believe the cause of all these abuses lies in the degradation of woman."
The Revolution, 1(5):1, Feb. 5, 1868

"There must be a remedy even for such a crying evil as this. But where shall it be found, at least where begin, if not in the complete enfranchisement and elevation of women?"
The Revolution, 1(10):146-67, Mar. 12, 1868

Emma Goldman
"The custom of procuring abortions has reached such appalling proportions in America as to be beyond belief. . . . So great is the misery of the working classes that seventeen abortions are committed in every one hundred pregnancies."
Mother Earth, 1911

Mattie Brinkerhoff
"When a man steals to satisfy hunger, we may safely conclude that there is something wrong in society — so when a woman destroys the life of her unborn child, it is evidence that either by education or circumstances she has been greatly wronged."
The Revolution, 4(9):138-9, Sept. 2, 1869

Victoria Woodhull (the first female U.S. presidential candidate)
"The rights of children as individuals begin while yet they remain the foetus."
Woodhull's and Claflin's Weekly 2(6):4, Dec. 24, 1870

"Every woman knows that if she were free, she would never bear an unwished-for child, nor think of murdering one before its birth."
Wheeling (West Virginia) Evening Standard, Nov. 17, 1875

These quotes, especially coming from pioneers and radicals whose lives were clearly dedicated to the rights and well-being of women, may sound odd to our contemporary ears. The story we are told today — especially in the privileged world of media, public policy, and academia — has changed. We are now told (often by male talking heads) that abortion rights are necessary for women in today's culture. What has changed since the days of Susan B. Anthony and Elizabeth Cady Stanton? How did such a dramatic shift take place? In answering these questions, I rely on the important work of the Democrat activist Kristen Day. Hers has been a voice crying in the wilderness on these matters, and it deserves a much broader audience.[24]

Before the Costanza Strategy

Day recalls the pivotal moment of the 1968 Democratic convention in Chicago. Democrats were a deeply divided party over the Vietnam War, but "immediate withdrawal" activists were well-organized, loud, and even violent. They did not hold a majority of the delegates, and they were enraged about the fact that their voices were not being heard. This explosive situation led to the now famous "Chicago riots" outside the convention hall. The Democratic Party was unable to unite itself around its nominee for president, Hubert Humphrey, who would go on to be defeated by Richard Nixon. In response to this defeat and in an attempt to have a more unified approach, party leaders reformed the nominating process to be more inclusive and broad so that everyone — even the activist groups — would feel that they were heard. Day argues that this resulted in aggressive and organized activists gaining more power over the platform and nominations. The broad base of the party was not as energized and aggressive, and the message was dominated by the activists.

At that time — obviously unlike today — being Democratic or Republican was not a predictor of how one would vote on abortion. In fact, when the state of New York passed the first sweeping abortion rights law, it was signed by none other than Republican governor Nelson Rockefeller. The law was repealed by the state legislature two years later, but it remained law when the repeal was vetoed by Gov. Rockefeller. In 1972, George McGovern was the Democratic candidate for president; he ran strongly and clearly against the Vietnam War. He rejected an attempt to add an abortion rights plank to the party platform, calling abortion a "no win issue" and claiming that it should be left up to the states. McGovern had the chance to appoint two vice-presidential candidates, and his choices were quite telling. The first was Thomas Eagleton of Missouri, a Catholic "pro-life" Democrat. When Eagleton stepped down, McGovern chose Sargent Shriver, another "pro-life" Democrat. Though "pro-choice" momentum was building in the party, and McGovern did receive some criticism for choosing "pro-life" running mates (along with serious concerns about Shriver's marriage to Eunice Kennedy, who was vehemently anti-abortion), this sentiment had not yet taken over the party's power structures.

Meanwhile, though Republican governor Ronald Reagan was supporting and signing the bill that legalized abortion in California, Richard Nixon and other national Republican figures were attempting to convert Democratic Catholic voters into Republicans. For decades they had been an essential part of the liberal base, but now "pro-life" Catholic Democrats were sensing the shift in the party. Republicans took full advantage. According to Day, Nixon specifically courted Catholic leaders, such as the archbishop of New York, Terence Cardinal Cooke, with his position against abortion. Rather than simply leaving it to the states, as McGovern proposed, Nixon at least claimed to support equal protection of the law for all prenatal children.

The shift toward the Costanza strategy had begun.

The Turning Point

In 1973, *Roe v. Wade* made abortion broadly legal in all fifty states. Of the nine justices (all men), Justice Bryon White (who was appointed by a Democratic president, John F. Kennedy) was one of only two dissenters and one of the most outspoken critics of the decision. Only one of the six justices who had been appointed by Republicans voted against *Roe*. Justice Harry Blackmun, appointed by Richard Nixon, wrote the majority opinion.[25] Day notes that this monumental decision gave the "pro-choice" camp serious momentum, and they worked even harder to add an abortion plank to the Democratic Party's platform. Indeed, they would attempt to exclude anyone who was "pro-life" from calling themselves liberal. In 1976, over the objections of their presidential nominee, Jimmy Carter, they successfully got abortion rights into the platform. Carter said he would have worded the plank differently because "abortions are wrong," and as president he planned programs to minimize them.

Republicans responded by pushing even harder in the other direction. Day relates how Republican leadership, and particularly that of Paul Weyrich and Henry Hyde, led the charge to unite with people like Jerry Falwell and the Moral Majority of the Christian right.[26] The abortion battle had been joined in earnest, and this was the crucial turning point. Day claims that Democrats, if they were to stay true to their principles, should have sided with Carter. They should have maintained that abortion was wrong and worked to give women the resources to resist the pressure (often applied by men) to get abortions. Instead, by going all in with the abortion-rights activists, they created an opportunity for Republicans to steal "pro-life" votes from the Democrats. In 1976 there were an astonishing one hundred twenty-five self-identified "pro-life" Democrats in Congress. Day recounts something that Democratic congressman Jim Oberstar used to say: people who opposed abortion didn't stop sending people to Congress, "they just stopped sending Democrats."

The Costanza strategy was now in full force, but it took some time for the party leopards to change their spots. This was clear when Republican Henry Hyde first offered his well-known amendment banning federal funding for abortion. President Gerald Ford, a Republican, initially leaned toward vetoing the bill; but when he heard that Jimmy Carter was going to support it, Ford claimed that he had the same position and would sign the bill. Despite this naked attempt to tie Carter to his party's stated position against the Hyde Amendment, it was Ford who would eventually go on to veto the bill. If this wasn't enough to show his true colors on abortion, Ford revealed himself as unabashedly "pro-choice" after his presidency when he decided to sit on the advisory committee of Republicans for Choice. As Kristen Day put it, "Neither candidate agreed with [his] prospective platform" when it came to abortion.[27]

Costanza Strategy Complete

The shift that had taken place within the Democratic Party could be personified in the person of Ted Kennedy. He had a strong "pro-life" voting record until the late 1970s, and once even said that abortion on demand was at odds with our basic civilizational values about respect for human life.

He compared abortion with other kinds of population control and eugenics. But by the time he challenged Jimmy Carter for the Democratic Party's nomination in 1980, he had totally switched course and ended up pushing Carter to become more clearly in favor of abortion rights. Senator Joe Biden, currently vice president of the United States, was also reliably "pro-life" until 1981. Democratic congressmen and presidential candidate Dick Gephardt had nearly a 100 percent "pro-life" voting record until the mid-1980s. Future vice president Al Gore, a Democrat, supported the Hyde Amendment and wrote constituents about his "deep personal conviction" that "abortion is wrong." Democratic activist Jesse Jackson, another former supporter of the Hyde Amendment, once said that "aborting a baby" affects the moral fabric of our nation. Even Democratic presidential candidate Dennis Kucinich very publicly claimed that he thought life begins at conception. Under pressure from the new party bosses, these and many others switched their positions. Day quotes the phrase coined by Kate Michelman, executive director of the National Abortion Rights and Action League: "If you're out of touch with the pro-choice majority, you're out of office." Democrats now had their orthodoxy on abortion, and dissenters were not permitted.

In the other political camp, we have already discussed how Ronald Reagan signed the bill that made abortion legal in California. Remarkably, this same person would go on to take the presidency away from Jimmy Carter largely because he was somehow able to siphon off "pro-life" votes from what would come to be known as "Reagan Democrats." His choice for vice president, George H. W. Bush, had such a clear "pro-choice" record that Reagan took serious flak from "pro-lifers" for choosing Bush. By 1988, however, when it came time for Bush to make his own run at the presidency, he had changed his position on abortion to "pro-life." This despite the fact that his first nominee for the Supreme Court was Justice David Souter, a reliable supporter of abortion rights. Most recently, we saw Mitt Romney, the former pro-choice governor of Massachusetts, take only three years to shift his position and become "pro-life" for his own presidential campaigns.

Day notes that Bill Clinton once told Arkansas Right to Life that he "was opposed to abortion and government funding of abortions." But by his 1992 campaign for president, our current abortion orthodoxy — in both parties — was fully entrenched, and Clinton was forced to switch his views. One of the few high-profile heretics who resisted this shift was the energetically "pro-life" governor of Pennsylvania, Democrat Robert Casey. Before the 1992 convention, Casey was reelected governor of Pennsylvania by more than one million votes and carried sixty-six of sixty-seven counties in the state. His opponent was a pro-choice Republican. On every other issue Casey was solidly liberal: whether it was appointing more women to his cabinet than any other governor, championing nutrition programs for low-income families, and even trying to pass universal health care in his state. He was one of the most courageous people in his party to directly reject the Costanza strategy.

Someone like Casey, a successful and popular governor of a major state, should have been expected to speak at the 1992 Democratic convention. But he was denied this chance because of his views on abortion. To add insult to injury, five other "pro-choice" Republicans (including a key supporter of Casey's primary opponent) were invited to speak at the convention. Some said that Casey was denied a speaking slot because he didn't endorse Clinton for president, but plenty of others who did not endorse Clinton (including the governor of California, Jerry Brown) did speak at that convention. Casey was a politician who spent his life in support of the government's defense of the vulnerable over against the typical Republican trump-card ideas of individual privacy, freedom, and autonomy. But he was publicly humiliated because he refused to cave in to a constituency that bullied weaker Democrats into "doing the opposite" of what was at the heart of their political philosophy. Unfortunately for Casey — and despite his best efforts — the battle was already lost.

Abortion Views and Politics Today

Our current abortion politics are part of a larger political structure and conversation. And at first glance, this structure looks hopelessly polarized. After all, it has been widely reported that Congress is now more polarized than at any time since the Civil War. But that description of Congress, much like our abortion politics, doesn't reflect the complexity of what Americans actually believe. A recent Gallup poll, for instance, found the following breakdown in political affiliation in the United States:[28]

9 percent	Very Conservative
31 percent	Conservative
35 percent	Moderate
16 percent	Liberal
5 percent	Very Liberal
4 percent	No Opinion

This is hardly a polarized group of people: only 14 percent are in the "extremes." Furthermore, a 2014 NBC News/*Wall Street Journal* poll found that a majority of Americans now refuse to identify as either Democrats or Republicans.[29] Indeed, Gallup also recently found that a record 42 percent of the electorate explicitly thinks of themselves as "independent," refusing to put themselves in either the liberal or conservative camp.[30] Portending the future, fully half of Millennials now identify themselves as independents.[31]

So the actual facts of what Americans believe about politics — unfiltered by the lazy binary "liberal/conservative" lens — is rather complicated. Most Americans are not extreme and cannot be put in a box: they will give you a "liberal" answer for one issue and then a "conservative" answer for another. The liberal/conservative binary just doesn't fit our complex political reality, and it will fit even less well going into the future. Indeed, as I argue in the conclusion to this book, the coming demographic changes in the United States suggest that a fundamental change in our politics is right around the corner.

This is also true of our abortion politics. At first glance, especially viewed through the lens of the media, we seem hopelessly polarized: as if this is somehow a fight between those who (1) want to ban abortion altogether in the name of stopping genocide and (2) those who want to make all abortions legal in the name of women's equality. While some of the loudest voices in our public abortion debates hold these views, and while the media tend to tell their stories this way in order to generate ratings, Americans have views on abortion that are even more complex than their political views in general. This should not be shocking, of course, given the bizarre way that our abortion political categories and "sides" came to be formed.

The poll numbers tell a very different story of what Americans actually believe.[32] According to a 2013 CNN poll, for instance, Americans thought abortion should be:

25 percent	Always Legal
11 percent	Legal in Most Circumstances
42 percent	Legal in Few Circumstances
20 percent	Always Illegal

This reality, of course, does not fit into our lazy and imprecise "pro-life" vs. "pro-choice" sound-bite rhetoric. It is interesting that a 2013 NBC

News poll found something similar, though they added some specifics to the question that will be very important for the argument I make in this book:

26 percent	Always Legal
19 percent	Legal Most of the Time
42 percent	Illegal Except in Cases of Rape, Incest, and Mother's Life
10 percent	Illegal without Exception

A CBS/*New York Times* poll, again, finds complexity. This was in response to questions about abortion availability:

42 percent	Abortion should be Generally Available
35 percent	Abortion should be Available under Stricter Limits
20 percent	Abortion should not be Permitted

One of the "stricter limits" that many Americans have in mind, for instance, is with regard to when in a pregnancy abortion should be legal. A 2013 Gallup poll found the following:[33]

First Three Months of Pregnancy

61 percent	Should be Legal
31 percent	Should be Illegal

Second Three Months of Pregnancy

27 percent	Should be Legal
64 percent	Should be Illegal

Final Three Months of Pregnancy

14 percent	Should be Legal
80 percent	Should be Illegal

Finally, there are situations in which Americans are absolutely clear that abortion should be legal. This according to a 2012 CNN poll:

"When the Woman's Life is in Danger"

88 percent	Legal
9 percent	Illegal

"When the Woman's Physical Health is in Danger"
83 percent   Legal
12 percent   Illegal

"When the Pregnancy was Caused by Rape or Incest"
83 percent   Legal
14 percent   Illegal

Hence, in summing up the views of Americans on abortion, we can safely draw at least two conclusions:

1. A very clear majority of Americans want to see abortion more restricted than it is now, especially the "middle" weeks of pregnancy.
2. An overwhelming majority of Americans, including many who identify as "pro-life," want to see abortion legally available in the exceptional 2 percent of pregnancies (rape or incest and a threat to the life of the mother).

We now have even more evidence that the categories we use to describe our abortion politics are woefully inadequate. Most Americans are "pro-choice" in some situations, and most are "pro-life" in some situations. In answering the question "Do you support abortion?" most Americans will respond, "It depends on the situation." Indeed, we learned above that 70 percent of Americans say the term "pro-choice" describes them somewhat or very well, and nearly 65 percent simultaneously say the term "pro-life" describes them somewhat or very well. American abortion politics, at least in the general electorate, are complex and actually not polarized in the "us vs. them" way they are commonly portrayed. Though some find themselves on the extremes of the debate, most are in the complex middle.

The (Brief) Return of "Pro-Life" Democrats

Don't get me wrong, the Costanza strategy is still alive and well in Washington, D.C. But we recently saw that, for a brief political moment, abortion politics could return to the complex — and more ideologically consistent — place they were before this strategy was used. After being soundly defeated by George W. Bush and the Republicans in 2004, Democratic Party leaders began to take a more inclusive approach and welcome "pro-life"

Democrats into their fold. The result was that these "pro-life" Democrats had a significant effect on public policy, especially during the health-care reform debates. Bart Stupak, a former congressman from northern Michigan, offered an amendment designed to supplement the Hyde Amendment in prohibiting federal funding of abortion in the new health-care system. And despite outrage from "pro-choice" interest groups, the amendment passed with a coalition of "pro-life" Democrats and Republicans; indeed, a full *one-quarter* of the Democrat caucus voted for it.[34]

However, the Senate would respond by passing a version of health-care reform that did not include Stupak's amendment and gave no impression that they would ever include it. Stupak, along with twelve like-minded Democrats (whose votes were required for the House version to pass), tenaciously negotiated for their "pro-life" principles against the Senate version. After months of back-and-forth politics, Stupak and other "pro-life" Democrats managed to work out a compromise. Appropriately, the compromise was brokered with Senate leadership primarily by Gov. Casey's son, Sen. Robert Casey Jr. It contained a remarkable number of "pro-life" provisions:[35]

- Coverage for abortion is specifically excluded from the standard package of benefits that all insurers would be required by law to offer.
- Existing restrictions on the use of federal funds appropriated via the HHS appropriations bill (the Hyde Amendment) are maintained.
- The federal government, acting in its capacity as both a civilian and a military employer, continues to exclude abortion coverage from the policies it offers to its employees.
- The new exchanges of private health-care companies are required to offer at least one policy that did not cover abortion, something not available in the individual policy market in many places.
- States have the option of preventing insurers in their state from offering plans through the exchange that cover abortion.
- Federal premium subsidies cannot be used to purchase insurance coverage for abortion.
- While individuals purchasing coverage through the exchange have the option to use their own funds to purchase abortion coverage, they have to make a separate premium payment to do so.
- Incorporation and passage of the Pregnant Women Support Act.[36]
- All of these elements are reaffirmed by the president of the United States in a high-profile executive order issued hours before the legislation's passage.

Several Republicans tried to claim that, in compromising with his opponents in negotiating the final deal, Bart Stupak and the "pro-life" Democrats had simply sold out their "pro-life" credentials. One even shouted out "baby killer!" as Stupak addressed the House a final time to assure passage of the bill. But much of the pro-choice lobby stood strongly against not only this kind of regulation of private insurance companies who participate in the health exchanges (because of the worry that insurance companies would drop abortion coverage altogether), but also against the Hyde Amendment itself. Indeed, despite campaigning for president as a candidate who was against the Hyde Amendment, Obama signed an executive order that effectively gave it legal status such that it now no longer needs to be renewed with each budget.[37] This was a substantial victory for "pro-lifers."

However, the realignment in Washington was short-lived. The old-guard "pro-life" movement found itself unable to imagine that it could work with Democrats, and movement leaders waged a multimillion-dollar political offensive, teaming with Republicans, to defeat "pro-life" Democrats in the midterm elections of 2010. This strategy worked: the caucus of "pro-life" Democrats was devastated, cut by more than 50 percent. Though Republicans had "their issue" back, this certainly did not mean that passing "pro-life" legislation was more likely. Indeed, given that they once again lost the inroads they had made with Democrats, "pro-lifers" lost the chance to repeat the bipartisan example of the health care-debates. Though there are moments outside the national scene that continue to buck the trend, the conventional wisdom appears to have returned to abortion politics.[38] At least for now, the two national parties have their issues right back where they want them.

What about Roe?

Some may find of all this interesting, but nevertheless will return to the bottom line: *Roe v. Wade* is the law of the land, and a clear majority of Americans support it.[39] According to a 2013 Quinnipiac poll, a very solid 63 percent agree with the decision. But to what, exactly, are these people agreeing? In a Pew Forum study done on the fortieth anniversary of *Roe v. Wade,* we learned that only 62 percent of Americans even know that this Supreme Court decision *is about abortion.*[40] And it is even more shocking that among those younger than thirty years old, this number falls to 44 percent! Furthermore, of those who know that *Roe* was about abortion, many don't know what the decision actually said or did. Many wrongly believe, for instance, that overturning *Roe* would mean making abortion illegal — instead of merely returning the issue to be decided by the states. To make matters worse, the questions asked in these polls themselves often misunderstand how *Roe* impacts abortion public policy.[41] So, what do the 63 percent who agree with the decision actually believe about abortion policy? The only honest answer is: We don't really know.

It is also worth mentioning that many people, even those who strongly support abortion rights, think that *Roe* was a bad law and even wrongly decided. Linda Greenhouse, who covered the Supreme Court for the *The New York Times* from 1978 to 2008, had the following to say about the decision:

> To read the actual opinion, as almost no one ever does, is to understand that the seven middle-aged to elderly men in the majority certainly didn't think they were making a statement about women's rights: women and their voices are nearly absent from the opinion. It's a case about the rights of doctors — fellow professionals, after all — who faced criminal prosecution in states across the country for acting in what they considered to be the best interests of their patients.[42]

To be clear, Greenhouse herself is a clear supporter of abortion rights. But she is dismayed that the opinion itself, which was decided by all men, has little to say about the rights and flourishing of women. She is joined by another important supporter of abortion and women's rights, Supreme Court Justice Ruth Bader Ginsburg. What follows is from the Associated Press story on her 2013 appearance at the University of Chicago Law School:[43]

> U.S. Supreme Court Justice Ruth Bader Ginsburg says she supports a woman's right to choose to have an abortion, but feels her predecessors' landmark *Roe v. Wade* ruling 40 years ago was too sweeping and gave abortion opponents a symbol to target . . . . Ever since the decision, she said, momentum has been on abortion opponents' side, fueling a state-by-state campaign that has placed more restrictions on abortion.
>
> "That was my concern, that the court had given opponents of access to abortion a target to aim at relentlessly," she told a crowd of

students. . . . "My criticism of Roe is that it seemed to have stopped the momentum that was on the side of change."

The ruling is also a disappointment to a degree, Ginsburg said, because it was not argued in weighty terms of advancing women's rights. Rather, the *Roe* opinion, written by Justice Harry Blackmun, centered on the right to privacy and asserted that it extended to a woman's decision on whether to end a pregnancy.

Princeton's Peter Singer agrees with both Greenhouse and Ginsburg, despite the fact that, as I mentioned above, he is a supporter of the right to abortion and infanticide. Nevertheless, at the aforementioned Princeton conference aimed at finding common ground on abortion, Singer courageously countered the "pro-choice" activists present and argued that *Roe v. Wade* was a bad decision.[44] He argued that, instead of continuing to short-circuit the legislative process, the United States should have an actual national and legislative debate about abortion and have it come to some finality. Singer cites Europe and his native Australia as examples of places where this has happened, and the "pro-choice" position is basically settled without much opposition.

These three thinkers, along with many other folks who think that *Roe* is bad law, may get the chance to make the law better by having it returned to the states for a legislative process. As we will see at several points in this book, the legal standing and basis for *Roe* has shifted and changed so much over the decades that it is not clear what is holding the decision together. The court is divided 4-4 on abortion, with Justice Anthony Kennedy being the swing vote. In some ways, the abortion policy in the United States rests on his evolving views. But that is a question for our current court. Even more important than this, perhaps, is what the trends indicate for the future of American abortion politics.

Trends and Looking to the Future

Those who attempt to limit abortion in the United States are often described by their opponents as "moving backwards." In the summer of 2013, for instance, the Texas legislature moved to ban abortion after twenty weeks and to require all abortion facilities to offer women easier access to hospitals should the abortion go wrong. Jamila Bey, writing in *The Washington Post,* spoke for many "pro-choice" people when she claimed that

Texas was trying to "turn back the clock" on women's rights.[45] But those who view Europe as more progressive than the United States is on social issues like abortion might be surprised to learn that the Texas law is rather tame by comparison to European restrictions. Belgium, Denmark, France, Germany, Greece, Ireland, Italy, Holland, Spain, and Sweden, just to name a few, restrict abortion to well before twenty weeks. Many countries draw the line at twelve weeks, and many require that the procedure be done in a hospital.[46]

Spain may make their abortion laws even more restrictive — allowing them only in cases of rape or when the life or health of the mother is in danger.[47] How does the government justify this new legislation? The Spanish justice minister, Alberto Ruiz-Gallardón, claimed that the proposed law change is an attempt to push back against "structural gender violence against women." He said that "the mere fact of pregnancy" creates "pressure" which causes women to abort. "I think [about] the fear of losing the job or not getting a job as a result of pregnancy. . . . I think women in these situations lack public support to freely choose an alternative to termination of pregnancy."[48]

U.S. Trends

Health care. Paid maternity leave. Commitment to international treaties and laws. Ecological concern. Especially for progressives, Europe stands for ideas and policies to which many hope the United States will also aspire. But with the Costanza strategy in effect, our political parties "do the opposite" here as well. Conservatives, who often criticize attempts to use Europe as a model for social issues, are pushing our abortion laws to be more like those in France and Sweden. Liberals, who often evoke Europe as a place of social progress, imagine such changes to be moving backwards. But the reality is that we are slowly becoming more like Europe when it comes to abortion restrictions.[49] Despite the fact that there is no serious attempt to make abortion totally illegal, many dozens of bills have passed in recent years that significantly restrict abortion. Here are just a few:[50]

- Thirty-three states have passed informed consent laws (twenty-four include an ultrasound requirement);
- Thirty-one states have passed abortion clinic regulations;
- Thirty-eight states have passed parental notification/involvement;

- Thirty-eight states have wrongful-death laws that treat the unborn child as a person; eleven of these protect the fetus from fertilization onward. Thirty-seven states have fetal homicide laws, and twenty-five of these extend the protection from fertilization.
- Virtually every state today has prenatal-injury laws that compensate for prenatal injury at any time after conception.
- The pregnancy care centers allied with Care Net (a pro-life support network for women with difficult pregnancies), for example, grew from approximately 550 in 1999 to 1,130 in 2010; by contrast, the number of abortion clinics declined from 2,200 in 1991 to 689 in 2011.
- With the passage of the previously mentioned Texas law, that state became the thirteenth state to ban abortion beyond twenty weeks.[51]

The trend shows no signs of slowing down. For instance, the year 2013 saw the second highest number of "pro-life" state laws passed in American history.[52] It is surpassed only by the year 2011, which holds the record.[53] As this book goes to press, there are many more in the pipeline.[54] One of the few attempts to change the law in the *other* direction was recently defeated in even the liberal state of New York. Toward the end of June 2013, both Republican and Democratic legislators rejected Gov. Cuomo's attempt to expand access to late-term abortion.[55]

So let's be absolutely clear: There has been a broad and dramatic shift, especially in the last fifteen to twenty years, toward more abortion restrictions in the United States. And though almost no one suggests that abortion will be banned altogether, this trend of European-style restrictions will almost certainly continue for at least another generation.

The Future of Abortion Politics

Perhaps we should begin with the obvious. The laws just mentioned continue to be passed by legislatures because they have the support of the people. But our actual abortion practices, to which these laws are reacting, are totally out of step with what most Americans believe about abortion. Recall the following:

- Sixty-two percent believe that abortion should be legal in "few" or "no" circumstances (CNN, 2013)
- Forty-two percent believe that abortion should be illegal except in

cases of rape, incest, or a threat to the life of the mother; 10 percent believe that it should be illegal without exception (NBC, 2013).

- Abortion should be legal in —
  - » first trimester: 61 percent
  - » second trimester: 27 percent
  - » third trimester: 14 percent (Gallup, 2013)

Contrast this with abortion practices in the United States:

- Thirty-three percent of women will have an abortion in their lifetimes.
- 1.2 million abortions are performed every year.
- Twenty percent of pregnancies end in abortion (40 percent in New York City).
- Ninety percent of fetuses diagnosed with Down syndrome are aborted.
- 120,000 abortions are performed in the second and third trimesters.

Though our current political parties are using the Costanza strategy in order to raise money and turn out their base (because their stated views on abortion run so counter to their core political beliefs), little has been done by either national party to change abortion law. But it will not stay this way forever; eventually the will of the people about abortion will be reflected in our national public policy. This seems virtually undeniable, especially as we think about the coveted voters of the next generation: Hispanics, Millennials, and women.

Hispanics are now the majority ethnicity in California; Texas will soon follow, along with much of the rest of the country. Though Hispanics disproportionately vote Democrat, they are certainly not reliable "pro-choice" voters. Far from it. As Dr. Victoria M. DeFrancesco Soto of *NBC Latino* mentioned during the heat of the 2012 elections, "On the issue of abortion Latinos are significantly more pro-life than non-Latinos."[56] For instance, Hispanics are 10 percent more likely than are whites to think that abortion should be made broadly illegal.[57] Dr. Soto also noted that Latino opposition to abortion changes little whether they identify as Democratic, Republican, or Independent. As Hispanics rightfully assume more positions in the power structures of the United States in the next generation or so, look for our abortion politics to change dramatically.

Yet the most obvious way that the electorate will shift over the coming ten to twenty years will come from the rise of the Millennials. That young people are trending "pro-life" is well known, and it was the primary reason for the 2013 resignation of the NARAL's sixty-one-year-old president, Nancy Keenan.[58] This issue has been on the radar screen of "pro-choicers" at least since the appearance of a 2003 article in *The New York Times* entitled "Surprise, Mom, I'm Against Abortion."[59] Then trends were clear:

> A study of American college freshmen shows that support for abortion rights has been dropping since the early 1990s: 54 percent of 282,549 students polled at 437 schools last fall by the University of California at Los Angeles agreed that abortion should be legal. The figure was down from 67 percent a decade earlier. A New York Times/CBS News poll in January found that among people 18 to 29, the share who agree that abortion should be generally available to those who want it was 39 percent, down from 48 percent in 1993.

A 2003 Gallup poll also found that well over 70 percent of teenagers thought that abortion was "morally wrong."[60]

If the last two generations are anything to go by, people get more skeptical of abortion as they get older, and it is thus unsurprising that this trend has continued. In 2010, for instance, Gallup found that "support for making abortion illegal was growing fastest among young adults." They found this to be "a sharp change from the late 1970s, when seniors were substantially more likely than younger age groups to want abortion to be illegal."[61] For all Millennials in 2012, only 37 percent consider abortion to be morally acceptable.[62] As I was writing this chapter, there was a debate brewing in Texas and in the U.S. House/Senate about whether to ban abortion beyond twenty weeks gestation. In stories on these events, *The Washington Post* noted that, of people who were fifty years or older, 44 percent supported such a ban, while 52 percent of those eighteen to twenty-nine supported it.[63] Unsurprisingly, given that Catholics tend to be similar to the broader culture, this trend holds for young Catholics as well. A 2013 *New York Times* poll asked Catholics the following question: "Should the next pope be for or against legalized abortion?" In the age group forty-five to sixty-four, only 49 percent said "against," but among those eighteen to forty-four, that number rose to 58 percent.[64] Finally, "pro-choice" groups such as EMILY's List and NARAL are very publicly worried about something they call the "intensity gap."[65] Of young people who identify as "pro-life," 51 percent claim that abortion is an important issue. But for young people who identify as "pro-choice," that number plummets to 20 percent. As with Hispanics, the abortion discourse in the United States will change dramatically as Millennials gain positions of power.

Finally, consider the all-important demographic of women. It is the commonly assumed wisdom that women are the group most opposed to "pro-life" policies; after all, aren't women the ones primarily affected negatively by restricting abortion rights? During the 2012 elections, some Democratic political operatives even suggested that these stances were part of a "war on women." But it is at least odd to claim that a particular policy stance is part of a war on women when more women than men support the policy. Returning to the *Times* poll that asked whether the new pope should be for or against legalized abortion: 60 percent of women said "against," compared to only 52 percent of men. With regard to the twenty-week ban, 50 percent of women were for it, compared with only 43 percent of men. In a 2013 Pew Forum study that asked whether having an abortion was morally acceptable, 49 percent of women said it was not, compared with 45 percent of men.[66] Once again, the conventional wisdom on abortion is called into question by the actual facts on the ground.

I want to finish this section by highlighting two things that deserve close watching. The first is the Costanza strategies of the political parties. With the Internet and social media virtually taking over political campaigns, it is unlikely that the party bosses will be able to hold on to power via political sleight of hand — and, at times, outright dishonesty. This shift has happened to a certain extent already in 2009 with the Stupak Health Care Reform and "pro-life" Democratic movement. We are already starting to see a shift in the abortion debate toward "libertarian vs. non-libertarian" rather than "Democrat vs. Republican." Those who are opposed to abortion will realize that they need "pro-life" Democrats, while the "pro-choice" movement will continue to enlist Republicans in their cause. The Costanza strategy is unsustainable, especially in the Internet age, and will not last forever.

But the other factor to keep in mind doesn't require speculation. Many believe that the "pro-life" laws that the states are enacting are unconstitutional. In a May 2013 article for *The New Yorker* entitled "The Abortion Issue Returns," Jeffrey Toobin notes that a few of these have already been struck down by lower courts.[67] These judges most often claimed that such laws posed an "undue burden" on women, something prohibited by *Planned Parenthood v. Casey,* the major Supreme Court abortion case that came after *Roe v. Wade*. Toobin notes that the holdover from that 1992 decision is Anthony Kennedy, who will likely be the swing vote once again in another likely 5-4 decision. Would he uphold a state law with a twenty-week (or earlier) ban? Mandatory ultrasounds? More abortion clinic regulations? It isn't clear that he thinks they are "undue burdens." Toobin points out that in another abortion case, *Gonzales v. Carhart* (2007), Kennedy upheld federal law against late-term abortions and reflected a very different sensibility from his opinion in *Casey*. Kennedy wrote: "The State may use its regulatory power to bar certain procedures and substitute others, all in furtherance of its legitimate interests in regulating the medical profession in order to promote respect for life, including life of the unborn." What counted as an "undue burden" for him when he helped decide *Casey* in 1992, Toobin noted ominously, looked very different to Kennedy fifteen years later. What will it look like when these state laws come before the Supreme Court? We don't know, but it deserves our very close attention.

Conclusion

Given current trends, the positions of key future demographics, and the legal challenges on the horizon, the question is not *if* the American national abortion policy will undergo a substantial change, but *when*. Though this may favor "pro-lifers," my view is not the result of special pleading or rose-colored glasses. Longtime "pro-choice" activist Frances Kissling of Catholics for Choice has been saying something similar for years. Accusing "pro-choice" activists of being out of touch with trends in the debate, she argued in a 2011 *Washington Post* op-ed that the rhetoric of "choice" and "freedom" — especially when combined with the view that abortion is just like any other medical procedure — is losing the argument in American culture.[68] Here she lays out the challenge rather directly:

> We can no longer pretend the fetus is invisible. . . . We must end the fiction that an abortion at 26 weeks is no different from one at six weeks. These are not compromises or mere strategic concessions, they are a necessary evolution. The positions we have taken up to now are inadequate for the questions of the 21st century. We know more than we knew in 1973, and our positions should reflect that. The fetus is more visible than ever before, and the abortion-rights movement needs to accept its existence and its value. . . . Very few people would argue that

there is no difference between the decision to abort at 6 weeks and the decision to do so when the fetus would be viable outside of the womb, which today is generally at 24 to 26 weeks.

Still, it is rare for mainstream movement leaders to say that publicly. Abortion is not merely a medical matter, and there is an unintended coarseness to claiming that it is. We need to firmly and clearly reject post-viability abortions except in extreme cases. . . . Those kinds of regulations are not anti-woman or unduly invasive. They rightly protect all of our interests in women's health and fetal life. Even abortions in the second trimester, especially after 20 weeks, need to be considered differently from those that happen early in pregnancy.

When hardcore "pro-choice" activists like Frances Kissling suggest changes with which many "pro-life" activists are likely to agree, this is good reason to think that they will happen. When we refuse to let the extremists rule the debate, we can see that Americans have a large amount of overlap when it comes to what they believe about abortion. We truly are on the cusp of a new moment for public discussion of abortion in the United States.

My view is that the best arguments about these matters happen to be very consistent with what a majority of Americans do believe — and will continue to believe in even stronger numbers — about abortion. In the next four chapters I will unpack the complexity of the abortion debate and deal with each major issue separately, and in a way in which each chapter builds on the previous one. I hope this chapter has convinced you that the arguments we will explore are not the abstract claims of yet another ivory-tower intellectual writing for the very few people in the world who can decipher what he is doing. Instead, because we are on the verge of a major cultural and legal shift on these matters, how the following arguments play out is of the utmost practical importance. The lives of millions and millions of prenatal children, as well as the fundamental freedoms of their mothers, hang in the balance.

CHAPTER TWO

Who or What Is the Fetus?

"A week-old baby is not a rational and self-aware being, and there are many nonhuman animals whose rationality, self-awareness, capacity to feel and so on exceed that of a human baby a week or a month old. If . . . the fetus does not have the same claim to life as a person, it appears that the newborn baby does not either."[1]

Peter Singer, Princeton University

"The Chinese consider themselves one year old when they are born as they count the period in the womb as well."[2]

Lim Chooi Kwa, Tunku Abdul Rahman University

Introduction

In the previous chapter I tried to clear space for a new kind of argument about abortion. But now I want to actually engage the argument. Where should I start? "With the woman," some would say without hesitation. "After all, it is her body that is at stake here — her autonomy, her choice." While these are absolutely essential concerns, concerns that require very careful attention, they are not the place to start the abortion debate. No serious person is arguing — in the developed world of the early twenty-first century, at least — that women are less than full persons with equal protection under the law. Instead, we argue about what their personhood and equal protection under the law *means*. On the other hand, many "pro-choice" arguments rely heavily on the claim that the prenatal child is not a person and does not deserve equal protection of the law. This fundamental, contested question about moral status and value must be explored before we can actually move on to speak about a woman's bodily autonomy. Only after coming to a conclusion about the moral status and value of the prenatal child do we have the moral insights necessary to discuss what this means for her pregnant mother and for how we should think about abortion more broadly. Therefore, this chapter is not about abortion per se, but rather only about the moral status of the prenatal child. A discussion of the act of abortion comes later, as does a discussion concerning what the law should be.

Language and word choice is an important concern throughout this book, but it is particularly important in this chapter. For the reasons already discussed, I will alternate between the use of "fetus" and "prenatal child." But there are other important word choices to consider. For instance, "pro-lifers" often make the following claim:

"The fetus is a human being."

But what this sentence means is not clear, and the several ways it can be misunderstood has led to much of the confusion in the abortion debate. Unpacking and explaining various interpretations will also help us organize this chapter so that we can overcome the confusion. The person making the above claim might be saying, "The prenatal child is a human organism, a member of the species Homo sapiens." But he also could be saying, "The fetus is a person, a being of irreducible value with a right to life." (Of course, he might be saying both things.) The first claim is one about science and biology, and — at least beyond the first few days of development — it is relatively easy to prove or disprove. The second claim, however, is more complex because it involves appeals to contested ideas about morality and ethics. When does a person become a person? When the sperm is finished fertilizing the egg? When she can live outside her mother's body? When she develops a certain trait — such as the capacity to feel pain? Something else?

One final word before we jump into discussion of these questions. Some of my students ask, "Why should we care about moral status or value at all?" The answer is complex, but here's one way to think about it: a being's moral status or value makes it more or less wrong to kill or otherwise harm her. For instance, imagine that someone drowns three different kinds of beings: (1) a tree, (2) a dog, and (3) a human person. What you will think of that person's actions in each case depends on the moral status or value of each being. You might think that a person's drowning a tree is wrong, if he did it "for fun" or some other silly reason. But for an important reason, such as rerouting a small river so that a town could have access to drinkable water, you would likely say that he did nothing wrong in drowning the tree. You will probably think that drowning a dog is terrible, and that there is likely no good reason at all for doing it. You might even suggest (and I'd agree) that a person should go to jail for such a cruel act. And if he drowns a person, unless he was acting in self-defense, most people would rightly say that he should be charged with and convicted of murder. He has done something far more serious than either of the first two acts: that is because a person has a higher moral status than the other two creatures.[3]

We can see how this will impact our discussion in the next chapter about killing (and refusing to aid) the prenatal child. Insofar as one thinks that the fetus has a moral status similar to that of a tree, a dog, or a person, one will also be likely to think that killing (or refusing to aid) a prenatal child is more or less wrong — depending, of course, on the reasons and circumstances for the killing. And we will explore the difficult questions raised by various reasons and circumstances in the next chapter. But we must first explore the more fundamental question: Who or what is the prenatal child?

Is the Fetus a Human Being?

If by human being we mean "human organism" or "member of the species Homo sapiens," then the answer to this question is given by science. Some argue that the prenatal child is "mere tissue" or "part of her mother," but the biological facts about the fetus tell a very different story. The prenatal child has different tissue from that of her mother, and in fact has a distinct genetic structure. Her mother's body releases special antibodies in order to protect the fetus, who would otherwise be attacked by her mother's white blood cells as foreign tissue. While the mother's body provides energy and the right *external* environment for her to live, the prenatal child is a different and self-organizing animal. To use the fancy biological term, the fetus has "homeostasis": her *internal* environment, along with the coherence of her bodily structure and the direction and organization of her growth — though obviously impacted by the environment of her mother's

43

body — is directed and organized by the prenatal child herself. We see this quite clearly at the embryonic stage, for instance, when embryos grow in a fertility lab without their mothers. And we see it later when fetuses are born early and continue, also without their mothers, to grow and develop during months of prematurity. Like all human animals, prenatal children need energy and the appropriate environment in order to survive, but their internal organization and growth is *self-directed*. Fetuses are individual human organisms, and it is simply biologically incorrect to say that they are "mere tissue" or "part of their mother."

Furthermore, prenatal children do things we expect from human animals. They feel, see, and hear. Though we aren't sure at exactly what stage these various senses "kick in," a fetus can feel pain, hear and recognize sounds, and react to different kinds of light. Pregnant women describe their prenatal children as able to recognize and react to the voice of their mother and father, dance to music (and remember the tune when the same songs are played to them after birth),[4] and even to follow a light source around the room. Particularly with the increasing study of twins, we are learning even more about the kinds of interactions fetuses are capable of. Researchers at the University of Padova, for instance, found that by week fourteen prenatal twins start reaching for and touching the other one — even more often than they touch themselves. The study found that they even used distinct gestures when reaching for their twin. Their hands lingered when they touched each other. The study was clear: "Performance of movements towards the twin is not accidental."[5]

Many readers will not be surprised by these biological facts. Especially with the development of new social media and other technologies, the human reality of the prenatal child is more present to us than ever before. For many new parents, the realization that they have a prenatal child comes when they first hear their child's heartbeat, and smartphone apps now allow parents to listen to that heartbeat (which begins just over forty days into pregnancy) outside of the clinic.[6] With 3-D and 4-D imaging of fetuses in the uterus, we can all see for ourselves that this prenatal child is a human organism. These are the kinds of photos that are now put on Facebook and Twitter for all to see. Often these fetuses already have names and decorated rooms. Relatives and others interact with them before birth. And those who do surgical procedures on a prenatal child get a live, unscreened, and stunning look at their human biological reality.

At this point, those who claim that the fetus is not a human being are in a difficult position. They must contradict science and biology, photographs, and the experience of parents. But almost no one who is educated and informed about the science (including many who are "pro-choice") denies that the fetus is a human organism. Instead, the claim is that mere scientific or biological facts cannot lead us directly to moral truth. The fact that prenatal children are human organisms does not necessarily make them human *persons*. One could argue that, while all persons have a right to life, this is not necessarily the case for all human organisms. After all, beings like the fertilized egg and a brain-dead human on a ventilator are also human organisms; but many people, even those largely against abortion, find it strange to think of them as persons just like you or me. While no one can deny that the fetus is a human organism, there is still work to do to if one wants to show that she is also a person.

Must a Person Be "Independent"?

Some argue that a prenatal child cannot be a person until she is "independent." By this they usually mean that she is not a person until she can live outside her mother's body. This is sometimes called "the viability standard," and it played a large role in the *Roe v. Wade* decision. It was after this stage in pregnancy, the Supreme Court said, that individual American states could begin to regulate abortion. Just to be clear, one reason that the Supreme Court may have thought that this was an important line to draw was because they believed a mother's *moral duty* to the fetus changes when the latter can live outside her mother's body. (This is a question I will save for the next chapter.) Again, we cannot explore what duty a mother may (or may not) have to her prenatal child until we first determine the moral status or value of that child.

So does the moral value of the fetus change based on whether or not she can live outside of her mother? Answering affirmatively pushes us in some odd directions. Imagine a twenty-four-week-old fetus — is she a person? The answer would seem to be yes, for a prenatal child of this age could easily live outside her mother. But if we imagine that the year is 1916, the answer would have to change, because in 1916 a fetus of that age would not be able to live outside her mother. On the other hand, suppose that the twenty-four-week-old prenatal child is living in our current time, but lives in the developing world without the benefit of medical technology. Is she a person? The answer would seem to be no, because a fetus in that situation could not live outside her mother.

Studies also show that prenatal children who are both female and of African descent can live outside their mothers significantly earlier than fetuses who are male and white.[7] This prompts the question: Do black females become persons before white males? Do prenatal children in the United States become persons before those of the same age in a developing country? Could a fetus be a person in the United States, only to have her mother travel to a developing country, where she ceases to be a person? Could a twenty-four-week-old prenatal child born in Chicago's Mercy Hospital be a person today, but not have been a person in Chicago's Mercy Hospital in 1916? Of course not. A being's moral status and value doesn't change based on race or gender; or on the decade into which one happens to be born; or on whether one happens to live in the developed or developing world.

Furthermore, being "totally dependent" doesn't appear to affect moral status or value in other, nonabortion circumstances. For instance, the birth of a prenatal child doesn't change her level of dependency: a newborn infant is just as dependent on someone else for her survival as she was before she was born. Also, suppose that a relative of yours needs to go on a ventilator temporarily to help him breathe while he has surgery. Does he cease to be a person because he is now totally dependent on this machine? Or how about an astronaut who goes on a spacewalk and is totally dependent on her tether to the ship for oxygen and temperature control? Does she have a different moral value than she has on earth or while safely inside the ship? Of course not.

And at least from the perspective of Christianity, feminism, and several other schools of thought, an individual who is totally dependent deserves *special* attention and protection. Christianity claims we must imitate Jesus' concern for the vulnerable and dependent. Not only are dependent human beings not worth less; in some sense they are worth more. Most secular feminists, long concerned with the vulnerability of women in a culture dominated by more powerful men, agree that we should have special protection for the vulnerable more generally. The dependence of a prenatal child, therefore, does not make her worth less. Again, if anything, her dependence should cause us to give her special attention and protection.

Now, let us try to identify the public confusion about what the real concern is when someone talks about the dependence of the prenatal child. What many people actually have in mind is *the mother's duty* (or lack thereof) to the prenatal child. They are not discussing moral status or value. They might say something like, "Well, when a child is born she is totally dependent, yes, but when she is inside her mother she is totally dependent specifically and only on her mother." This will be an important consideration in the next chapter, when we look at whether a mother has a duty to sustain a child with her body, but a being's *moral status or value* does not change based on her relative dependence on her mother, a doctor, a spaceship, or anyone or anything else.

"Trait X"

Many who reject the idea that the fetus has the moral value of a person do not use either of the arguments we just considered. Instead, they challenge the very idea that "being human" is really what matters for being a person at all. It appears our culture got the idea that "all human beings are persons" from the Bible, which tells us that humans have this value because they are made in the image and likeness of God. But if you believe that our public debates about abortion should be secular and should avoid the use of explicitly religious doctrine — and especially if you also reject the doctrine itself — the idea that all human beings are persons because "God made it so" is obviously not going to work.

One of the most important people to make this point is the aforementioned Princeton philosopher and activist Peter Singer. Singer points out that, before Christianity started to dominate the Western world, we didn't believe that all human life was sacred. The only human lives that mattered had developed *certain traits.* Singer argues that rationality and self-awareness is what mattered to the ancient Greeks and Romans, which is why they permitted not only abortion but also infanticide. No prenatal child is rational and self-aware, but neither is any newborn child. Neither of them was considered a person, notes Singer, until Christianity became the dominant cultural force in the West. And as our culture becomes more secular, we have seen a return to this way of thinking. That we can admit that the fetus is a human being but not a person means that a new Copernican revolution is already in progress. We have already rejected the theological idea that the earth is the center of the *physical* universe, but Singer argues that our culture is in the process of rejecting the theological idea that the human being is the center of the *moral* universe.

Is Singer right to say that what many value in the fetus is not her humanity but rather her having certain traits? I think he's on to something. Those who are educated about biology know that the prenatal child is a fellow human being, but many "pro-choicers" nevertheless reject the idea that she is a person like you or me. Why? Often it has to do with the fact that at least the early fetus does not have certain traits and abilities: to feel pain, to move around, to engage in relationships, to act rationally, to become aware of one's self, to develop a moral sense, and so on. Once human beings develop these traits, many believe that their moral status increases. Fetuses who can feel pain are worth more than those who cannot; fetuses who can engage in relationships are worth more than those who cannot; fetuses who are rational and self-aware are worth more than those who are not. And so on.

But while Singer is right that many people think this way about the fetus, almost no one is willing to be consistent and apply his or her view to other beings. Suppose you think that a prenatal child becomes a person with a right to life when she can feel pain. Are you willing to say that *any* being that feels pain is a person with a right to life? Dogs? Pigs? Chickens? Rats and mice? We've already established that merely being a human organism is not what's doing the work, because otherwise even the very early fetus would count. Or perhaps you think the prenatal child becomes a person when she can engage in relationships, such as when she reacts to the sound of her parent's voice. But plenty of nonhuman animals are far more relational than this. The pig whose flesh many of you ate for lunch yesterday, for instance, is capable of far more sophisticated relationships than any human fetus.

But suppose you up the ante here and choose a more sophisticated trait. Perhaps a fetus does not become a person until she is rational and self-aware, or capable of free and moral choice. Perhaps you invoke very sophisticated traits like these specifically to avoid the possibility that pigs and mice have a right to life. But not only is it true that no *fetus* has these traits; no *newborn infant* has them either. We don't think that children are morally or legally guilty of a crime until they are capable of rationality, morality, and free choice, and that doesn't take place until many years after birth. We can tell that a child is self-aware when he can recognize himself in a mirror, but this doesn't happen until several months after birth. Furthermore, elephants, dolphins, and the great apes all pass the mirror test and would thus count as persons on this view as well.

So the problem with the "Trait X" approach to moral status and personhood is that you are forced into two strange claims that almost no one wishes to accept. Either you pick a "lower-end" trait and end up claiming that animals like mice and rats count as persons with a right to life, or you pick a "higher-end" trait and end up claiming that not even newborn infants are persons. Some are willing to bite these bullets. The prestigious international *Journal of Medical Ethics,* published at Oxford University, recently released a special issue entitled "Abortion, Infanticide, and Allowing Babies to Die." Remarkably, several authors argue not only that the prenatal child fails to count as person, the same should be said of a newly born child. In fact, a *fetus* of thirty-four weeks might have significantly more value than an *infant* born prematurely at twenty-four weeks.[8] Some hardcore animal-rights activists are also willing to say that we should never kill mice and rats because doing so is akin to murder.

But most of us are unwilling to go to either of these places.[9] As an alternative, you might be tempted to simply go back to the beginning and identify personhood with the species Homo sapiens. But this is also problematic. Again, we cannot leap from the *scientific and biological* fact that the fetus is a human being directly to any kind of *moral* truth. And while explicitly religious claims about the value of human beings being made in the image of God might be persuasive to Christians (along with Jews and Muslims), they don't seem to work very well with non-Christians or in our secular discourse. Furthermore — and especially for the Abrahamic religions — it isn't clear that we want to limit personhood to human beings. Angels, for instance, are nonhuman persons. And if we ever meet aliens who are like us, they will be additional examples of nonhuman persons. Indeed, the head of the Vatican Observatory was asked, at a 2010 astrobiology conference (hosted by the Catholic church!), about the existence of aliens, and he replied that it would be acceptable to baptize an alien "if he asked"[10] — a position reaffirmed by Pope Francis.[11]

The Argument from Potential

Fortunately, there is an alternative approach. And it builds on an important difference between the prenatal human child and the kinds of nonhuman beings that I have used in the above comparisons: the *potential* of each being. Suppose you think a person is someone who can create and pursue a life of meaning. Or someone who is capable of creating and appreciating art. Or someone who can love God and neighbor. Excepting (perhaps) some very, very sophisticated animals, the overwhelming majority of nonhuman beings on this planet cannot do any of these things. And they never will be able to. On the other hand, a human fetus or infant, if she or he is allowed simply to develop and fulfill the potential inside of her/him, *will* do all of these things. This potential, I would argue, is why both prenatal children and newborn infants are persons.

Is that enough? Does invoking "potential" mean that we've solved the problem of the moral status of the fetus and can now pack up and move on to the next chapter? Not at all. Many thinkers reject the argument from potential, and they push us to see how far we will take such an argument. Do we really want to say that *all* potential persons should count as full persons like you and me? If we follow this principle wherever it goes, what should we think of a fertility lab tech who rinses spare sperm and egg cells down the drain? It looks as though what he destroyed had the potential to be a person. Did he do something terribly wrong? Furthermore, in light of cloning technology, we now know that each of our human body cells has the potential to be turned into an embryo. If I scratch the outside of my hand and kill some skin cells, am I killing a bunch of persons? After all, they have the *potential* to become persons, don't they?

This would seem to be a devastating response. What serious person could believe that killing skin cells or disposing of semen down a drain are murderous acts? And yet, if these entities have the "potential" to be persons, then it looks like the argument from potential is forced into this kind of absurd territory. And if a direct implication of an argument is absurd, then we must abandon the argument itself as also absurd.

But is the argument from potential really in such bad shape? The problem, rather than actual disagreement, largely comes from confusion over the meaning of the word "potential." Quite sensibly, the Greek philosopher Aristotle distinguishes between two different senses of this concept that the English language confuses. The first understanding is something like what we mean by "probability," or "chance." In this view, a being has the potential to become X if that being has a percentage chance *greater than zero* of becoming X. But the second understanding refers to potential of a different kind: what *already exists* inside a being as the kind of thing that it already is.

Those who have never considered this point before may understandably find it to be complicated, but it is absolutely essential, so let's explore two examples that may help illustrate the difference. Someone who is very morbid, perhaps in an attempt to induce you to get off the couch and become more active, might say, "You need to remember that you are a potential corpse and will die someday. Get out there and live!" But perhaps you have had a coach or a parent, also in an attempt to get you off the couch and live life, who said, "You have so much potential! Don't waste it!" Both statements use the English word "potential," but they mean two different things. In the first example, yes, your *body* has a certain percentage chance (approaching 100 percent!) of becoming a corpse, but it isn't true that *you* become a corpse. In fact, if you die, the whole point is that you are not the corpse. On the other hand, when your teacher says that you need to work hard to "reach your potential," she is speaking of the potential that already exists inside of you. It is part of who you are as a human person. It is potential based on the nature of the kind of thing that you already are.

Are you still unsure about this distinction? Here are two more examples to help make the point. Suppose a carpenter says that "a tree is a potential desk," and a biologist says that "a sprouting acorn is a potential oak tree." Again, the word "potential" is used by both people, but in two very different ways. A tree has a certain percentage chance of becoming a desk, and in that sense is a potential desk. But it makes no sense to treat a tree as if it is a desk. In fact, in order for a tree to become a desk, it must be cut down into little pieces, carved up, screwed and glued together, and so forth. It ceases being a tree and *becomes a new kind of thing.* The fancy phrase I like to use for this process is a "nature-changing event." But what about the sprouting acorn's potential to become an oak tree? Does it need to become a new kind of thing to reach its potential? Not at all. It just needs energy and the right environment to become the kind of thing it already is. No "nature-changing event" is necessary. In a very real sense — and especially from the perspective of biology — a sprouting acorn is *already* an oak tree. Indeed, if a certain kind of oak tree had special legal protection, one could be prosecuted for killing such a tree even at this early stage.

We can now see how this distinction responds to those who wish to reduce the argument from potential to the absurd. "Pro-lifers" should agree that potential in the first sense of "mere probability" or "percentage chance" is not morally significant when it comes to moral status or value. Skin cells and sperm-egg pairs have the potential to become persons, yes, but they would have to undergo a nature-changing event. Skin, sperm, and egg cells would have to cease to be cells that are part of another organism and would have to become a *brand-new organism,* a new member of the species Homo sapiens. This is not true of the human fetus or newborn infant. These entities are already human organisms, and thus they already have this potential inside them based on the kind of things that they already are. Based on their nature. No "nature-changing event" is necessary. They only require energy and the right environment to express their potential to become *the kind of thing they already are.* Indeed, we already acknowledge this kind of potential when we say that a prenatal child or newborn has a "disease" or "injury." Something accidental to her nature is frustrating her ability to express the potential that exists inside of her. If we find a way to heal the disease or injury, we don't consider this to be anything like a nature-changing event. We say that the potential that always existed inside her was finally able to be fully expressed. A diseased or injured person, when healed, is finally able to fully express who he already was the whole time.

Problems for Those Who Reject the Argument from Potential

But suppose you still aren't convinced. (More could certainly be said about all of this, and I have done so in another recent book.[12]) If you reject the argument from potential, then you are stuck with very serious problems. For if *actually expressing* "Trait X" (rationality, self-awareness, moral responsibility, having a life plan, and so on) is necessary for someone to be a person — and not just *potentially* expressing it — there are several very big bullets to bite. We have already discussed the newborn human infant as one important example. If we reject her potential for the future, there is no good reason to see an infant as a person. Her actualized and expressed traits are no more significant than those of a chicken.

For many, the prospect of being forced to admit that the newborn baby is not a person with a right to life would be enough to accept the argument from potential. But this is just the beginning of the problems with the "antipotential" position. Suppose my physician puts me into a medically induced coma so that I heal faster after surgery. While in this coma, of course, my morally significant traits (rationality, self-awareness, and so on) are potential rather than actual. Is there a reason to consider me different from a chicken, a snail, or even a plant? And what about other times when my rationality and self-awareness are merely potential rather than actual? Suppose I get drunk and pass out. Or I fall into a deep and dreamless sleep. Could someone kill me in any of these situations and fail to kill a person? If you reject the argument from potential, it looks like the answer is yes.

Also consider a severely mentally disabled human being who has the cognitive and mental capacities similar to those of a high-functioning dog. Why should that human being be treated in a different way than the dog is treated? In my view, the answer comes from the argument from potential. This severely disabled human being is the same kind of being as anyone reading this book; but he has a disability that frustrates his capacity to express the kind of being he is. This fact, again, is implied by calling what he has a "disability" in the first place, rather than thinking of him as a different kind of being altogether. A disability frustrates his ability to fully function as the kind of being he is: a person like you and me. But if you reject the argument from potential, it is unclear we should treat him and other severely disabled humans like other humans who are higher-functioning. Consistency seems to require treating them like lower-functioning animals.

These are troubling implications. One could, I suppose, simply accept them as the price for rejecting the argument from potential. And a tiny few, such as Peter Singer, have done this; but that view forces them into supporting choices like infanticide and euthanasia of the mentally disabled. If you reject Singer's conclusions, you must reject the argument that produced them, and this means accepting the argument from potential. If we accept the argument from potential, consistency requires that we must consider all prenatal human children to be persons — just like you and me.

Or does it? There remains one more complicating factor to consider.

Gray Area between Person and Nonperson?

Whichever understanding of personhood one has, there will always be a transition phase from a nonperson (sperm-egg, or fetus, or infant) to a person. But just how should we think of that transition? Our current rhetoric in the abortion debate imagines that there are only two possibilities or categories: it often suggests that there is one "moment" where we have a nonperson and a next "moment" where we have a person. Indeed, we often hear from "pro-lifers" that the prenatal child is present from the "moment" of fertilization.

But fertilization isn't a moment; it is a *process*. There is a gray area during which the egg cell is being fertilized and reprogrammed into an embryo. Something similar could be said about when a prenatal child becomes "viable" and can live outside her mother. There is a time where this definitely could happen, and a time where it definitely could not happen; and then there is a gray area where we can't be sure. This is also true about the "moment" of birth: we have a definite time before, and definite time after, but what about when birth is *in process?* Back in 1999, in a debate on the floor of the U.S. Senate about partial-birth abortion, then Senator Rick Santorum of Pennsylvania pressed Senator Diane Feinstein of California about when, precisely, a baby was born and had legal protection. Would a baby not be born, and be a full person, Santorum asked, even if "her toe" was still inside her mother? Feinstein was flustered because it seemed absurd to think that a toe being inside the mother mattered, but she was arguing against the only other option she could imagine: that a prenatal child was a person just like you and me. Even Peter Singer's threshold of self-awareness has this problem. A newborn is not self-aware, and a two-year-old definitely is, but how should we think about the time in between?

So, regardless of where you think the transition from nonperson to person takes place, you must deal with this gray area. There is always a transitional stage in which it will be impossible to say whether it is one thing or the other. In a less morally serious context, we see this in the transition from day into night. We have the category of "dusk," which is neither day nor night. Or it is both day and night. Many popular movies and books over the last few years have featured stories about zombies and vampires. These beings are also neither alive nor dead, or both alive and dead. They are "undead."

How should each of us, wherever we think the gray area between person and nonperson exists, think about the moral status or value of beings in the gray area? One way to respond is via what is sometimes called the "precautionary principle." According to this view, the idea is that we treat any individual in this gray area as a person "just to be safe." (This at least appears to be the view of the Roman Catholic Church on the early embryo: the church does not commit itself to the arguments about the early embryo's personhood one way or the other, but instead claims that an embryo should be treated "as" a person.[13]) But this doesn't seem to apply to what I'm suggesting the gray area actually is. Almost by definition, a being in the gray area *cannot* have the value of the thing before the transition; nor can it have the value of the thing it will become after the transition is complete. We will never figure out whether we should treat "dusk" as (1) night or (2) day by letting the arguments play out or having more evidence presented. That's because asking "Is dusk day or night?" is asking the wrong question. By definition, dusk is neither day nor night.

So where do we find this gray area in the transition from person to nonperson? For most "pro-lifers," it takes place during the fertilization of the egg cell; for some others, it is the formation of the future brain and spinal cord in the early embryo; for others, it will be viability or even birth. For a rare few, it will be the formation of capacities for rationality and self-awareness after birth. We have already addressed each of these arguments as thresholds for when personhood "kicks in," but how should we think about the moral status of an entity in this "in between" stage, in whatever place we happen to think that stage exists? Maggie Little, director of the Kennedy Institute of Ethics at Georgetown University, argues that a being at this stage is "on its way" to becoming one of us, and thus "has a claim on us, but not a full one."[14] This provides a very important opening for common ground. For instance, suppose that a certain "pro-choicer" believes that a fetus at twenty-one weeks is not a person but instead a being in transition from nonperson to person — and that she has a high moral status with a serious claim on our behavior. There is important common ground here between this "pro-choicer" and a "pro-lifer" who believes a twenty-one-week-old prenatal child is a person with a full right to life. Both could agree, for instance, that abortions *for certain reasons* at this stage are wrong. The "pro-lifer" would say they are wrong for the same reason that all killing of humans is wrong; but the "pro-choicer" would say that the reason for the abortion (say, wanting to cover up an affair or a one-night stand, as opposed to a more serious reason like responding to a health concern) could also make it wrong. (These considerations will become more important as we think about specific compromise proposals in chapter 6.)

Conclusion

"Science" is often the trump card laid in debates about morality and public policy. When we ask, "Who or what is the fetus?" a biologist will say, "a human organism." But science (at least when it is functioning within its proper boundaries) refuses to make judgments of moral value between human organisms at different stages or circumstances of life. A prenatal child at twelve weeks is a human organism, as is a human being in a persistently unconscious state, as is any person reading this book. Mere scientific facts cannot directly give us moral truth. Value judgments must evaluate and incorporate scientific claims. Christians are committed to the claim that all human beings are made in the image of God and are thus persons; but some others disagree. Hence, we must move beyond science in answering the *moral* question: "Who or what is the fetus?"

In moving beyond science, some argue that only an *independent* human being, one who can live outside her mother's body, can be considered a person. But we also saw that this has some ridiculous implications, including that one's personhood could be determined by race, gender, time period, sophistication of technology in one's community, or even ability to travel to another community. Furthermore, it appears that in contexts other than pregnancy we don't consider "dependence" to be lower moral status. A newborn infant, a medical patient on a ventilator, and an astronaut on a spacewalk are all "dependent," but this dependence does not lower their moral status of value. Indeed, from some perspectives, such dependence means that they deserve a special level of attention and protection.

A good number of people take the "Trait X" position. They say that when a fetus has "Trait X," she becomes a person; before that time she is not a person. This also has strange implications. If you pick a "low" trait, such as the capacity to feel pain, then it looks like rats and mice count as persons. But if you pick a "high" trait, such as self-awareness or capacity to make moral choices, then it looks like newborn infants and severely disabled humans do not count as persons.

I argue that the solution is to consider all beings with *the natural potential* for "Trait X." Personally, I would pick two traits: the capacity to know and the capacity to love (but it works for other kinds of traits as well). This includes both newborn and mentally disabled human beings, but it excludes beings such as chickens and rats. It also includes those who are in an induced coma and those who are passed out drunk. Significantly for our topic in this book, it includes the prenatal child.

But what does it mean to say that the fetus is a person? It means many things, some of them complex, and we will take them up as the book unfolds. But we can say one simple thing up front: as persons, our prenatal children deserve equal protection of the law, including a *right to life*.[15] History is filled with injustices under which certain kinds of persons were not given equal protection of the law. But whether we are talking about women, people of color, or gays and lesbians, the argument is always brought back to the question of justice. Justice demands that all persons receive equal protection of the law. Those who are interested in social justice, in particular, know that the marginalized — those whose equal dignity under the law poses a serious problem for those in power, who find their dignity inconvenient — need our special attention so that they receive equal protection. Like other kinds of civil rights movements, the movement to give our prenatal children equal protection of the law will be resisted by both men and women who see such protection as a threat to their power, a threat to their ability to live life as they would prefer. Such people (as we will see, they are often men) benefit from the fact that the dignity of the prenatal child remains largely invisible in our culture. But those of us who are interested in justice cannot let the powerful keep us from working for equal protection of the law for all people, especially for the most vulnerable and dependent.

Despite the complex arguments we have just engaged, the view that the fetus is a person (at least in many contexts) is common sense and is reflected in our laws and the way we speak. We saw above that thirty-seven states already have laws against fetal homicide. The doctor says that the "baby" is doing fine. The mother says the "baby" is kicking. We tell stories about pregnant women, described as "mothers" who are "with child." Nor is this somehow necessarily a Christian or religious idea. Plenty of secular people (led by perhaps the most famous public atheist of the last generation, Christopher Hitchens) agree that the fetus is a person. Even the very secular (and non-Christian) Chinese culture records the age of a person *from fertilization* — so that, when she is born, a baby is described as already one year old.

Resistance to calling a fetus a person is often less about what one believes about the moral status of the fetus and more about what one believes about the rights of women. This is perhaps the best explanation for why the same person will call the prenatal child a "fetus" in the context of abortion and a "baby" in the context of a wanted pregnancy. Indeed, the moral status of the prenatal child, while foundational, is only the first major issue one must explore in order to engage the abortion debate. There is much more to discuss.

In contexts other than abortion, for instance, many believe that it is legitimate to kill a person — in very rare circumstances, such as self-defense. Even more believe that it is legitimate to refuse to sustain or aid a person even when we know that person will die without our aid. (Each day sees the death of many hundreds of people whom we could aid with our excess resources, most of which we spend on needless luxuries.) Every person may have equal protection of the law, but it doesn't follow that every person has the right to be sustained and aided — especially when such sustainment and aid requires another person to take on a huge and devastating burden.

In the next chapter we move on to discuss this next set of issues in the abortion debate. Given the moral status of the fetus, how should we understand the duties of her mother? Does she have an exceptionless duty not to kill her prenatal child? A duty to sustain and aid her? In what circumstances? Those who believe that a prenatal child is a person should absolutely refuse to compromise on the view that she deserves equal protection of the law. Indeed, we should be even more insistent on this fact. But at least if we are committed to exploring abortion in all its complexity, there are many important questions to ask that go beyond the moral status of the fetus.

CHAPTER THREE

Aiming at Death or Ceasing to Aid?

"Among all the crimes which can be committed against life, procured abortion has characteristics making it particularly serious and deplorable."

Pope John Paul II, *Evangelium Vitae*

"Forced pregnancy requires a woman to provide continuous physical service to the fetus."

Dawn Johnsen, National Abortion Rights and Action League

Introduction

If you thought that the issues considered in the previous chapter involved confusion and people talking past each other, well, you haven't seen anything yet. In this chapter, where we will examine the reality and morality of the act of abortion, we again find that people engaged in the arguments are often not even discussing the same idea. For instance, those who see most abortions as *directly killing* an innocent child are mystified by those who speak about the "right" to do something they consider so horrible. On the other hand, those who understand most abortions as a *refusal to aid* a fetus are quick to the point out that bodily autonomy and freedom are essential for the right of self-determination, something that has been shamefully denied to women throughout most of history.

In this chapter I will unpack the confusing and polarizing results when these two very different groups, with two very different understandings of abortion, try to engage each other. The first half of the chapter considers how a principle held by almost everyone — "aiming at the death of an innocent person is wrong" — should (or should not) be used to describe abortion. I will focus significant attention on whether and in what circumstances a fetus should be considered "innocent." In the second half of the chapter I will focus on abortions that do not appear to aim at death, but are better understood as refusing to aid the prenatal child. Especially in the Catholic moral tradition, "refusing to aid" is a different kind of action, and it could be justified if one has a proportionately serious reason.[1] In exploring this subject, we will begin by looking at cases of indirect abortion already accepted by the church, and then try to reason consistently from these cases, exploring whether similar reasoning should be used in other cases.

Aiming at Death

It is gravely wrong to kill. This moral principle goes back as far as we have written records and transcends multiple religions and cultures. Most of the controversy and complexity in our public discussion of abortion comes from determining (1) *who or what* is wrong to kill, and (2) *what it means* to "kill" in the first place. The issues present in the first topic were the subject of the previous chapter, but let's briefly revisit them here. Persons are not "things," or "objects," with merely *contingent* value based on how we use them. Persons are beings with *irreducible* value that should not be used as mere objects. It is therefore wrong to radically reduce a person's dignity to a mere means to some other end, with killing a person being the most egregious example of this kind of reduction. It may also be wrong to kill beings who are not persons, but killing a person is of the utmost seriousness because of that person's irreducible moral value.[2]

The Roman Catholic Church, along with almost every other moral and legal system in history, strongly prohibits the killing of persons. If you get up one morning, and your roommate is really annoying you, it may serve your interests if he were to meet an unfortunate end. But our culture rightly says that it would be very seriously wrong to kill him. You may not radically reduce the dignity of your roommate by killing him, even if your roommate is a huge burden on you. The church goes so far as to say that every example of killing, at least when that person is "innocent," is wrong *without exception* (more on this below). We have already seen one reason for this prohibition: persons simply don't have the kind of contingent, reducible value that can be weighed against our wants and desires. Philosophers call this kind of confused comparison a "category mistake."

But there is another reason for the prohibition, and it involves a focus on vulnerable populations. History has seen innumerable vulnerable populations killed (sometimes on a massive scale) even in societies where killing was against the law. Loopholes and exceptions were created to get around the rule, and these have been exploited by those who found the irreducible value of such people to be inconvenient. Once we allow exceptions to the rule that it is always wrong to aim at the death of an innocent person, we know that the powerful will use them to kill the most vulnerable in our culture. Especially if we care about social justice for these vulnerable populations, we should be very skeptical of attempts to create exceptions.

But back to the topic of this book: Is abortion aiming at death? For many the answer is obviously yes. But for others the answer isn't so clear. The philosopher Maggie Little, whom I cited in the previous chapter, is one of several thinkers who argue that abortion lies between "direct killing" on the one hand and merely choosing "not to aid" on the other. In her view, therefore, abortion is not aiming at death. However, when we examine the act of *direct* abortion ("indirect" abortion, as we shall see, is another matter), Little's view seems implausible. While one could say that the *end,* or goal, of abortion might be to stop aiding a prenatal child, the *means* by which that end is accomplished is a clear example of direct killing. It is difficult and even heartbreaking to describe the reality of the process of abortion, but any authentic and honest discussion of these issues should face the reality of the procedure head on. This is especially true when we are attempting to discern the all-important question of whether an abortion is an example of killing or a refusal to aid. So let us do the difficult but necessary work of describing the reality of abortion.

In the first trimester of pregnancy, a procedure called Suction Dilation and Curettage is most often used to terminate the pregnancy. In this kind of abortion, the mother's cervix is dilated and a hose-like instrument called a cannula is inserted into her body. The hose is attached to a powerful vacuum and maneuvered by the physician so it can suck out the fetus, placenta, and amniotic fluid. Sometimes, however, the hose does not get all the body parts of the prenatal child, and a curette is used to scrape the uterus to make sure every last limb and organ has been recovered.

Later in pregnancy, however, the fetus is too large for this method to be effective, so a different procedure, called Suction Dilation and Evacuation, is used. What follows is the congressional testimony of an abortion provider who has performed Suction Dilation and Evacuation over a hundred times. It makes for difficult reading, but, again, if we are to deal honestly with abortion, we must not shy away from its medical and clinical reality.

> With suction complete, look for your Sopher clamp. This instrument is about thirteen inches long and made of stainless steel. At the business end are located jaws about 2½ inches long and about ¾ of an inch wide with rows of sharp ridges or teeth. This instrument is for grasping and crushing tissue. When it gets hold of something, it does not let go. A second trimester D&E abortion is a blind procedure. The baby can be in any orientation or position inside the uterus. Picture yourself reaching in with the Sopher clamp and grasping anything you can. At twenty-four weeks gestation, the uterus is thin and soft, so be careful not to perforate or puncture the walls. Once you have grasped something inside, squeeze on the clamp to set the jaws and pull hard — really hard. You feel something let go and out pops a fully formed leg about six inches long. Reach in again and grasp whatever you can. Set the jaw and pull really hard once again and out pops an arm about the same length. Reach in again and again with that clamp and tear out the spine, intestines, heart and lungs.[3]

I will spare you further testimony about the challenges he sometimes faced in retrieving the head of the fetus. This description makes the reality of the procedure quite clear.

Perhaps at this point some of you are wondering just what the point of these gruesome descriptions has been. Isn't this just a manipulative way of trying to move the argument in a "pro-life" direction? When I wrote about animal ethics and factory farming in an earlier book, I was similarly questioned and criticized for describing the horrific conditions and practices of such farms. Some thought those descriptions were also a manipulative attempt on my part to push for animal protection. And it is true that no final moral conclusions follow directly from a negative emotional reaction to these descriptions. Some people, after all, have similarly negative emotional reactions to gruesome descriptions of battlefield surgeries. All by themselves such reactions don't tell us very much. We should, however, honestly name and describe the reality of abortion, and if we have a negative emotional reaction, that is at least a good reason to pay close attention and try to figure out why we are reacting this way.

So what should we make of Little's claim (made by many others as well) that direct abortion is not direct killing? Given the clinical facts of direct abortion described above, this understanding of direct abortion cannot be defended. The procedures described above are direct and clear *attacks* on the life of the prenatal child. Again, while the goal or end of the action might be described as "refusing to allow the fetus to use my body," the *means* by which that goal is accomplished is the active, direct killing of the fetus.

Furthermore, our public discussion of abortion — obscured with misleading language about "reproductive choice" — often hides the fact that even the *end* of many abortions (and not merely the means by which the end is accomplished) is simply the death of the prenatal child. For instance, when adoption is presented as an alternative to abortion, some women (and often the men who are pressuring and even coercing them) will decline. Their reason for having the abortion is not about ending their pregnancy, but about not wanting the child to exist beyond pregnancy. Anecdotally, I've had very frank conversations with a good number of people who explained why they chose abortion over adoption. Some made this choice because they (and/or their parents) couldn't bear to think about the child being raised by someone else, while others were afraid of the public stigma of supposedly "avoiding responsibility" for raising their child. Also, when we know that 90 percent of fetuses diagnosed with Down syndrome (or other mental disability that makes them unacceptable to their parents) are killed via abortion, it is also a clear example of where the aim is the death of the prenatal child. So whether it is the means by which the end of their action is accomplished or the actual end itself, a direct abortion aims at the death of the fetus. And because persons are beings who cannot have their dignity reduced in this way, these direct abortions are always wrong.[4]

Tough Cases

For many, the claim that "all abortions are wrong" is so implausible as to be absurd. As we saw in chapter 1, an overwhelming majority of Americans — even those who describe themselves as "pro-life" — support abortion to save the life of the mother. Can we really say that such abortions are wrong without exception? Don't we allow the use of deadly force in other contexts to save one's life? What would make the abortion context different? For almost everyone in the abortion debate, abortion to save the life of the mother is an exception that seems to directly contradict the claim that "all abortions are wrong."

But *is* it a contradiction? In order to figure it out, we'll have to roll up our sleeves and do some hard work unpacking the contested and complex meaning of several key ideas mentioned above. The discussions that follow (especially if you are unfamiliar with philosophical and/or theological ethics) may seem abstract and legalistic, but they are of the utmost importance in the abortion debate. In fact, if the argument I'm about to make works, then we do not have to choose between defending the innocent and acknowledging a mother's right to self-defense. This would be a huge step forward.

Recall the moral principle we are examining: "It is always wrong to aim at the death of an innocent person." First, let's think more precisely about what it means to "aim at death." Direct abortions, like the ones described above, are examples where death is either the goal of the act or the means by which the goal is accomplished. But not all abortions are like this. *Indirect* abortions of pregnancy that do not aim at the death of the child are different. Indeed, even the Catholic Church allows this kind of abortion for a proportionately serious reason. Suppose a pregnant woman is given the devastating diagnosis of cancer of the uterus. According to Catholic teaching, she may abort her pregnancy by having her uterus removed if the goal of her action, as well as the means by which she accomplishes it, do not involve the death of the prenatal child.

When teaching this distinction to my students, I use something they affectionately call the "Camosy pissed test," which may help determine whether someone is aiming at death. Take the case cited above of the removal of the cancerous uterus: Would the mother be upset (i.e., "pissed") if the child lived through the procedure? Of course not. She would be overjoyed. The goal of her action is to save her life, and the means by which she accomplished this goal is by removing the uterus — not by killing the prenatal child. Contrast this with the cases above in which either the goal or means is clearly death. After all, it is meaningless to ask "What if the fetus lived?" after Suction Dilation and Evacuation. The very nature of the procedure itself aims at death.

Another example often used to make a similar argument about indirect abortion involves the tragic situation in which the prenatal child has implanted in the fallopian tube rather than the uterus. If permitted to grow, the prenatal child will often kill both herself and her mother. Once again, even very strict and traditional Catholic teaching clearly allows for an *indirect* abortion in this case: removal of the tube with the fetus growing inside it to save the life of the mother. But especially if the woman still wants to have biological children, or if she is so sick that surgery would endanger her life, the removal of the tube could be a devastating and risky means by which she defends her life. Wouldn't it be better simply to take a drug like methotrexate, which expels the prenatal child from the tube, rather than risk her fertility and perhaps her life? An increasing number of "pro-life" theologians claim that taking this drug actually causes an *indirect* abortion, and that the death of the child is not intended — either as the goal or means of the action.[5] Others believe that taking methotrexate in such a situation aims at death by its very nature, and because it always wrong to aim at the death of a fetus, taking the drug even to save the mother's life cannot be justified.

Some theologians, even those who are strongly committed to Roman Catholic Church teaching, make a very interesting argument against the idea that the "very nature" of an act can aim at death. One good example is the famously orthodox Catholic moral theologian Germain Grisez. (Fair warning: we are about to get even deeper into the weeds of our complex argument, but I will try to keep it as simple as possible without sacrificing the complexity of the issue. Another warning: the argument deals with a case that is difficult and disturbing to think about. But again, we do ourselves no favors by shying away from the reality of abortion.) Grisez asks us to think about a case that has become uncommon in the developed, technologically sophisticated world, but one that still happens in remote areas and developing countries. Suppose the head of a fetus is too big for her to exit her mother's body. If the pregnancy and labor are allowed to go forward, without modern medical technology that makes a cesarean section safe for the mother, she will likely die. In such a desperate and tragic situation, some believe a "craniotomy" is medically indicated. In this procedure, the prenatal child's skull is crushed so that she can be removed from her mother's body.

At first glance, anyway, this surely looks like it violates the principle that it is always wrong to aim at the death of an innocent person. But Grisez challenges that first reaction by asking us to consider what the physician who performs such an action really intends.[6] Is it possible to describe the act as "altering the size of the fetus's head" rather than aiming at her death?

The death of the fetus, after all, contributes nothing to either the goal of the act (which is to save the mother's life) or the means to get to the goal. Indeed, the same procedure would likely be performed even if the prenatal child was *already* dead. Could we say that the baby's death, though foreseen, is not intended? In traditional Catholic theology, then, this would be a case of double effect — that is, where the death can be permitted if there is a proportionately serious reason. And the mother's likely death if we do not act is precisely this kind of reason.

To many, this sounds a lot like academic sleight of hand. Can someone's intention really change the commonsense understanding of an act like this? If doing a craniotomy can be described as something other than killing a baby, then what other redescriptions of commonsense acts can we do? In sixteenth-century Japan, samurai would sometimes test the sharpness of their new *katana* swords on unsuspecting innocent people. It was called *tsujigiri,* which means "crossroads killing," because the samurai would often wait at a crossroads for their unsuspecting victims. Now, it is difficult to imagine a more horrific act than this, right? (Incidentally, the example of *tsujigiri* is an excellent challenge to cultural relativists who insist that there are no ethical rules that apply universally.) But suppose a Grisez-influenced samurai objects to our moral judgment and says that he was "merely aiming at testing the sharpness of his new katana," and that the death of the person was "not the aim of his act at all." Indeed, suppose he told us that the person he just killed was slouched on a bench, fast asleep, when the samurai approached him from behind. The samurai could argue: "It didn't matter whether he was alive or dead. All I wanted to do was test the sharpness of my blade on his neck. I would have done the same thing if it was a dead body slouched on the bench."

Except that it wasn't a dead body, and he knew it. The very structure and nature of the act (cutting off a living person's head) involves killing of an innocent human as the means to the end of testing the sharpness of his blade.[7] The samurai cannot evade the charge of aiming at death because the very *nature of the act* of involves death. The same is true in the craniotomy case. The crushing of the prenatal child's skull has a *nature* and *structure* built into it that cannot be separated from aiming at death.

So where does this leave us? If we reject Grisez's argument, we seem to be left with two terrible options: either (1) we insist that the mother accept death, or (2) we abandon the principle that it is always wrong to aim at the death of an innocent person.[8] But I don't think we need to make this choice, and I will now attempt to explain why.

What Does It Mean to Be Innocent?

In general, what it means to be "innocent" is not that complicated. An innocent person must, at the very least, not wrongfully harm another person. What allows defenders of just war and just policing to accept the use of deadly force (without giving up the principle that it is always wrong to aim at the death of an innocent person) is the fact that those who seriously and wrongfully harm others are *not* innocent. But very young children, of course, are always innocent; therefore, aiming at their death in war or in a police action is always wrong. So if the human fetus is an innocent person, then aiming at her death is always wrong.

Or is it? Aren't there some (rare) exceptions to these rules? Consider a six-year-old child soldier who has been brainwashed and forced to kill. Or what about an adult who, through no fault of his own, takes a drug that causes him to go completely insane and embark on a deadly shooting rampage? Is an adult soldier or police officer morally justified in using deadly force to defend innocent lives against either the child soldier or the insane shooter? If the answer is yes, then it looks once again as though we must abandon the principle that it is always wrong to aim at the death of an innocent person. But maybe we don't have to; instead, we could think more carefully perhaps about what "innocence" means.[9]

Surely, on one level, both the juvenile soldier and the insane shooter are innocent. At the age of six, the child certainly can't be held morally responsible for his actions, especially if he was brainwashed or otherwise coerced. Whatever part of his will might be involved, it is certainly not a will that is morally guilty of anything. The child's will is innocent. The insane shooter's will, having been totally compromised by the drugs, is not operative and thus also cannot be guilty of anything. But there is more to consider in this story. In many different situations, Catholic morality makes an important distinction between the "formal" and the "material," and it may be that this distinction should be invoked here. For example, in deciding whether or not one is permitted to cooperate with wrongdoers, the church makes the distinction between "formal" cooperation (where our will is aligned with the wrongdoer) and "material" cooperation (where our will is not so aligned).

How might this distinction impact our understanding of innocence? It may be the case that someone could be *formally* innocent but nevertheless remain a mortal threat *materially*. Both the child soldier and the insane shooter, we must agree, are formally innocent. An evil or unjust will is not involved in either action. Indeed, from a moral perspective, I think we should say that neither the child nor the adult performed an action at all; they were coerced by forces beyond their ability to control. Nevertheless, both are a mortal threat materially, and it may be acceptable (though certainly not morally required) to use defensive deadly force against them. Interestingly, the history of the word "innocent" connects better to the material sense of the innocence than the formal one. It comes from the Latin *innocentem,* which means "not" *(in)* "harmful" *(nocentem).*[10] Indeed, we get our current English word "noxious" from this Latin root. The insane person and the child soldier, though formally innocent, are nevertheless noxious or harmful.

So, in light of these insights, how should we think about a fetus who threatens her mother's life? She is also as *formally* innocent as she could possibly be. I agree with Popes Pius XI and John Paul II that it would be wrong to think of the prenatal child as an "unjust aggressor."[11] Because her will is not involved, she is not performing an action at all, and so descriptors like "aggression" or "unjust" simply don't apply to her actions. However, tragically, she is *materially* a mortal threat to her mother's life.[12] If one may use deadly force to defend against the deadly threat of an innocent juvenile soldier and an innocent shooter, then perhaps a mother may choose to use deadly force against the deadly threat of an innocent prenatal child who threatens her life.[13] Notice that we can say this *without* giving up the absolutely essential moral principle that it is always wrong to aim at the death of the innocent. The key is to more precisely define what is meant by "innocence" within that principle.[14] If the principle refers to those who are innocent (that is, "not noxious" or "not harmful") in both formal and material senses, it may be permissible for a pregnant woman to use deadly force to save her life in the face of a material mortal threat and remain true to this principle.[15]

Practical Application

Now, as I warned you, much of the argument we just explored made abstract use of analogies.[16] Does it have any *practical* relevance? Notice that if we preserve both (1) the principle that it is always wrong to aim at the death of an innocent person, and (2) the right of a mother to defend herself when pregnancy threatens her life, we not only preserve two very important moral principles but we are also in an excellent position to make authentic progress in the abortion debate. I've already mentioned the horrors that have resulted throughout history when we abandon the principle of defense of the innocent: the most vulnerable among us are marginalized and killed by those who find their dignity inconvenient. Furthermore, while martyrdom should be an option that mothers of prenatal children are able to choose, it is essential to give women their inherent right to act in self-defense against a mortal threat. That we can have both is no small thing.

But at this point we should highlight a very important caution. Like other use of deadly force in defense of self or another, this tragic act must be the last resort.[17] And if it really is the last resort, then these kinds of abortions will be extremely rare, especially when compared with the hundreds of thousands of birth-control abortions performed every year in the United States. Consider also that when a woman is later in her pregnancy, a physician who wants to save her life often does not have the luxury of waiting the dozens of hours necessary to dilate the mother for a direct abortion. In such situations, termination of pregnancy can be completed via an indirect abortion (such as cesarean section), which is both (1) not aiming at the death of the prenatal child and (2) is often better for the mother.[18]

Some respected groups (such as the International Symposium on Excellence in Maternal Healthcare) will even argue that it is *never* medically necessary to perform a direct abortion to save the life of the mother.[19] But this seems too strong. Consider a situation where the mother has a very serious disease, such as pulmonary hypertension. In this case even an otherwise normal pregnancy can be deadly. The disease makes surgery of any kind so risky that it may also pose a serious threat to her life. An indirect abortion via cesarean section is thus ruled out. Could labor be induced? Perhaps. But again, that takes precious time and (especially in combination with hypertension) could cause the mother to lose her life. Especially if it is an emergency situation, here again I think we may at least explore the possibility that a mother may use deadly force in defense against a material mortal threat to her life.

In concluding this first part of the chapter, let me return to a very important caution. The cases that could require direct abortion to defend a mother's life are extremely rare, especially when we put them in context with the far less serious reasons for which most abortions are sought and (often) coerced. We should not tiptoe around the fact that deadly force is being used, nor around the moral duty to make this kind of abortion the absolute last resort. This is important not only for showing the prenatal child the moral respect she deserves, but for finding alternatives to protect women's lives. Thomas Cavanaugh points out that, historically, alternatives to craniotomy were pioneered by French Catholic physicians who were intent on baptizing the child, while their Protestant counterparts in Britain lagged far beyond when it came to development of a safe cesarian section.[20] It is possible to make room for the very rare cases in which direct abortion is necessary to save the life of the mother while also working hard to discover new techniques that do not aim at the death of the prenatal child.

Ceasing to Aid?

At least in my experience, a good number of "pro-choicers" will open their discussion of abortion with some version of the following idea: "A woman has the right to do what she wants with her body." This is a puzzling claim for those of us who are skeptical of abortion, for surely such a right doesn't extend to killing an innocent person. Of course, as we saw in the previous chapter, many times the disagreement is about whether the prenatal child is, in fact, a person. However, more often than we might expect, the disagreement is about the process of abortion itself. Dawn Johnsen's claim at the beginning of the chapter is telling: she sees pregnancy as a mother providing a "service to the fetus." According to this understanding, abortion is a choice to *refuse to aid* the fetus rather than a choice to kill. In this context the claim that abortion is about the right of a woman to do what she wishes with her body makes much more sense.

We saw above that for most surgical abortions, however, this is just a misunderstanding of what is actually happening in the act itself. Perhaps the *goal* of the abortion is to stop aid to the prenatal child, but the *means* by which that is accomplished is killing the fetus. It is the "direct and deliberate" killing of a person to which John Paul II refers in *Evangelium Vitae*.[21] But we have already seen that not all abortions involve "direct and deliberate" killing as the means of ending the pregnancy. For instance, removing the cancerous uterus of a pregnant woman obviously aborts the pregnancy, but even for most serious "pro-lifers" (including the institutional Catholic Church) it is a *justified* abortion. And for two reasons. First, it is an indirect abortion that is not aiming at the death of the child: the death of the child is neither the goal nor the means by which the goal is accomplished; indeed, the mother would be overjoyed if the child survived the procedure. Second, there is a proportionately serious reason for permitting (though not intending) the death of the child: the mother's life is at serious risk.

But what if the fetus is preterm and cannot live outsider her mother?

Isn't this aiming at death? After all, *you know* that there is no way the child can survive once you remove the uterus. In answering this very important question, let me ask you to think about something that will at first seem unrelated to our discussion: all the children who will die of easily preventable diseases this year. Once you have that idea squarely in your mind, think about all the needless luxuries on which you (likely) spend money: vacations, going out to dinner, perhaps living in a house rather than an apartment, and so on. You could likely save several thousand dollars a year if you avoided these needless luxuries, and you could come to the aid of many sick children by donating the money you save to places like Oxfam and Catholic Relief Services. But suppose, like most of us, you don't do this. Suppose you refuse to aid these children and foresee — but don't intend — that several will die without your aid. Are you aiming at death? After all, *you know* that these children will die without your aid. Leaving aside the question about whether it is right or wrong for you to refuse to aid these children, you were certainly not aiming at their death — even if *you know* that they will die without your aid. In a similar way (though parents obviously have a stronger obligation to their own children than we do to children overseas), a mother who makes a choice to refuse to aid her prenatal child is not necessarily aiming at her death.

But even if it doesn't aim at death, one needs a proportionately serious reason to refuse to aid a child that will die without such aid. From the case of the mother with the cancerous uterus, the proportionately serious reason is that her own life is at risk. The *Ethical and Religious Directives* given out to Catholic hospitals by the U.S. Conference of Catholic Bishops confirms that this would be a proportionately serious reason to refuse to aid even a preterm fetus.[22] In these situations, however, one can easily see how the reason is proportionate: the issue at hand is "life vs. life." I'll leave it for you to decide whether taking vacations or going out to dinner count as proportionately serious reasons to refuse to aid children who, without your aid, will die of easily treatable diseases.

Other Examples of Refusing to Aid

Refusing or ceasing to aid the fetus, at least when death is not intended, is not *intrinsically* evil because it does not aim at the death of an innocent person. But neither is it necessarily morally acceptable, because such a refusal requires a proportionately serious reason. Though pregnancy is obviously not medical treatment, well-established ways of thinking about moral choices at the end of life can help us here. Euthanasia is wrong because it aims at the death of an innocent person. But refusing or ceasing to aid a patient, even when one knows that patient will die without such aid, is not necessarily wrong — as long as their death is not intended and there is a proportionately serious reason for choosing not to aid. For example, even at a Catholic hospital, a "do not resuscitate" order can be accepted for a newborn child who is about to die. A refusal to aid such a child by doing compressions on her easily breakable chest bones is not aiming at death, and the proportionately serious reason should be obvious.

But are there examples of abortion that are better described as refusals to aid rather than direct killings? Again, for some, a focus on this distinction might sound like legalism — an academic distinction without a common-sense moral difference. But we have already considered the example of the removal of the fallopian tube or the cancerous uterus with the prenatal child still inside. These kinds of abortions, because the death of the child is not intended either as a goal or means of reaching the goal, are refusals to aid rather than direct killings. And they are done for what almost everyone agrees is a proportionately serious reason: a serious threat to the life of the mother. Other indirect methods might include induction of labor or cesarean section. Again, as long as one is not aiming at death, a refusal to aid is not necessarily intrinsically evil — though it does require a proportionately serious reason.

Beyond the Life Exception?

So far, the only acceptable reason for refusing to aid the prenatal child we have discussed involves a serious threat to the mother's life. Could there be others? Thinking again about end-of-life decisions, Catholic teaching allows life-sustaining aid to be withdrawn or refused for many different kinds of reasons. One must never aim at the death of an innocent person, but Catholic hospitals are, of course, permitted to honor requests to refuse or withdraw ventilators, dialysis machines, and chemotherapy — and for many different kinds of reasons. Such aid might be judged too painful, too burdensome, or even an unjust use of resources.[23] In such cases, Catholic teaching allows for aid to be refused or withdrawn, even if the foreseen (but unintended) consequence is going to be death.

What does this have to do with abortion of pregnancy? "Pro-life" thought leaders have apparently not been comfortable asking whether there could be any other proportionate reasons — beyond the danger to the mother's life — that could justify an indirect abortion. Perhaps they are afraid that such an opening might lead to abuse of the principle and to justification of abortion on demand. I share this concern, but refusing even to consider the question fails to apply our moral principles consistently across all issues. If we actually believe our principles are *objectively correct* (rather than just a means of getting to a comfortable conclusion, decided before carefully engaging the issues) then we must be willing to follow our principles wherever they take us. An old philosophy professor of mine once told our class that our moral principles are like buses rather than taxis. You don't get to tell a principle where you want it to go, but instead you must follow it wherever it leads.

So where do our principles lead on the matter of indirect abortion? Let's begin our investigation by looking at a case that was first written about in *America* magazine back in 2009.[24] Here is a summary of the case:

> The diagnosis, at 21 weeks, was Potter syndrome. This prenatal child had no kidneys, an insufficient amount of amniotic fluid, underdeveloped lungs and no ability to breathe on his own at birth. There was no cure, and the fetus would either die in utero or shortly after birth. The parents asked that their child be delivered as soon as was morally and legally possible. Why? They gave several reasons:
>
> > They wanted the baby baptized.
> > They arranged for a photographer to take pictures of them as a family.
> > They wanted to have footprints and handprints made of him.
> > They wanted to hold him.
> > They wanted to try to feed him.
> > They wanted to give him his first bath.
>
> And it turned out that their baby boy was born in the dark of early morning, and died that same day, shortly after his first sunrise. During the three hours he was alive, the baby was photographed and footprinted, held and fed, bathed and baptized. He died in his parents' embrace.

What should we think about this case? If labor was not induced early, it is possible that he could have lived a bit longer at birth. But it was also possible (and even likely) that the child would have died before being born. Is this case of early labor induction an example of an abortion that aims at death? Not at all. To return to the "pissed test," the child's parents would have been absolutely overjoyed if a diagnostic mistake was made and the child lived through the procedure. In fact, as the details above clearly demonstrate, the early induction of labor was a way to honor the goodness of their child's life. It looks as if the parents had proportionately serious reasons for early induction of labor, especially true from a Catholic perspective, with our special concern for baptism and embodied relationships. In this case we have a morally acceptable example of early induction of labor for a reason other than the mother's life being in danger.

The family in the case above decided to wait until "term" (viability outside the womb) to induce labor early. But imagine a different scenario. Suppose that, because the prenatal child was about to die while still inside his mother, they induced labor at twenty weeks rather than twenty-two. Should this change our moral evaluation? Whether the child was born at twenty weeks, twenty-two weeks, or thirty-six weeks, he had no chance of living more than a few hours. We have already seen that the removal of a cancerous uterus is morally acceptable, even if the baby is pre-term.[25] If the reasons for inducing labor above count as proportionately serious reasons for a "term" child who is about to die, then they are also proportionately serious reasons for a pre-term child who is also about to die.

But this is where some of my fellow "pro-lifers" might start getting nervous. Once you allow intentional pre-term delivery of a fetus for reasons that go beyond saving the life of the mother, where do you draw the line? How are we to determine what a proportionately serious reason might be? Instead of the horribly unjust situation of direct abortion on demand, aren't we left with the horribly unjust situation of *indirect* abortion on demand? While this worry deserves careful attention, I believe we can make clear distinctions such that indirect abortion is permitted only for a proportionately serious reason — a reason that would take into account the mother/child relationship in pregnancy as different from other kinds of relationships. In making my case, I turn to the most famous attempt to show that indirect abortion on demand is morally acceptable.

The Violinist Case

In 1971 the "pro-choice" philosopher Judith Jarvis Thomson wrote an article destined to be read by hundreds of thousands of undergraduate students for decades to come. In the article, which she titled "A Defense of Abortion," Thomson (for the sake of argument only) gives "pro-lifers" the concession that our prenatal children count as persons. Nevertheless, she arrives at a generally "pro-choice" conclusion. Her argument relies on the following analogy:

> You wake up in the morning and find yourself back to back in bed with an unconscious violinist. A famous unconscious violinist. He has been found to have a fatal kidney ailment, and the Society of Music Lovers has canvassed all the available medical records and found that you alone have the right blood type to help. They have therefore kidnapped you, and last night the violinist's circulatory system was plugged into yours, so that your kidneys can be used to extract poisons from his blood as well as your own. The director of the hospital now tells you, "Look, we're sorry the Society of Music Lovers did this to you — we would never have permitted it if we had known. But still, they did it, and the violinist is now plugged into you. To unplug you would be to kill him. But never mind, it's only for nine months. By then he will have recovered from his ailment, and can safely be unplugged from you." Is it morally incumbent on you to accede to this situation? No doubt it would be very nice of you if you did, a great kindness. But do you have to accede to it? What if it were not nine months, but nine years? Or longer still? What if the director of the hospital says, "Tough luck. I agree, but now you've got to stay in bed, with the violinist plugged into you, for the rest of your life. Because remember this. All persons have a right to life, and violinists are persons. Granted you have a right to decide what happens in and to your body, but a person's right to life outweighs your right to decide what happens in and to your body. So you cannot ever be unplugged from him."[26]

Thomson asks us to examine our intuitions about such a situation. Would you be guilty of murder if you decided to disconnect yourself from the violinist? Thomson assumes that most of us would say that we can remove ourselves without being guilty of murder, despite knowing that the violinist will die without our aid, and despite the fact he is a person with a right to life.

You can probably guess Thomson's next move. A pregnant woman who winds up with an unintended pregnancy is analogous to you being attached to the violinist. Even if we can agree that both the violinist and the fetus are persons with a right to life, should we conclude that removing one's self from such a person is morally acceptable? Thomson says that if you choose to be a "good Samaritan," it is of course within your right (and the woman's right) to stay connected and give aid, but you do not have a *moral duty* to do so.

Now, partly because Thomson's article is so famous, there has been a mountain of response literature to her argument (along with many responses to the responses). I cannot hope to do justice to those responses here. Fortunately, however, many of the responses are not our concern. For instance, much has been made of the fact that "removing yourself from the violinist" is an *indirect* action that may not aim at death, while the overwhelming majority of surgical abortions are *direct* killings of the innocent. We have already moved well beyond that point in our discussions, and we are now focusing primarily on what reasons (beyond the danger to the mother's life) might serve as a legitimate basis for indirectly removing the prenatal child from one's body.

Thomson believes that it is just common sense for you to remove yourself from the violinist for virtually any serious reason. Perhaps if the burden on you was extremely small (say, only having to stay connected for an hour before a transplant becomes available), you might have an obligation to stay connected; but if being connected creates a substantial burden, then you should be morally and legally free to remove yourself. In doing this you have not killed a person; you have simply refused to aid a person (indeed, someone who did not have a right to the use of your body) for a proportionately serious reason.

In response to Thomson, some have claimed that one does have a moral duty to stay connected to the violinist. (One of them, somewhat surprisingly, is Peter Singer, though he, of course, refuses to give up the claim that a fetus is something other than a person with a right to life.) Christians will recall that Jesus' command in the parable of the Good Samaritan is that we should "go and do likewise" and act with the same kind of self-sacrificial love. But many of us — especially if we reject or qualify these specifically Christian obligations — would agree that it would be morally acceptable to remove oneself from the violinist for a serious reason. Does it follow that one should also find it morally acceptable to remove the prenatal child via an indirect abortion for virtually any serious reason?

I don't think so. Thomson claims that she is granting "pro-lifers" the claim that a prenatal child is a person with a right to life; but many of us are not so sure that she is. Most "pro-lifers" understand personhood as something very different from the individualistic, "choice"-centered understanding that Thomson's analogy implies. The fetus inside the mother's body is not an unrelated, foreign parasite that, like the violinist, suddenly shows up one day. "Pro-life" thinkers like Francis Beckwith and Gilbert Meilaender have pointed out that Thomson hasn't really given us our claim that the fetus is a person, because most "pro-lifers" understand personhood to be a much more relational, embodied concept.[27]

Furthermore, most of us have rights and obligations that exist outside of any "choice" we make to have or accept them. We have rights and obligations with respect to our parents and children, despite often not having control over this embodied relationship's coming into existence. In thinking about the obligations of fatherhood that are not chosen, for instance, consider the situation of many forty-something single, professional men in New York City, where I work. It is certainly not unusual to see these men trolling the bars and clubs looking for a meaningless hookup. Now, suppose one of these men, ten months later, gets a call from his partner in one of those one-night stands explaining that she has given birth to their daughter and that she is now asking for child support.

How should we react if he refuses to support his child? Our culture would refer to him as a "deadbeat dad" and treat him as a criminal until he paid what he owed. (Our laws in this area are so strong that a man can be held responsible for child support even if the sexual encounter did not involve intercourse.[28]) But suppose this man defends himself by claiming that he never chose to have a child, and certainly never chose to give up 30 percent of his salary for the next two decades to a woman he barely knows. (In New York this could easily end up being several million dollars.) Would such a defense be enough to get him off the hook? Of course not. His choice to have sex brought with it the natural obligation to aid any children that might result, even if having such obligations was the last thing on his mind when he was pursuing the hookup.

This insight highlights a major difference between the violinist case and pregnancy. One does not have a *natural* obligation to the violinist; but a parent does have a natural obligation to his or her child — even if the woman never intended to bring about the child.[29] We do not freely choose our natural obligations (and rights) as parents with respect to our children, just as the rights (and obligations) of our children with respect to us have nothing to do with their choice. Far from a parasite, the fetus is actually welcomed by a healthy female body, which has been created (by God and/or natural selection, depending on your point of view) with the specific capacity to protect, nurture, and sustain a prenatal child. As I have observed above, the mother's pregnant body even makes special changes to protect the fetus from white blood cells attacking the fetus as foreign tissue.

Both fathers and mothers have a natural obligation to aid their children. For fathers, this could amount to several million dollars' worth of support and could come about merely from having made a single sexual mistake; for mothers, this could mean becoming pregnant and either giving the child up for adoption or caring for her (in ways, as we shall see, that require great sacrifice) after birth. In both cases, the natural obligation to aid one's biological child cannot be ignored simply because one finds it inconvenient or burdensome. Thomson's attempt to link our intuitions about the violinist situation with abortion fails. A parent, in choosing not to aid his or her child, violates a natural duty that all parents have. (Though, again, it must be said that it is not always clear where the actual guilt lies — often it is with a coercive father who does not want to be responsible for his child.) This duty cannot be overridden for the reasons Thomson thinks justify abortion. Indeed, our culture demands seriously burdensome sacrifices of both men and women in fulfilling this duty.

Exceptions beyond the Life of the Mother?

So we know that indirect abortion must not be "on demand," especially given that parents are morally obligated to make huge sacrifices for their children. Beyond the "life of the mother" exception, could there be a proportionately serious reason to refuse or cease to aid a fetus via indirect abortion? We have already seen one case which may count: where death of the prenatal child is imminent and the decision is made to do a baptism and to allow both parents a chance to show embodied love in the midst of a terribly tragic situation. If we accept this as a proportionally serious reason, then we have already established that an exception can go beyond the "life of the mother."

Could there be other such reasons? Again, given that our natural duties to our children require very high levels of sacrifice, they would be extremely rare. What about circumstances in which the mother's life is not in serious danger, but her *health* is threatened? All parents know that meeting one's obligations to your children sometimes requires sacrificing your health for their benefit — whether that is not getting enough sleep, adding dozens of new sources of stress in your life, being unable to exercise consistently, and so forth. This is especially true if one is a single mother or father without a good support system in place. Issues related to mental health, though real and deserving of more attention, are also generally poor candidates for abortion exceptions.[30] All parents of children (both prenatal and postnatal) have their psychological health dramatically affected. If there is going to be a health exception that allows for indirect abortion, it must rise above the substantial health risks that many parents of older children are forced to take every day. For a health exception to count as a proportionately serious reason, the risk would have to be such that the mother is in serious danger of death; but, as we saw above, this is already covered with the life-of-the-mother exception.

"What about rape?" This very direct and difficult question was put to a colleague and friend of mine several years ago when he was participating in an abortion protest. His response was: "I'm against it." This brief exchange manages to reveal two very important things about the abortion debate. First, many who have critical questions about a "pro-life" position on abortion often have in mind difficult cases like rape, where a woman has been assaulted and is using abortion as a way of defending herself from one of the consequences of that assault. Second, the "I'm against it" joke reveals that far too many "pro-lifers" are often flippant and disrespectful when it comes to discussing the rape exception. While it is true that the prenatal child should not be punished for the horrific behavior of her biological father, it is not clear that a woman who has been raped has the same obligation to aid a fetus as someone who has had consensual sex. That this question has not been given more thoughtful consideration within the public leadership of many "pro-life" communities is just the latest example of our culture's refusing to take sexual violence against women seriously. Not least because nearly one in five women can expect to be victims of some kind of sexual violence during their lifetimes, we must be willing to have new and difficult conversations about abortion in these cases.

In fact, the difference between abortion in the case of consensual sex and in the case of rape comes out in the response most of my students have to Thomson's violinist analogy. Being kidnapped in the middle of the night and attached to the violinist, they say, is much more like becoming pregnant as the result of sexual violence than the result of consensual sex. Whether it is the forty-something looking for a hookup in New York City, or the person who consents to the hookup, everyone knows on some level that one biological point of a man and woman having sex is to produce children. Biologically speaking, that is a central part of what the sex organs were created to do. This is why we can and do ask both men and women to "take responsibility for their actions" when it comes to supporting children who result from consensual sexual activity.

But our duties are much less clear when pregnancies come about as a result of sexual violence.[31] Suppose the NYC man, instead of being the aggressor, was given a date-rape drug and sexually assaulted by the woman. Does he still have a moral and legal duty to pay millions of dollars in child support? If it is not clear that he does, then it is not clear why we should ask a woman to support a child with her body who was similarly conceived. It is true that the father's financial support may not be necessary to keep the child alive, while (at least preterm) the mother's support is so required. But does this really mean that the mother's duty is different from the father's? Perhaps. But if you accept this distinction, you need to be very, very careful, for it has consequences you may not be ready to accept.

If it is true that a special duty to aid a child exists simply because a person will die without your help, this has dramatic moral implications in other areas of your life. Anyone in the United States with a middle-class lifestyle who is reading these words can put the book down — right now — and pick up his smart phone or laptop and save a life by pressing some buttons. Again, children all over the world are dying of easily preventable diseases by the millions, and they could be saved if you donate to Oxfam or Catholic Relief Services. Does the fact that these children will die without your aid give you a strong obligation to get on your smart phone right now and do this? How strong a duty? Are you guilty of murder if you do not aid these children who will otherwise die?

Traditional Christian theology, along with the teaching of the Catholic Church, claims that one does have a very strong duty to aid such children. Indeed, if we use our excess money on luxuries rather than simply on what we need to flourish as human beings, both the church fathers and the Catholic *Catechism* say that we are guilty of *indirect homicide*.[32] But again, refusing to aid does not mean that we are guilty of direct killing. And determining whether we have a proportionately serious reason for spending money on, say, a modest vacation rather than a donation to an aid organization must be done on a case-by-case basis. Again, though mothers (and fathers) have a stronger duty to aid their own children than to aid the children of others, something similar should be said about a woman who must decide whether or not to aid a prenatal child who appeared in her body as a result of sexual violence. Some women will have a duty to aid such a child, but perhaps others will have a proportionately serious reason for ceasing to aid via indirect abortion.[33] It does not appear to be something we can decide in the abstract.

Methods of Indirect Abortion

Let us remind ourselves that, in thinking harder about these exceptions, one does not compromise the beliefs of most "pro-lifers" (and the settled doctrine of the Catholic Church) that it is always wrong to aim at the death of an innocent person. We are discussing *indirect* abortion, where the aim of the procedure (both end and means) has nothing to do with the death of the fetus. The choice is to refuse or cease to aid the prenatal child, and the death of the child is "foreseen but not intended." Of course, there must be a proportionately serious reason for allowing the death to take place, and we have seen that such reasons are very, very rare.

We have already discussed a few different methods of indirect abortion. One can abort pregnancy by the induction of labor, removing the uterus, or cesarean section without aiming at the death of the fetus. These are morally different from direct abortions, which by their very nature attack the prenatal child. But while these techniques are suited to circumstances that arise later in pregnancy, they don't seem to work well for situations early in pregnancy.[34] Suppose, for instance, that a victim of sexual violence finds out she is pregnant, and at an early stage she discerns that she has a proportionately serious reason for ceasing to aid the fetus. What methods would be available to her?

For starters — and even at an orthodox Catholic hospital — she may be given the drug known as "Plan B." This may surprise some readers familiar with the church's teaching against contraception, but the idea here is that victims of sexual violence are in a special, exceptional situation. They have the right essentially to defend themselves against becoming pregnant as a result of rape. Thinking about taking Plan B as "defending against pregnancy" makes good sense if the drug stops ovulation such that an egg is prevented from being there to meet the rapist's sperm. But what if an embryo has already been created? Isn't Plan B an "abortifacient," which can also stop an embryo from implanting into the uterus?

The Connecticut Catholic Bishops responded to this concern in the following way:

The administration of Plan B pills in this instance cannot be judged to be the commission of an abortion because of such doubt about how Plan B pills and similar drugs work and because of the current impossibility of knowing from the ovulation test whether a new life is present. To administer Plan B pills without an ovulation test is not an intrinsically evil act.[35]

This view is bolstered by several respected "pro-life" bioethicists, including the renowned Dan Sulmasy, who claims that the chances of Plan B refusing to allow an embryo to implant are vanishingly small.[36] But the views of Sulmasy and the Connecticut Bishops are contested, not least because the marketers of Plan B previously advertised the fact that it would refuse to allow an embryo to implant in the uterus.[37] Another drug sometimes administered after sexual violence, Ella, works up to five days after sex and is much more likely than Plan B to have an abortifacient effect if an embryo is already present. How are we to think of the use of drugs that refuse the embryo the chance to implant in the uterus?

For starters, we should say that such use is not (necessarily) aiming at death. Returning to Thomson's case, taking an abortifacient drug in the case of rape would be analogous to fighting off the attempts of the Society of Music Lovers to attach your body to that of the violinist. In doing so, you do not intend the violinist to die (though you foresee it will happen); rather, you defend your body against being forced to sustain the body of the violinist. If being the victim of sexual violence could serve as a proportionately serious reason for having an indirect abortion, there seems to be nothing intrinsically evil about giving rape victims Plan B or even Ella in their attempts to defend their bodily integrity after a rape.

But even Ella works for only a few days after pregnancy. It often takes a victim of sexual violence substantial time simply to come to grips with what has happened. Would there be indirect options available to a pregnant victim of sexual assault? In theory there could be a hysterectomy or even cesarean section, but these involve intense surgical procedures that carry substantial risk. Sometimes Plan B and Ella are confused with the "abortion pill," otherwise known as RU-486. One result of this confusion is that few know how RU-486 actually works. Basically, it cuts off the pregnancy hormone (progesterone), which then detaches the fetus from the uterus and flushes it from the woman's body by inducing a period. This can abort a pregnancy in the United States through week eight.

Is taking RU-486 a direct abortion? Recall that the act of surgical abortion of its very nature involves a direct attack on the body of the pre-natal child. The drugs present in RU-486, by contrast, do not, by their very nature, appear to attack the fetus. Instead, the drug cuts off the pregnancy hormone, and the fetus is detached from the woman's body. Back to Thomson's analogy: using RU-486 is like removing yourself from the violinist once you are already attached. You don't aim at his death, but instead remove yourself because you don't think you have the duty to support his life with your body. Remaining attached to the violinist is a huge burden, and you find yourself in this situation as a result of violence. If you choose to remove yourself, the violinist's death is foreseen but unintended. Perhaps we should think similarly about the case of a victim of sexual assault taking RU-486.[38] She need not aim at the death of the prenatal child in order to choose to cease to aid the child with her body. And though we should pay attention to the many stories of women who have found pregnancy in the case of rape to be a blessing,[39] we should also accept the experiences of women who are burdened by such pregnancies at least as much as someone forced to remain attached to the violinist.[40]

Conclusion

We began this chapter by noting that many who engage in the abortion debate are speaking past each other on these matters. "Pro-lifers" understand abortion as direct killing of an innocent child, and they cannot imagine how this could be justified by claims about the "right" to do whatever a woman wants to with her body. On the other side, many with "pro-choice" views see abortion, not as direct killing, but as refusing to aid the fetus; they, in turn, cannot imagine how one could consider women to have the right to self-determination without having the right to bodily integrity.

We can now see, however, where much of the confusion is coming from. "Pro-lifers" are correct in saying that the overwhelming majority of surgical abortions are direct killings and aim at the death of the prenatal child. However, the "pro-choice" insight is also important: some abortions are indirect and better understood as refusals to aid. Even according to strict "pro-life" Catholic ethics, indirect abortions could be morally acceptable for a proportionately serious reason. Furthermore, if we apply our moral principles from other contexts consistently, it looks like a woman could use deadly force against a fetus who was threatening her life. Yes, this prenatal child is formally innocent, but materially (and tragically) she is a mortal threat to her mother.

But let us keep in mind that the incredibly strong expectations our culture has for parents to care for their children. The exceptions discussed in this chapter (life of the mother and rape) constitute a tiny minority of the 1.2 million abortions procured each year in the United States. We should never forget that most prenatal children are killed via abortion because they are inconvenient. Especially if you are concerned about those with power using violence to radically reduce the dignity of vulnerable, voiceless people on the margins, this simply cannot stand. Basic respect for persons requires that we root out such radically unjust practices and defend the dignity of those voiceless, helpless persons who cannot defend themselves.

But we should never be lured into making a defense of the fetus that causes us to neglect the equal value and rights of her mother. Despite the difficult and tragic nature of the exceptional cases where a baby threatens her mother's life, or when a mother becomes pregnant as a result of sexual violence, loving both mother and child means that we must energetically and carefully explore the difficult issues presented in this chapter. And I am not alone in this point of view. Both Pope Benedict XVI and the Congregation for the Doctrine of the Faith have encouraged Catholic ethicists to explore the question of the "life exception" in more detail.[41] There must be no retreat from the view that every one of our prenatal children are full and equal persons who deserve equal protection of the law. But what that protection means in these exceptional circumstances poses difficult and disputed questions.[42]

CHAPTER FOUR

The Challenge of Public Policy

Introduction

Suppose you are pretty much on board with the arguments I've made up until this point. Maybe you agree that the prenatal child is a person with moral full status and deserves equal protection of the law. Perhaps you also agree that one should never aim at the death of the fetus (except in self-defense) and, except for a proportionately serious reason, that one is morally obligated to care for and sustain a prenatal child. Does it follow directly from these claims that abortion must be made broadly illegal? Not at all. Doing so requires us to ask further questions. What aspects, if any, of these very personal matters should be legislated in a culture that guarantees freedom of (and from) religion? Might the criminalization of abortion actually produce more harm than good? Is effective and coherent enforcement of such a public policy even *possible*?

That it might be reasonable to agree with the "pro-life" arguments I've made in the previous two chapters, and yet give "pro-choice" answers to these questions, is even more evidence of the inadequacy of these categories. Indeed, it shows quite clearly, not only that one could be "pro-choice" on multiple levels and for multiple reasons, but also that not everyone who describes herself as "pro-choice" is "pro-abortion." One could absolutely despise abortion, considering it a very serious evil, and yet reluctantly conclude that we have no good way of reflecting such judgments in U.S. law.

The Catholic Church, it turns out, is broadly aware of this next level of complexity in the abortion debate:

However, if the reasons given to justify an abortion were always manifestly evil and valueless, the problem would not be so dramatic. The gravity of the problem comes from the fact that in certain cases, perhaps in quite a considerable number of cases, by denying abortion one endangers important values to which it is normal to attach great value, and which may sometimes even seem to have priority. We do not deny these very great difficulties.[1]

One very difficult consideration, most often raised by "pro-choice" advocates, is the possibility that the equal moral standing of women in our culture could be threatened by any broadly "pro-life" public policy on abortion. (This very important and complex topic deserves its own detailed and intense consideration, and that discussion follows in chapter 5.) Our discussion in this chapter begins by engaging the view that religious conclusions about abortion should not be the basis of public policy, particularly in view of the strong guarantee of religious freedom afforded by the United States. Next we will explore when and if public policy should reflect moral claims about abortion. Could a public policy banning abortion actually fail to prevent abortion and merely serve to harm the health of women? We now have evidence that suggests that a culture's laws helps teach that culture right and wrong. What role should this play in crafting abortion public policy? This chapter concludes by exploring what it might mean to have just legal punishment for those involved in obtaining an abortion.

Religion and Public Policy

Religious ideas and perspectives are strongly connected to our American public discourse on many topics, but they appear to play a special role in the abortion debate. Religious organizations so dominate the public "pro-life" movements that, despite the existence of many secular groups, many simply assume that one must have strong religious beliefs to take a position that calls abortion into serious question. The previous two chapters discussed very deep and "thick" moral ideas: what it means to be a person, what it means to kill, and so on. Answers to these questions just seem to be based on personal values that are fundamentally religious. The well-known secular philosopher Michael Tooley, for instance, recently claimed the following:

About the only alternative to a philosophical approach to ethics is an appeal to revealed religion, and so it is that many antiabortionists appeal to some book that they consider sacred, or to the teaching of their own religion or sect, or to some personal religious experience, either as a source of some relevant moral principle, or in support of some theologically orientated claim about the nature of human beings — such as that humans have immaterial souls.[2]

Tooley, as you may be able to tell, is not happy about the "great gulf" he believes exists between the approaches of the good guys (philosophers) and the bad guys (religious folks) on abortion-related questions. Indeed, he specifically calls out those who take a philosophical approach for not being as forthright as they should be about why those who take a religious approach should be rejected — especially in the American abortion public debate. He argues that any claim concerning some "alternative source of revealed truth" should be severely critiqued by those who use philosophy rather than religion to discuss abortion.[3]

But especially in today's postmodern world, Tooley's criticism of the religious approach as somehow fundamentally different from his own actually risks undermining his own secular approach. A moment's thought reveals that there is no purely secular "view from nowhere" from which someone can look at *any* ethical issue, but especially one as complex as abortion. The best philosophers and theologians over the past two generations have demonstrated that so-called "secular" or "philosophical" approaches also work within traditions that appeal, without argument, to fundamental first principles.[4] If you ask such thinkers why they accept such principles, they usually appeal to some sort of authority, faith, or intuition. As we saw in the introduction to this book, secular utilitarians rely heavily on two foundational faith claims: (1) our fundamental moral duty is to calculate and maximize good outcomes, and (2) in making this calculation, one person counts only one and none more than one. These secular doctrines are understood as true without argument and come from the authority of several magisterial figures in the utilitarian tradition (Bentham, Mill, Sidgwick, Singer, and so forth) and from an accepted, authoritative group of texts understood to belong to the utilitarian canon. Explicitly religious concepts like "faith" or "the sacred" are not generally used, but Tooley's "great gulf" between secular and religious approaches to abortion is simply imagined. If the authoritative first principles of secular utilitarians are fair game for use in our public debate over abortion, then authoritative religious moral principles should be welcomed as well. This doesn't mean we must accept either set of principles, but it does mean that neither set of principles can or should be ruled out of the discussion of abortion public policy.

But a slightly different concern about the relationship among religion, abortion discourse, and public policy has been raised by the Christian ethicist Paul Simmons. He argues, from the legal tradition of religious freedom in the United States, that "no group should seek to impose its own moral/theological beliefs on others who hold differing beliefs regarded as equally personal and sacred." Instead, our public policy should have "tolerance" for multiple points of view on abortion.[5] Simmons has special skepticism about laws that "rest on abstract metaphysical opinion." Wouldn't forming public policy on this basis be a classic example of infringing on the religious freedom of others? In a culture that values such freedom, we must first come to some consensus about issues like the moral status of the prenatal child — and not through "abstract metaphysical speculation" but through a "democratic process in which every perspective is subject to critical analysis."[6] Much like Tooley, Simmons believes that when "pro-life" advocates appeal to the authority of their foundational moral principles, it rules them out of our public, pluralistic culture — one that should be governed instead by democratic consensus.[7] The largely religious principles that support "pro-life" views, therefore, should not be the basis of an American public policy on abortion given that they attempt to impose an authoritative understanding that undermines the religious freedom of those who do not share this understanding.

But Simmons makes a mistake similar to Tooley's. While he criticizes the use of authority in the method of his "pro-life" religious opponent, he misses how authority functions in his own point of view. In a paragraph that immediately follows his insistence that a democratic process be followed, Simmons says the following:

> Part of the genius of *Roe v. Wade* (now affirmed by *Casey*) was putting forward the standard of viability: that stage of development at which the fetus has sufficient neurological and physiological maturation to survive outside the womb. Prior to that, the fetus simply is not sufficiently developed to speak meaningfully of it as an independent being deserving and requiring the full protection of the law, i.e., a person. The notion of viability correlates biological maturation with personal identity in a way that can be accepted by reasonable people. It violates

no group's religious teachings or any premise of logic to provide protection for a viable fetus. The same can hardly be said for those efforts to establish moral and legal parity between a zygote (fertilized ovum) and a woman, which create substantive First Amendment issues.

We have already seen several of the deep problems with using viability to determine the moral status of the fetus, including the fact that viability seems to be a function of whatever time or social situation in which the prenatal child happens to be living. Furthermore, it is not clear why Simmons's claim about biological maturity correlating with the development of the person is something that "can be accepted by reasonable people," while the "pro-life" claim that all members of Homo sapiens, regardless of age or condition of dependency on another, are persons "creates substantive First Amendment issues." Both are abstract metaphysical claims about the understanding of the person. Both are claims about which reasonable people agree and disagree. In fact, those people who reject Simmons's understanding of the person could and should claim that his view imposes on *their* liberties and those of the prenatal children they are trying to protect. Such a person might also argue that Simmons's understanding of the person undermines her view that the most vulnerable human beings — especially those who are completely dependent on others — deserve special moral and legal protection. Note that even a "pro-choice" advocate interested in defending late-term abortion might claim that Simmons should not be imposing his "abstract metaphysical point of view" about the fetus after viability. He might reply that he is not imposing it, and that this is simply the view of the Supreme Court in *Roe* and *Casey*; but again, authoritative judicial fiats (like those about viability) impose precisely the kind of "abstract metaphysical point of view" that Simmons says should be avoided. The Supreme Court cases he cites circumvented the very democratic process that he advocates.

To drive this point home, let's consider two other cases of public policy that involve abstract metaphysical and religious claims about vulnerable populations. Peter Singer, as we saw in chapter 2, argues that our views about human infants are largely based on ideas from a Christian era (and its ethic of the sanctity of human life) that are now well beyond their sell-by date. Indeed, it wasn't until Christianity came to power that the West came to see anything wrong with infanticide. Because a newborn infant is not rational and self-aware, and because mere membership in the species Homo sapiens isn't morally significant, Singer argues that the idea

89

that a newborn infant is a person (and that a parent should be forced to support this individual) is also essentially based on a religious principle. Our culture simply isn't fully aware of it just yet.

Second, consider the debate over slavery. The first country in the West (unless one counts ancient Ireland after its evangelization by St. Patrick)[8] to morally and legally condemn the slave trade was Great Britain, a country whose abolition movement was led by an unapologetic and ferociously evangelical Christian, William Wilberforce. He said:

> Let us not despair; it is a blessed cause, and success, ere long, will crown our exertions. Already we have gained one victory; we have obtained, for these poor creatures, the recognition of their human nature, which, for a while was most shamefully denied. This is the first fruits of our efforts; let us persevere and our triumph will be complete. Never, never will we desist till we have wiped away this *scandal from the Christian name* [emphasis added], released ourselves from the load of guilt, under which we at present labour, and extinguished every trace of this bloody traffic, of which our posterity, looking back to the history of these enlightened times, will scarce believe that it has been suffered to exist so long a disgrace and dishonour to this country.[9]

Time and time again Wilberforce used hardcore Christian theology at the heart of his "abstract metaphysical claims" about the moral status of African slaves. This would eventually lead to his leading an abolition movement, and this movement would change the public policy of Great Britain regarding slavery. But this was not accomplished without a number of political fights. And many of Wilberforce's opponents argued that the Africans sold into slavery, though clearly Homo sapiens, were examples of human beings who were "slaves by nature" and not fully rational and autonomous persons. They certainly did not accept the "abstract metaphysical views" of Wilberforce and the other abolitionists.

If we were to accept Simmons's views of religious freedom, how should we think about making public policy that addresses infanticide and slavery? The shift of law in the West to reflect the dignity of infants and slaves imposed an abstract metaphysical view of the person on many who did not accept this view. The first shift dramatically affected the religious and reproductive freedom of Roman families who understood "social birth" of children to take place several weeks after biological birth. The second shift dramatically affected the religious and economic liberty of slave traders with families and communities who depended on this line of work. Indeed, there are even those around today with an "abstract metaphysical view" that rejects the idea that infants or people of color have full personal dignity. It looks as if Simmons must claim that these shifts of policy in the West, precisely because they impose a contested view of the person — which comes explicitly from a religious tradition not shared by all — were mistaken and violated the religious liberty of those who disagree.

I hope that almost all of us reject this approach. Our postmodern world has called into question the neat and clean divisions between "secular" or "philosophical" ideas that can be accepted by "reasonable people" on the one hand, and "religious" ideas or "abstract metaphysics" on the other. *No one,* whether she is making a case for abortion or any other public policy, has a "view from nowhere" in which the first principles of her particular moral tradition are accepted by all "reasonable people." At least if we care about justice for the most vulnerable, we simply cannot reflect and respect all points of view in our law and public policy. If justice is to prevail, one set of values about who counts as a member of a vulnerable population (and what is demanded of us in supporting those individuals) must defeat another set of values. It is up to those who would like to see our set of values prevail to convince others of our point of view.[10] In thinking about how this process of debate and persuasion works, we must not rule out certain values simply because they are associated with a "religious" tradition rather than a "secular" tradition. Doing so relies on a kind of bigotry directed against those who are open and honest about the fact that faith and intuition are the basis of their foundational views. They should not be marginalized simply because they admit something that is true of every person in our public debates, whether religious or secular.

Practical Considerations

But suppose a set of moral values and principles has, in fact, prevailed in our public sphere. What should the relationship be between such values and principles and our society's public policy and law? The Catholic moral theologian and legal scholar Cathleen Kaveny has argued that we cannot simply have a knee-jerk reaction that attempts to reflect every moral principle in our public policy. Indeed, Kaveny argues that if we follow Saint Thomas Aquinas on this question, there needs to be "a proper distance" between moral and legal claims if we want to achieve the common good.[11] Kaveny uses Thomas's thought to argue for a view of the law that is "quintessentially practical," one that is sensitive to politics and other factors specific to the context in which law is made (p. 357). Law should not and cannot be understood in a contextless vacuum without reference to a particular situation and context.

For instance, Kaveny worries that a drastic change in settled law might destabilize a "firm sense of the Constitution" and even "the binding power of the law" altogether (p. 358). Whatever goods could come from changing a law, the decision to change it must be weighed against the harm that could come from the change. She also asks us to consider the possibility that a law or public policy would not, in fact, "deter, detract, and punish" the relevant harm it is intended to address (p. 376). For instance, a law may reflect a good moral principle but require a level of personal strength so high that most people will end up breaking the law. This might actually work against the common good, and even against the very goods the law was attempting to protect. Kaveny notes that Aquinas himself argued against enforcement of a particular law that, though it attempted to defend a good moral principle, would actually result in greater evils that were present in the situation the law was trying to remedy. Not everything that is true about the natural moral law, he says, should be reflected in the positive law issued by government. This leads Thomas to claim that even actions that are intrinsically evil, like prostitution, should not necessarily be prohibited by law.[12]

Kaveny wants to apply each of these insights to public policy about abortion. Would a change in our abortion law violate the "settled" nature of our public policy? Especially around the time of Senate confirmation hearings for a nominee to the Supreme Court, we are often told that the law that has come from *Roe v. Wade* is, in fact, "settled" and cannot (or should not) be changed. I will say more about the reality of the Supreme Court's views on abortion in chapter 6, but there are several reasons to question the idea that our abortion law is "settled."

At the time this book goes to press, for instance, there are four Supreme Court justices who at least appear to support the central conclusion of *Roe,* there are four who do not, and one (Justice Anthony Kennedy) who appears to have a more complicated view. If another justice who is skeptical of *Roe*'s conclusion were appointed, or Kennedy began leaning in an even more "pro-life" direction, *Roe* would likely be dramatically changed — or even overturned. Furthermore, it is not at all clear just *what kind* of law has supposedly been settled. As Kaveny points out, the Supreme Court's decision in *Webster* significantly restricts the central finding of *Roe* by allowing states to limit abortion rights in various controversial ways (p. 344). Paul Simmons was very concerned that the Court's decision in *Casey* not only defend *Webster*'s restrictions (such as mandatory informed consent and waiting periods for those seeking abortions),[13] but also essentially rejected two key aspects of *Roe:* the trimester system and the use of a constitutional right to privacy as the essential legal consideration, which gives rise to abortion rights.[14] Furthermore, we now have a record number of state laws attempting to restrict access to abortion.[15] They range from "personhood" amendments designed to give equal protection of the law for prenatal human beings, to banning abortion coverage in government-sponsored insurance policies, to limiting abortion after a fetus could possibly feel pain. Abortion law is hardly "settled" in the United States. Indeed, part of the reason there is an opening for a book like the one you are reading is that American law and public opinion surrounding abortion are currently in a state of confusion and flux.

But what about the worry that it is simply impractical to enforce a law protecting prenatal human life? Kaveny suggests that

> under no circumstances would criminal sanctions ever be sufficient to ensure the well-being of the unborn. The project of giving birth to a healthy baby requires the active cooperation of the mother in a way which could never be secured by penal prohibitions. She must eat right, rest and exercise properly, abstain from drugs and alcohol, and obtain adequate medical care. A pregnant woman must acquire, sometimes in tremendously difficult circumstances, many of the virtues of a mother, often putting the good of the one she carries ahead of her own wishes and desires. (p. 376)

Along with the Congregation for the Doctrine of the Faith, we should admit that there is no denying these great difficulties. But they need to be balanced against our culture's central interest in fundamental justice — particularly when it involves protecting all persons equally under law, and particularly when a certain set of persons are vulnerable to violence from those who find their dignity inconvenient. Consider that Kaveny's point also applies not only to a pregnant mother, but also to a mother who has just given birth. Those who think like Peter Singer or Michael Tooley could use their reasoning to claim that not only are the rights of newly born human beings contested, but also that under no circumstances would criminal sanctions ever be sufficient to ensure the well-being of the *newly born*. The project of taking care of a healthy baby requires the active cooperation of the mother in a way which could never be secured by penal prohibitions. She must give the baby proper food and medical care, spend sufficient time with the child, make sure that the child learns how to do all the things that flourishing human beings need to learn. She must acquire, sometimes in tremendously difficult circumstances, many of the virtues of a mother, often putting the good of her child ahead of her own wishes and desires. (p. 376)

Surely these considerations, while important, should have absolutely nothing to do with whether newborn children deserve equal protection of the law. Nor should they have any implications for whether prenatal children deserve equal protection of the law.

But Kaveny highlights another important question: Should the law "recognize that it is sometimes beyond the capacity of women of ordinary virtue to carry certain pregnancies to term without condoning the destruction of fetal life?" After all, "recognizing that law is framed for the average person" might mean that some abortions that are morally wrong "nevertheless ought not to bring down upon those who obtain them the full weight of the criminal law" (pp. 378-79). These are certainly true statements as far they go, but we need to know more precisely what is meant by "certain pregnancies" and "some abortions." Using the arguments we examined in the previous chapter, what would be a proportionate reason for a mother to stop sustaining her child? How often would it be "beyond the capacity" of the average person to do this?

As we have seen, there are clear cases in which even strong "prolifers" would be sympathetic to this kind of reasoning, especially in the cases where the mother's bodily integrity has been assaulted by threats to her health or by sexual violence. But we saw in chapter 1 that the overwhelming majority of abortions are done in the name of birth control — and often even on the basis of a mental disability like Down syndrome. And if we consider that a substantial majority of others never have an abortion, it then seems that the number of pregnancies that are "beyond the virtue of the average person" to support (while certainly significant and worthy of our close attention)[16] are a tiny percentage of the 1.2 million abortions procured annually in the United States. Indeed, if one considers the prenatal child to be a person (who, again, is in a particularly vulnerable position), then it would take a very powerful reason indeed to decide to terminate such support. After all, one of the law's fundamental tasks is to protect the most vulnerable from those who have an interest in their dignity not being recognized and supported.

Kaveny's basic point is more convincing when it works *with,* rather than *against,* the law's duty to protect the most vulnerable. What if a law criminalizing abortion was unable to protect prenatal children, and its primary effect was to seriously threaten the lives of vulnerable women? Some argue that criminalizing abortion would not significantly change the number of women who procure abortions, and the huge number of now illegal abortions would put the health and lives of a large number of (especially poor) women at risk. Given the possibility that it might undermine the very good it is designed to protect — the lives of the most vulnerable — "pro-lifers" must honestly wrestle with the following question: Is criminalizing abortion the right approach if one wishes to defend the dignity of both the prenatal child and her mother?

Criminalizing Abortion: More Harm Than Good?

One person who makes a forceful version of the above argument is "pro-choice" activist Cristina Page. Like many others, she claims that, if abortion were to be criminalized,

> it's likely that a clandestine, illegal underground will emerge again to meet the need for abortions, a need that virtually no one believes will disappear. After all, research shows that even when abortion was previously illegal in the United States, women had abortions. Indeed, the number of women who had abortions has remained fairly constant over the decades. The only thing that legality changes is whether abortions will be safe.[17]

To the now familiar images of back alleys and coat hangers, Page adds bleach and castor oil injections, squatting in scalding hot water, and hammering one's stomach with a meat pulverizer. At best, we are told, we can expect illegal and unsafe abortions to be performed by less experienced and greedy physicians. These are frightening images and ideas, and when combined with trustworthy statistics about what happens when abortion is made illegal, they can become the basis of a powerful "pro-choice" argument. Especially if it would not change the number of women who get abortions, who could possibly advocate for a public policy that leads to such horrific situations?

But *do* we have trustworthy statistics? As early as 1970, the great "pro-choice" bioethicist Daniel Callahan argued that we do not:

> But how many illegal abortions and how many injuries and deaths? . . . [T]he available data from all over the world are poor. Rarely are illegal abortions reported to the public-health authorities, much less to the police . . . . Those strongly favoring liberalized laws are prone to cite very high estimates, and those opposed, to cite very low estimates. Most often, some very broad estimate is cited (e.g., 200,000-1,200,000 illegal abortions every year in the United States), so broad as to be all but useless in determining how extensive the problem of illegal abortions actually is.[18]

Indeed, Callahan notes that a statistics committee commissioned by a 1955 Planned Parenthood conference on abortion found that there was "no objective basis for the selection of a particular figure between these two estimates as an approximation of the actual frequency."[19]

With that limitation clearly in mind, let us examine some other data. As noted above, it is fragmentary and difficult to interpret, but in order for Page's very strong claim to be convincing, we should expect to find hard numbers from when abortion was illegal to be similar to those of the contemporary period. In the last decade or so, there have been about 1.2 million abortions per year in the United States; about 22 percent of all pregnancies during that time have ended in abortion.[20] More than 30 percent of American women have abortions by the time they are forty-five years old.[21] However, according to a study of 22,657 women from the late 1930s by demographer Raymond Peal, only about 1.4 percent of all pregnancies among white women (0.5 percent for black women) ended in illegal abortion. Despite taking place during a time when abortion estimates were being revised sharply higher, the Kinsey studies at Indiana University conducted in the 1950s found that only 22 percent of the women they surveyed had had at least one abortion by the time they were forty-five years old.[22] But perhaps the most telling trend could be found if we had statistics just after abortion was legalized in all fifty states in 1973, and could then compare them to the statistics a few years down the road. In that first year after *Roe v. Wade,* there were approximately 750,000 women who had abortions, or one abortion for about every four live births. However, just seven years later the numbers had risen dramatically to 1,600,000 women getting abortions, or one abortion *for every two* live births.[23]

Of course, if these are trustworthy statistics, one could argue that the abortion rates were lower before abortion became legal, not because of fear of criminal penalties or because it was more burdensome (cost, travel, etc.) to obtain an abortion, but because there was a stigma and public consciousness surrounding abortion that made people less likely to seek it. The apparent shift toward more abortions might have been not primarily a function of a more permissive public policy, but rather the result of changing social attitudes about abortion. But especially in light of Kaveny's important point about the law's capacity to teach our culture right and wrong, this argument cuts both ways.[24] Since the law is such a powerful teacher, recriminalizing abortion would certainly help form public consciousness about the morality of abortion — with much the same force that its legalization had on our culture.[25]

But what of the claims that the lives of women are seriously threatened by making abortion illegal? Daniel Callahan highlights a study claiming to show that illegal abortion accounted for one-third of all maternal deaths between 1957 and 1962. And another Guttmacher study done on New York maternal deaths suggested that illegal abortion was responsible for a whopping 50 percent of such deaths. But these numbers (and any conclusions drawn from them), says Callahan, need to be called into question in light of other data. Significantly, there was a steep drop in maternal mortality related to abortion between 1927 and 1945. By 1940 the known abortion death figures in New York City were half of what they had been in 1921.[26] The physician and public health scholar Mary S. Calderone, writing in 1960, claimed that abortion, whether legal or illegal, "is no longer a dangerous procedure." Indeed, while the maternal death rate related to abortion was going down "strikingly" from 1921 through 1957, we know that the population and birth rate were rising dramatically. How can both be true? Calderone explains:

> Two corollary factors must be mentioned here: first, chemotherapy and antibiotics have come in, benefiting abortion along with all surgical procedures as well as abortion. Second . . . 90 per cent of all illegal abortions are presently being done by physicians. Call them what you will, abortionists or anything else, they are still physicians, trained as such; and many of them are in good standing in their communities.[27]

What can we say about Page's argument at this point? At the very least, we can confidently say that the data that exist do not support her claims. Indeed, a strong case could be made that dramatically fewer women die from abortions today, not primarily because abortion is legal, but because medical technology has improved so dramatically. Yes, it is likely that there will certainly be a number of illegal abortions performed if it is recriminalized. But given that it would still be trained physicians doing the vast majority of such abortions — to say nothing of our improvements in emergency and other kinds of medical care — it is unlikely that the maternal death rate from abortions would rise significantly if most abortions were made illegal.[28]

Why, then, do we so often hear precisely the opposite in our American public discourse? Some "pro-lifers" speculate that inflated numbers are part of scare tactics used by some who support abortion rights. But we need not call it speculation when we have former abortion-rights activists to recount their actual practices. Bernard Nathanson was a physician who performed thousands of abortions (including one on his own wife) and co-founded the National Abortion Rights and Action League (NARAL). He later admitted that he and NARAL simply fabricated estimates of deaths from illegal abortions to aid their public "pro-choice" arguments:

> I confess that I knew the figures were totally false, and suppose the others did too if they stopped to think of it. But in the "morality" of our revolution, it was a useful figure, widely accepted, so why go out of our way to correct it with honest statistics? The overriding concern was to get the [pro-life] laws eliminated, and anything within reason that had to be done was permissible.[29]

Our Contemporary Situation

So, while I believe that we can draw some modest conclusions about the era of illegal abortion in the United States, we lack the hard data necessary to draw confident, sweeping conclusions. This is frustrating. But it is even more frustrating when those like Cristina Page try to draw something more than modest conclusions. Most hard conclusions about abortion during this time period rely, not on data, but on biased speculation in favor of one's already established position on abortion.

But what about our contemporary situation? Perhaps data are better now, and we can bypass this difficulty by focusing on more reliable contemporary evidence? A relatively recent commentary on studies about abortion maternal health done from 1995 to 2008, for instance, was published in a 2012 edition of *The Lancet*.[30] The article claims, "Although the legal status of abortion and risk associated with the procedure are not perfectly correlated, it is well documented that morbidity and mortality resulting from abortion tend to be high in countries and regions characterised by restrictive abortion laws, and is very low when these are liberal." This seems like a major problem for those who wish to claim that legally restricting abortion is the way to get fewer abortions. One problem with this claim, however, is that correlation is different from causation. Generally speaking, countries with permissive abortion laws are rich countries with comparatively excellent health care, while countries with restrictive laws tend to be poor and have comparatively worse health care. If we could examine contemporary Western countries similar to the United States in terms of health care, but with restrictive abortion laws, this would be a better comparison. And it turns out that we have two countries that may fit the bill: Ireland and Poland.

The Irish law against abortion dates back to British rule and the Offenses Against the Person Act of 1861, which criminalized the procedure in both Great Britain and Ireland. When Britain overturned this law in 1967, no such change occurred in Ireland. Roused by the aftermath of *Roe v. Wade* in the United States, Irish "pro-lifers" successfully resisted a similar movement growing on the Emerald Isle:

> Following a [1983] referendum, the Eighth Amendment, known as the 'Pro-Life Amendment', came into existence to deter the legalisation of abortion in the future. The amendment contained three assertions: the unborn's right to life must be protected; the unborn's right to life was equal to that of the mother; and, this right to life would be defended to the greatest degree practicable.[31]

Just two years later, a "pro-life" campaign began to push back against pregnancy groups giving out information about obtaining abortions outside of Ireland. Irish courts made distribution of such information illegal. More recently, the European Court of Human Rights in Strasbourg ruled on a challenge to these very restrictive Irish abortion laws. Though the Court ruled that Ireland needed to make more provisions for abortion in cases where a mother's health was in danger, the basic Irish public policy was upheld. The court found that there is no fundamental legal right to abortion and that member states of the European Union had the freedom to make their own public policies.[32]

The Irish policy, from the data we have, appears to be effective in deterring and reducing abortion. According to Planned Parenthood's research arm, the abortion rate in Ireland in 1996 was 5.9 per 1000 women. Contrast this with the rate across the water in England and Wales: it was almost triple that of Ireland, 15.6 per 1000 women.[33] No doubt cultural differences between the two countries contributed to this difference, but this is consistent with the power of the Irish law to be a moral teacher.[34] There is, however, the consideration that a number of Irish women travel to England to have abortions. The numbers are disputed, but according to the BBC in 2009 there were 4,600 women seeking abortions in Britain who gave an Irish address.[35] It is also worth noting that the trends are making such "abortion tourism" more and more rare: two thousand fewer Irish women sought abortions in Britain in 2009 than did so in 2001, for instance. The significant (though shrinking) numbers of Irish women who go elsewhere to obtain abortions, therefore, is unlikely to be a sufficient explanation of the difference in the abortion rate when comparing Ireland with England.

Despite its restrictive abortion laws, Ireland is one of the safest places in the world for pregnant women.[36] Induction of preterm labor to save the life of the mother, along with excellent prenatal and other health care, has led to very low maternal death rates. Ireland, it turns out, actually has better outcomes for pregnant women than even the United States and the United Kingdom do — both of which have broad access to direct abortion and similar quality of health care. All of these data suggest not only that restricting access to abortion need not harm health outcomes for women, it could even be associated with *better* outcomes.

We have less good information about Poland, but it is still an important example of a relatively rich country with good health care and very serious restrictions on abortion. The communist regime of the 1960s changed a previously restrictive abortion policy to one that legalized abortion on demand. But with the fall of communism, an elected parliament dramatically restricted abortions with a 1993 law prohibiting them in all cases except in case of rape or when the life of the mother was threatened. Not least because of the lack of good data, there is serious disagreement about the size of the gap between the abortion rate under communism and the rate under the restrictive law, but almost everyone agrees that a gap exists. As with Ireland, there is debate about how many Poles travel to other countries for abortion services. These incomplete data indicate that it is simply too strong to say that we *know* Polish abortion restrictions save lives; but the data are at least consistent with that point of view.

And considering *The Lancet*'s argument cited above, we might suspect that there is hard evidence for a significant number of illegal abortions in Poland itself, along with a significant number of women dying from said abortions, given its restrictive abortion laws. However, even according to the (strongly "pro-choice") World Health Organization, Poland had only *nine* maternal deaths from abortion during the three years 1999, 2000, and 2001.[37] Like Ireland, Poland is a dramatically safer place for pregnant women — the data show — than are the United States and the United Kingdom.[38]

Broad Conclusions from the Data?

Can we come to any substantive and responsible conclusions about what happens in a modern, developed Western democracy when abortion is criminalized? We need to take care in not going beyond the data, but I do think we can now say a few significant things. First, though it is not clear how much either the law or other cultural factors affect one's behavior (indeed, they seem to mutually reinforce each other), it is certainly possible for a Western country like the United States to criminalize abortion and have far fewer abortions than similar countries who have not criminalized it. The strong claim made by Page and others that the same number of abortions will take place in a given country whether abortion is criminalized or not — even if we acknowledge that there will be a significant number of illegal abortions or abortions women seek in other countries — is not supported by the data.

Second, we seem to have strong data showing that, before abortion was legalized in places like the United States and Western Europe in the late 1960s and early 1970s, the numbers of women dying from illegal abortions had become very low due to improved medical technology and the fact that trained physicians were the ones doing the overwhelming majority of illegal abortions. If the United States followed the example of Poland and Ireland and criminalized abortion, the vigorous claim by Page and others that large numbers of women would die from illegal abortions does not follow from the available data.

Abortion could be criminalized in the United States in such a way that the important public policy concerns raised by Kaveny and others are answered. The law, both as teacher of morality and with its threat of criminal penalty and financial liability, could protect large numbers of vulnerable prenatal children from being killed. It could achieve its goal without unduly threatening the common good. Let us remind ourselves that fetuses currently have little to no protection of the law and are killed to the tune of 1.2 million each year often simply because they are inconvenient. Though we absolutely should not minimize the significance of women dying from illegal abortions (especially when they are poor, desperate women who are often pressured and coerced by men), the millions and millions of prenatal children killed are the more vulnerable population.[39]

But as a final point to consider in this section of the chapter, let us assume that this is *not* the case. Let us assume for the sake of argument that criminalizing abortion would leave the abortion rate virtually unchanged and that many women would have their health and lives put dramatically at risk. Does it follow that the United States should therefore not criminalize abortion? In answering this question, let us do a somewhat historical thought experiment. Let us go back to a time explored in chapter 2 and imagine a situation in which a growing and influential Christian population is pushing to criminalize infanticide in early fourth-century Rome. Suppose some "pro-choice" supporters of infanticide respond by claiming that, if infanticide were to be criminalized, there would still be a similar number of newborn babies killed by their mothers. Suppose they also mention that under current law such babies are killed in a fairly systematic and pain-free way — and that the current policy even allows for some exposed babies to be adopted. But under the Christian plan of criminalizing infanticide, the killing would take place under the table and hidden from society in a way that would cause more suffering for the infants and throw away any chance they had of being adopted. It would do more harm than good.

Suppose — again just for the sake of argument — that all this was true. Does it follow that infanticide should have remained legal in ancient Rome? Of course not. The fourth-century Christians should have argued that equal protection under the law means that the empire should protect newborn children the same way it protects older human beings. Furthermore, while it is likely the case that infanticides will still happen, and even true that we will likely never be rid of the practice altogether (infanticide still happens in the United States, even today), those who accept the moral value of human infants need to work at changing the culture so that it begins to learn to respect the dignity of newborn infants, and part of th[...] involves using the law's ability to teach morality.

Dissenters like Peter Singer and Michael Tooley notwithstanding, contemporary Western culture sees it as a very good thing that this is precisely what happened. Over a relatively short time, infanticide went from totally acceptable, to illegal, to unthinkable.[40] Though we saw in chapter 3 that abortion is not directly analogous to infanticide, it seems clear that something similar could happen with abortion. The law is an important teacher.

Punishing Abortion Criminals?

Part of what makes a law good, as we saw above, is its capacity to be enforced. But shouldn't there also be coherence with regard to the violation of a law and any punishment that is given in response to its violation? If the law that is being proposed is simply incoherent, then shouldn't this be a reason to reject it? Many people on multiple sides of the abortion debate do think that the law, in the interest of justice, should punish criminals proportionately with the seriousness of their crime. But even very strong "pro-lifers," those who believe abortion involves the grave matter of killing of an innocent person, will rarely suggest that mothers who get illegal abortions (and, sometimes, even the physicians who do actually do them) should be subject to jail time for their actions. While campaigning for his wife's 2008 presidential campaign in Steubenville, Ohio, former President Bill Clinton responded to the challenge of some "pro-life" activists by calling them out on precisely this point:

> You want to criminalize women and their doctors and we disagree. If you were really pro-life, you would want to put every doctor and every mother as an accessory to murder in prison. And you won't say you want to do that because you know that you wouldn't have a lick of political support.[41]

Dennis O'Brien, in his book *The Church and Abortion: A Catholic Dissent,* pushes Clinton's argument even further.[42] He claims that the failure of "pro-life" groups to argue that both physicians and mothers should have punishment proportionate to what they describe abortion to be reveals an inherent contradiction. "The ultimate 'realism' of anti-abortion legis-

…tion," he says, "hinges on the plausibility of making the punishment fit the crime" (pp. 24-25). But according to O'Brien, "pro-lifers" seem to have no interest in the punishment of abortion fitting the crime of abortion. He notes that Catholics were urged to support South Dakota's HB 1215, which bans abortions in all cases except when there was a direct threat to the mother's life; but the bill also states specifically: "Nothing in this Act may be construed to subject the pregnant mother upon whom any abortion is performed or attempted to any criminal conviction and penalty." There were criminal penalties for the abortion provider, but they amounted to, at most, five to ten years in prison — hardly proportionate with the murder of a prenatal child (p. 24).

In a September 2011 exchange he had with Peter Steinfels and Cathleen Kaveny (in a *Commonweal* article titled "Can We Talk about Abortion?"), O'Brien noted that the church's support of this law seems out of step with other stated positions:

> The *Catechism of the Catholic Church* says that abortion is the killing of innocent human life; *Gaudium et spes* says "abortion and infanticide are abominable crimes." What laws and penalties would be appropriate for these stringent condemnations? In older legal codes, such as the British Offenses against the Person Act of 1861, both the abortionist and the woman were subject to a maximum sentence of life imprisonment. That would seem to be a proper penalty for an "abominable crime" . . . . It does not seem wholly off-base to say, then, as some Catholic spokespersons do, that abortion is murder or — escalating that condemnation because of the number of abortions — a form of "genocide." If abortion is "murder," "genocide," and an "abominable crime," that claim does not, to my mind, fit the specifics of HB 1215.[43]

Whatever we think of the punishment of the physician — even from a broadly "pro-life" perspective — the church is right and consistent to argue for leniency and mercy to the mother. After all, it is the physician who actually kills the prenatal child, and not the mother; so the latter should not be subject to the same penalties as the former. In response, O'Brien says this: "If abortion is murder, that would seem strictly analogous to hiring an assassin. Soliciting felony murder would make the woman as guilty, if not more guilty, than the one who pulls the gun or wields the scalpel" (pp. 27-28). The fact that even very serious "pro-lifers" do not think that women should be held responsible in this way, even when they craft the public policy themselves, is strong evidence that the rhetoric that some "pro-lifers" use about abortion being "murder" does not describe what abortion actually involves: the complex, intimate, bodily relationship between a woman and the prenatal child growing inside her.

As we saw in the previous chapter, even if one understands the fetus to be a person with full moral status, many kinds of abortions do not appear to involve the intentional killing of an innocent person. O'Brien may be right with regard to *these* kinds of abortions, and we will return to them in a moment. But let us first examine another important point made by Kaveny in the *Commonweal* dialogue — namely, that O'Brien artificially sets up only two positions. Either abortion must be murder, or the choice should be left up to the mother. She notes:

> The Anglo-American legal tradition has significant resources to resist all-or-nothing dichotomies. In order to do justice to the complexities of a moral dilemma like abortion, the law takes into account not only the status of the victim, but also the circumstances of the perpetrator, as well as other factors such as practical workability. As O'Brien notes, before *Roe*, abortion was a distinct class of offense. If *Roe* is ever overturned, and even if the law then acknowledges the full personhood of the fetus, there would still be good jurisprudential reasons to be extremely sparing in the use of the criminal law to punish those involved in abortions.

Kaveny argues that "O'Brien is mistaken in claiming that it would be hypocritical to punish abortion providers but not the women involved." She says that many "pro-lifers consider women to be abortion's second victims. They want the law to protect them too, not punish them." This point cannot be emphasized enough: most "pro-lifers" I know highlight the men (and often, as we will see in the next chapter, the male-created social structures) who pressure and coerce abortions, and the "pro-lifers" are loath to judge and blame the woman. Some of those with the strongest anti-abortion views are running programs like Rachel's Vineyard, a ministry dedicated to women who have had abortions.[44] Pope John Paul II insisted that "before being something to blame on the woman," abortion "is a crime for which guilt needs to be attributed to men and to the complicity of the general social environment."[45]

The physicians who perform such abortions are not subject to such coercion, and this is another reason to give them a stronger penalty. Indeed, Sean Cardinal O'Malley (head of the U.S. Catholic Bishops' Pro-Life Office) said the following when addressing the 2014 "March for Life":

> The Pro-Life Movement needs to be the merciful face of God to women facing a difficult pregnancy. Being judgmental or condemnatory is not part of the Gospel of Life. . . . The feelings of the woman in the Gospel must be like the young woman caught in a crisis situation of an unwanted pregnancy. She feels overwhelmed, alone, afraid, confused. We must never allow that woman to perceive the Pro-Life movement as a bunch of angry self-righteous Pharisees with stones in their hands, looking down on her and judging her. We want the woman to experience the merciful love of Christ.[46]

O'Brien is skeptical of this approach. For him, there are different levels of coercion that "may or may not offer excuse." Having an abortion "because a gun is at my head is one thing — giving in to pressure from a sex partner is another."[47] But this similar all-or-nothing response fails to understand the complexity of social forces at work in a woman's decision to have an abortion. She may feel pressure, not just from a "sex partner," but from many who hold sweeping and even intimate power over her life: her family, her husband or her boyfriend, even her university or place of employment. Women with children have abortions at a higher rate than those who do not, and in light of these considerations it is not difficult to understand why.[48] Many women feel pressure to have abortions especially from those upon whom they depend for various forms of support for their children. This kind of power imbalance is yet another good reason for distinguishing between women and physicians: the latter, as Cristina Page notes, will do illegal abortions for the money.

But there are also at least two good reasons for the "pro-lifers" mentioned above to support criminalization of abortion in a way that punishes abortion providers as guilty of something less than felony murder. The first is simply a prudential judgment about what is politically possible. From the perspective of a "pro-lifer" who wants to save and protect the lives of prenatal children, it is far better to have the deterrence of a law that threatens five to ten years in prison than to have no law at all. As we have seen above, the function of the law as a teacher of right and wrong can play an important role in creating a culture that comes to understand the equal value of all people — and therefore the need to protect all humans under the law.

But a second reason to punish differently comes from the different moral character of different kinds of abortions. Recall from the previous chapter that, while we discovered that most surgical abortions directly aim at the death of an innocent person, there are some abortions that are not this kind of act, such as those that remove both the fetus and a cancerous uterus, or doing a cesarean section before the child can live outside her mother's body. The Catholic Church will claim that these abortions, while not directly killing an innocent person, can only be performed for a proportionate reason. And saving the mother's life is certainly one such reason. But suppose that an indirect abortion was performed for a reason that was not proportionately serious. Is the refusal to sustain a person when one has a duty to do so the legal equivalent of first-degree murder? No, it is not. First-degree murder must involve the premeditated intent to kill. Perhaps an abortion provider who performs an indirect abortion without a proportionate reason is instead legally guilty of something like manslaughter or reckless homicide, in which case the lower penalty seems like it is proportionate with the seriousness of the crime. Indeed, there is a vast literature exploring the many ways in which different kinds of homicides are punished in the criminal law. I will say more about these matters in the final chapter of the book; but these important distinctions are missing in O'Brien's simplistic argument.

Conclusion

The difficult slog involved in moving from (1) conclusions about abstract moral claims to (2) enacting laws and public policy in a specific context is not discussed enough in our American abortion discourse. But as I think this chapter has shown, to the extent that it is discussed at all, it is often not discussed with honesty, clarity, and attention to complexity. The common arguments saying that religious principles have no place in the public policy of secular Western societies fail to understand that many different kinds of public policies — including the "pro-choice" public policy of the United States — are grounded in contested, abstract, faith-based claims about what a person is (and specific claims about why the fetus doesn't count), the right to privacy, bodily autonomy, and more. Furthermore, given the limited amount of data available to us about public policies on abortion in the past, its interpretation is too easily skewed in the direction of the biases of the interpreter. Strong "pro-choice" claims like "if abortion were criminalized in the United States there wouldn't be fewer abortions" are simply not supported by the data. Similarly, claims like "if abortion were criminalized, large numbers of women (who would otherwise live if abortion remained legal) will die from illegal abortions" are on weak ground. Abortion became the relatively safe procedure it is today well before it was legalized, primarily due to improved medical technology and the fact that well-trained physicians are the ones who do the overwhelming majority of illegal abortions.

Furthermore, the examples of Ireland and Poland show us not only that modern-day Western democracies can find a way to make restrictive abortion laws "work," getting excellent health results for women, while also building a culture that comes to understand the value of prenatal child. Finally, a public policy that gives prenatal children equal protection under the law need not punish women as murderers. The complexity of the act involved in various kinds of abortion, coupled with circumstances where women are coerced, means that our nimble legal tradition can use already-existing resources to nuance the way those who violate abortion laws should be punished.

But there are important considerations of law and public policy, essential to the argument I want to make in this book, which this chapter did not consider. One involves how our society could legally determine certain sets of circumstances in which a good majority of Americans — including many pro-lifers — would agree count as a proportionately serious reason for doing an indirect abortion. Building on the argument of the last chapter, suppose we consider the fact that the mother did not consent to sex as an example of a proportionate reason for getting an indirect abortion. How does this play out in a public policy? Can we legally determine when a woman has had consensual sex? Especially in situations of date/marital rape or of a dramatic power imbalance in the relationship, there often isn't much evidence to show that a particular pregnancy is the result of non-consensual sex. However, because these specific examples play key roles in the public policy compromise that I will call for in the final chapter, I will save the complicated arguments about them when we return to them at that point.

Another essential issue related to abortion public policy that is missing from this chapter was that of the moral and legal status of *women*. Of course, no one in the American public discussion of abortion questions the moral status of women in the way that the moral status of the fetus is being questioned. No one is arguing that women have virtually no moral status and may be killed on demand, including, as we have seen, merely because we find their lives to be inconvenient. However, this kind of argument is on stronger and more interesting ground when it claims that criminalizing abortion limits the sexual and economic freedom and autonomy of women, relative to men, in such a way that makes them de facto unequal in our culture. If abortion is criminalized, it will be women — and not men — who will bear a staggeringly disproportionate physical, financial, and psychological burden for the mutual sexual choices of men and women. This burden, especially when one thinks about it with respect to relationships and career/economic opportunities, effectively gives women a lower moral status than men.

This is a powerful argument. It is so powerful that it deserves a chapter all its own, and it is to that chapter we now turn.

CHAPTER FIVE

Abortion and Women

"If men could get pregnant, abortion would be a sacrament."

Florynce Kennedy, lawyer and feminist civil rights activist

"[Pro-choice feminists] should look rather to their own elitist acceptance of male models of sex and to the sad picture they present of women's lives. Pitting women against their own off-spring is not only morally offensive, it is psychologically and politically destructive."

Sidney Callahan, Hastings Center Distinguished Scholar

Introduction

Men have been deciding what happens to women's bodies for most of human history. Any man who is thinking and writing about abortion should always keep this fact squarely in the front of his mind. Some will go further (for reasons we will see below, and they are often men!) and claim that this history means that men should not offer their views on abortion at all. Or, at the very least, it means that a man's view doesn't "count" in the way that a woman's view should count.

At least at first glance, this would appear to be a classic example of the ad hominem fallacy. Rather than challenging the actual claims or arguments of the person with whom one disagrees, this looks like an attack on the *person* presenting the facts and arguments. In addition to being a fallacy, the attempt to stifle or dismiss the speech or views of a

certain group of people on the basis of their gender (or sexual orientation, race, and so forth) almost always emboldens them with an even
stronger sense that they have the correct position. After all, why engage
in personal attacks unless the facts and arguments aren't on your side?
Furthermore, though it is mostly "pro-choicers" who make this kind of
argument, men turn out to be stronger allies of the "pro-choice" position.
Recall the polls cited in chapter 1 that showed women as more skeptical
of abortion than men. In attempting to marginalize the male voices from
the abortion debate, some "pro-choicers" unwittingly cut off some of
their strongest allies.

But suppose this really isn't about the ad hominem fallacy of attacking men as men, but rather about the fact that men happen to be unable
to experience childbearing and thus cannot understand all the nuances of
what is at stake and are not as affected by abortion ethics and policy. But
this point of view also has implications for many women who are unable
to have the experience of childbearing. If this is truly not an ad hominem
argument against men, then the "lack of experience" argument applies to
both men and women.[1]

My view, however, is that we should reject taking any direction that
would shut certain voices out of the debate based merely on their lack of
personal experience. One does not need to have experienced something in
order to make a valid claim about it. I believe, for instance, that fast-food
corporations ought to pay all of their employees a living wage. Surely, I
should reject a claim made by one of their finance officers who might reply,
"Since you aren't a business owner, and you don't know what it's like to run
a business, you need to stay out of the minimum wage debate. Only those
with experience running a business get to be a part of the argument over
just wages." Slave-owners in the early nineteenth century could have made
a similar argument. So could those currently running child-sex-trafficking
rings. When it comes to those of us who are working for justice for the vulnerable — whether immigrant children, African slaves, McDonald's workers, or prenatal children — it is simply wrong to say that one must "have
experience" in order to critique unjust practices. Indeed, sometimes the
best justice-centered arguments come from those who stand outside this
kind of experience — which can bias and even blind one's point of view.
For instance, those who (unlike the finance officer) have no interest in
exploiting fast-food employees could be better at making justice-centered
critiques. Those who have strong interests connected to the practices being debated are, if anything, the voices of those we should be the most

skeptical about. They are the ones who find the dignity of the vulnerable population most inconvenient.

One of the more important things that this chapter will show is that our broader abortion practices and policies, on the whole, actually serve the interests of men and have had disastrous consequences for women. The Supreme Court justices who proclaimed abortion to be a constitutional right were all men and, as we will see, used legal reasoning that was anything but feminist. Furthermore — and despite being told by educators and the media at every turn that abortion is necessary for their flourishing in modern society — women remain more skeptical about abortion than are men. As we will see throughout this chapter, we should consider both prenatal children and their mothers as vulnerable populations — especially when evaluating our male-created American abortion policy. So while the views of men about abortion should not be dismissed out of hand simply on the basis of their chromosomes, it is absolutely fair game to be skeptical of certain points of view when they entrench the power of one gender and force the other gender into coercive situations.

The first person to really make this kind of argument was Sidney Callahan, whose marriage and professional relationship with fellow bioethics pioneer Daniel Callahan (mentioned several times in the previous chapter) nicely illustrates the point just made above. After briefly looking at their story, and Sidney's arguments, the chapter will then move to consider in more detail how our current abortion law was produced by men and how it serves the interests of men. We will then explore the counterintuitive fact that more choice does not equal more freedom, particularly when it comes to women and abortion rights. Finally, we will examine the view that women overall are hurt by abortion rights, and — far from "choosing" it — are most often pressured and even coerced by many different kinds of forces. Remarkably, we will see that, of the women who seek an abortion and are denied for various reasons, only 5 percent later end up regretting not getting the abortion.

The Story of Sidney and Dan Callahan

Sidney and Dan Callahan were pioneers. The efforts of this dynamic husband-and-wife team led to the founding of the Hastings Center, now the premier place in the world to study bioethics. A key moment came in 1968, when Dan received a grant from the Ford Foundation to do comprehensive research and produce *Abortion: Law, Choice and Mortality.* This came at a time when abortion was just heating up as a national issue, with *Roe v. Wade* (which would end up citing his book) coming a mere five years later. Month after month, day in and day out, Dan and Sidney would talk and argue about the ideas he was exploring in the book. After the research and arguing was complete, Dan came to a "pro-choice" conclusion, while Sidney decided that she was "pro-life." Indeed, after her husband's book came out in support of abortion rights, Sidney responded not only by providing the intellectual support behind the now widely popular and successful group Feminists for Life, but by responding to some of her husband's arguments.

Perhaps her most famous essay is entitled "Abortion and the Sexual Agenda: A Case for Pro-Life Feminism."[2] The essay begins by highlighting and explaining what she takes to be the four main principles of "pro-choice" feminism. In what follows, I summarize this section of her essay:

1. *The autonomous right to control one's own body*
   - A woman choosing an abortion is exercising a basic right to do what she wishes with her body. If she does not want to be pregnant and give birth, she should not be compelled to do so. Just because it is her body that is involved, a woman should have the right to terminate her pregnancy.
   - This is an especially important right in a society in which women cannot count on medical care or social support in pregnancy, childbirth, or child rearing.
2. *Personal responsibility and reproductive freedom*
   - In order to plan, choose, and exercise personal responsibility, one must have control of reproduction. A woman, therefore, must be able to make yes-or-no decisions about a specific pregnancy according to her present situation, resources, prior commitments, and life plan.
   - Abortion is necessary to guarantee women this freedom. Without abortion rights, women's personal moral agency and human consciousness are subjected to biology and chance.
3. *The contingent value of fetal life*
   - A woman must want and value the fetus for it to be considered of moral worth. After all, the process by which a fetus gains social and moral significance can only take place in the body of the woman.
   - The meaning and value of fetal life are constructed and defined by the woman. Without this personal conferral, the only thing left is

a biological process. Thus fetal interests or fetal rights can never outweigh the woman's prior interest and rights.

4. *The right to full social equality*
   - Female social equality depends on being able to compete and participate as freely as males can in the structures of educational and economic life. If a woman cannot control when and how she will be pregnant or rear children, she is at a distinct disadvantage, especially in our male-dominated world.
   - Women should enjoy the basic right of everyone to the free exercise of full sexual expression, separated from procreation. No less than males, women should be able to be sexually active without the constant fear of pregnancy. Therefore, it is necessary for abortion to be available in order for women to participate in our culture on an equal footing with men.

Upon examining the arguments she was having with "pro-choice" feminists, Callahan began to realize that the categories, assumptions, reasoning, and goals with which she was being confronted were not feminist at all. To the contrary, her opponents simply borrowed the categories, assumptions, reasoning, and goals of "pro-choice" men. Indeed, it turned out that the arguments she was hearing from most "pro-choice" feminists were very similar to the ones her husband was making.[3]

In response, Sidney Callahan maintained that each of the above principles must be changed — or even abandoned altogether — if we are to incorporate the insights of an authentic feminism. Again, what follows is my summary of this part of her essay:

1. *A shift from talk about "autonomous control" over one's "own body" to a more inclusive focus on justice and a nonviolent focus on the vulnerable*
   - In pregnancy, a woman's body no longer exists as a single unit but as nurturer and protector of another's life. Pregnancy is not like the growth of cancer or infestation by a biological parasite. It is the way every human being enters the world.
   - Debates similar to those about the fetus were once conducted about the personhood of women and girls. A woman was once viewed as incorporated into the "one flesh" of her husband's person; she, too, was a form of bodily property. In all unjust patriarchal systems, lesser orders of human life are granted rights only when wanted, chosen, or invested with value by the powerful. As

114

recent immigrants from "nonpersonhood," feminists have traditionally fought for justice for both themselves and others who have
their personhood threatened by the powerful.

- Rejecting male aggression and destruction, feminists seek alternative, peaceful, ecologically sensitive means to resolve conflicts. It
is a chilling inconsistency to see pro-choice feminists demanding
continued access to assembly-line, technological methods of fetal
killing. It is a betrayal of feminism, which has built the struggle
for justice on the bedrock of women's empathy and nonviolence.

2. *A shift from "personal responsibility and choice" to a deeper and more
authentic sense of reproductive freedom*

- Morality is sometimes thought of as a matter of human agency and
decisive action, but feminists know that we have moral duties we
do not choose. Morality is hardly limited to contracted agreements
between isolated individuals.
- A pregnant woman, whether or not she has explicitly consented
to the existence of the child, has a moral obligation to the now-
existing and dependent fetus. No pro-life feminist would dispute
the important observations of pro-choice feminists about the extreme difficulties that bearing an unwanted child in our society can
entail. But the stronger force of the fetal claim presses a woman
to accept these burdens: the fetus possesses rights arising from its
extremely vulnerable situation.

3. *A shift from the "contingent value" of human life to a justice-centered
respect for its intrinsic and irreducible value*

- Human beings, from the beginning to the end of their development, have intrinsic value that does not depend on meeting selec-
tive criteria or tests. Human rights arise from human needs, and
it is the very nature of a right, or valid claim upon another, that it
cannot be denied or rescinded by more powerful others.
- It is particularly odd for feminists, who otherwise have justice-
centered concerns to protect the vulnerable from the powerful,
to hold that in the case of the fetus it is the pregnant woman alone
who has the power to bestow or remove her rights.

4. *A shift of our understanding of "full social equality" to reflect an authentically feminist perspective*

- Permissive abortion laws do not bring women freedom, social
equality, sexual fulfillment, or full personal development. They
are based on male models of sex, which have long been used to

subjugate women. This male-centered understanding pits women against their own offspring in a way that is not only morally offensive but psychologically and politically destructive.

- Women's rights and liberation are linked with fetal rights. If a woman claims the right to decide by herself whether the fetus becomes a child or not, what does this do to paternal and communal responsibility? Why should men share responsibility for child support or child rearing if they cannot share in what is declared to be the woman's sole decision? Furthermore, if explicit intentions and consciously accepted contracts are necessary for moral obligations, why should men be held responsible for what they do not voluntarily choose to happen? Abortion on demand, often advocated as a response to male irresponsibility, *legitimates* such irresponsibility.

- In our male-dominated world, what men don't do doesn't count. Pregnancy, childbirth, and nursing have been characterized as passive and debilitating. Pregnancy is likened to a disease or impairment that handicaps women in the "real" world. Many pro-choice feminists, deliberately childless, adopt the male perspective when they cite the "basic injustice that women have to bear the babies," instead of seeing the injustice in the fact that men cannot give birth to children. Women's biologically unique capacity and privilege has been denied, despised, and suppressed under male domination. Rather than accept this view of the world, women should argue that pregnancy is an exercise of life-giving power that men can never know.

- Instead of being empowered by their abortion choices, women are instead merely attempting to survive the debilitating reality of not being free to bring a baby into the world in terms that respect their difference from men. A new kind of pro-life feminism is needed in which all of women's reality is accorded respect. This time, instead of conforming to male models and ideas, women must demand that society must make room for the biological reality of women.

When it comes to the insights of pro-life feminism, though she was expanding on what the first American feminists had already said about abortion, Sidney Callahan began the movement in the contemporary era. And, for me at least, her arguments remain the best ones out there. The rest of this chapter rests squarely on the foundation of her groundbreaking work.

Our Current Abortion Law as a Product of Men

Sidney Callahan's views provide numerous jumping-off points, but let's begin by focusing on the central idea in her argument: that abortion rights serve the interests of men and actually hurt the interests of women. This can be a difficult idea to accept, even if one finds her other points persuasive, because our American discussion of abortion presumes just the opposite. How could what we are constantly told is the most sacred of women's rights actually be at the service of men? It becomes easier to accept when we think about some of the major players who were pushing new abortion policies in the United States in the 1960s and '70s. We already saw, for instance, that Dr. Bernard Nathanson was a founder of NARAL. Don't forget the "pro-choice" activism of Hugh Hefner and his Playboy Foundation, including his direct sponsorship of the lower court cases that led to *Roe v. Wade.* (Interestingly, Hefner claims that he "was a feminist before there was such a thing as feminism."[4]) It is also rarely pointed out that *Roe v. Wade* was decided when the Supreme Court had all male justices. Were these men sensitive to women's issues and realities? Did they decide the law based on justice concerns for women?

Recall Linda Greenhouse, a strongly "pro-choice" journalist who covered the Supreme Court for the *The New York Times,* claiming that "the seven middle-aged to elderly men in the majority certainly didn't think they were making a statement about women's rights"; rather, authentically female concerns were "nearly absent from the opinion."[5] We saw that a current Supreme Court justice, Ruth Bader Ginsburg, agrees: speaking at the University of Chicago, she said that *Roe* was a disappointment because it focused on privacy rather than on advancing women's rights.[6] Justice Harry Blackmun, writing for the majority in the *Roe* decision, was a former lawyer for the Mayo Clinic. Greenhouse noted the unsurprising fact that his decision was particularly focused on the concerns of male physicians.

Aside from this fairly obvious (though overlooked) example, the influence of male perspectives and ideas on *Roe* and its successors is more subtle in that it connects with issues that aren't directly about abortion. These men of the Supreme Court based their opinion on many concerns that "nested" with abortion: sexual freedom; marriage; the meaning and place for parenting; and the role of women in society. As legal scholar Helen Alvare notes, the Court pontificated on these very complex and delicate matters in an "urgent and authoritative" manner, especially about the harms they believed women suffer without access to abortion.[7] Callahan shows in some detail how the model they used for thinking about how women suffer was not feminist. It did not, for instance, offer a feminist critique of an individualist, disconnected, hierarchical, autonomy-focused view of the person. Indeed, far from critiquing it, that was *precisely the view of the human* that the justices used. Women were imagined to be disconnected and isolated individuals — in a more privileged position on the hierarchy of value than their prenatal children — who must be given the private space to make individual, autonomous decisions about their reproductive lives.

Toward this end, the *Roe* court sought a solution that made women "free" to act like men: to imagine themselves as able to live sexual, reproductive, economic, professional, and parental lives and concerns as men did. On this model, pregnancy and childbirth are a burden and cause of distress relative to one's economic gain, professional advancement, and sexual autonomy. In *Planned Parenthood v. Casey,* the Court reaffirmed *Roe*'s general framework and this understanding of the person. They looked back at the American social landscape since *Roe* was decided in 1973 and offered the following assessment:

> For two decades of economic and social developments, people have organized intimate relationships and made choices that define their views of themselves and their places in society, in reliance on the availability of abortion in the event that contraception should fail. The ability of women to participate equally in the economic and social life of the nation has been facilitated by their ability to control their reproductive lives.[8]

What did the Supreme Court claim, then, was essential for women to participate equally in society? Equal pay for equal work regardless of whether a woman chooses to have children? Nope. Mandatory pregnancy leave and child care for female students and workers? Nah. Strict antidiscrimination laws in hiring practices? Sorry. What is essential for women's equality, it turns out, is that they are able to end their pregnancies when those pregnancies constitute a burden on their economic and social interests.

But being pregnant and having a child is often so burdensome for women precisely because our social structures have been designed by and for human beings who cannot get pregnant. Notice how, in this context, the recourse to abortion ends up serving the interests of men. The patriarchal social structures that serve their interests remain unchanged. If we were interested in offering women genuine reproductive freedom, we would change our social structures in ways that honor their differences from men. Men offering women the so-called "freedom" to pretend that their social, economic, and reproductive lives can flourish in social structures designed for people who can't have babies is preposterous and insulting.

Unsurprisingly, recent history indicates that "pro-choice" men in power will sacrifice women's genuine social equality in favor of attempts to protect abortion rights. In 2013, New York's outspokenly "pro-choice" governor, Andrew Cuomo, introduced what he intended to be women-friendly legislation. Indeed, it was a "ten point plan" that he called the Women's Equity Act. The ten points included lots of absolutely wonderful and (at least in New York) largely uncontroversial provisions: pay equity, banning pregnancy discrimination, and so on. However, Cuomo insisted on including expansion of late-term abortion in the bill. "Pro-lifers" — both Republican and Democrat — defeated the abortion expansion and offered to pass the other nine provisions instead. Cuomo refused, and thus he let the whole bill fail. Rather than pass nine key women-friendly laws, Cuomo decided to stick to his abortion guns and let the whole bill go down in flames. Tellingly, his decision occurred in the same legislative session in which he pushed a budget that cut funding for a successful program supporting low-income and teenage mothers.[9] Cuomo let everyone know that his true loyalty was to abortion rights and not women's equality.

Many times, however, the coercive influence of men is less about subtle and abstract matters like social structures and understandings of humans. Sometimes the coercion is more direct: multiple studies, for instance, have found a strong correlation between abortion and "intimate partner violence," especially when a woman has had multiple abortions.[10] Of a disturbingly large number of examples that could make the point, consider the story of Tanner Hopkins, who, in response to his girlfriend's refusal to submit to his pressure to have an abortion, pulled up next to her in his vehicle at an intersection and fired two shots into her without saying a word. And blatant male coercion of abortion goes well beyond physical violence. Consider the recent story about NBA player J. J. Redick and the "abortion contract" he signed with his former girlfriend. According to *The Huffington Post,* the leaked contract revealed that his ex was pregnant, and he stipulated that she end the pregnancy and provide proof of the abortion. The two would then be legally mandated to maintain a social relationship for another year. If Redick bowed out of the relationship before that time, the contract indicated that he would pay her $25,000.[11]

The people with whom I've shared this story have found it shocking and disgusting. We could not find a better example of Callahan's point that abortion rights legitimate the irresponsibility of men and pressure/coerce the choices of women. But *should* we find it shocking? Isn't this simply making public and explicit what is already the informal understanding in our culture? Men like Reddick don't want to be burdened — economically or socially — with the prospect of raising and/or otherwise supporting a child. The social expectation that a privileged male's sexual partner will get an abortion is built into his lifestyle. It may shock us that someone would make this unstated social expectation so explicit in a legal document, but the idea that men expect women to get abortions as a necessary component of their sexual lifestyle is hardly new. At this point it might be helpful to remember something we discovered from chapter 1: more than half of women who abort their pregnancies cite "being a single mother" or "having relationship problems" as a reason.[12]

In the stories of Charlotte, Heather, and Madeline recounted in the introduction, we saw the effect of pressure, not only coming from the sexual partners of these women, but also coming from their family members. The coercive role that parents (and particularly fathers) play in the decisions of pregnant women and girls is worth far more attention than it currently receives. In 2013, for instance, a pregnant teenage girl brought suit in Texas against her father for pressuring her into getting an abortion. A copy of the lawsuit claimed that he "was going to take her to have an abortion and that the decision was his, end of story."[13] During the very same year, another man sued his girlfriend's family for pressuring her to have an abortion.[14] In the complaint he claimed that not only was she in favor of keeping the child, but that her family was of the view that her life would be "ruined" if she had a child with a "non-white man." Again, these stories merely highlight what we already know through experience and intuition: abortion serves the interests of parents who want to pressure and even coerce their daughters' reproductive choices. Especially when a young pregnant woman is financially and otherwise dependent, there is little to stand in their way.

No doubt our culture's laws should change to better protect women from these kinds of coercive situations (one could also invoke the numerous examples of pimps and sex-trafficking ringleaders who force women into having abortions), situations that make a mockery of the idea that women have the "freedom of choice" to have an abortion. But when "prolifers" propose legislation to protect women from these kinds of situations, it is often opposed by powerful "pro-choice" men. Two recent examples occurred in Canada. Prime Minister Stephen Harper opposed and defeated a 2010 bill that would have created serious penalties for anyone who co-erced a woman into having an abortion, and then he proclaimed that he would refuse to allow any abortion-related bill to come to a vote.[15] Justin Trudeau, leader of the Canadian Liberal Party in 2014 and a candidate for prime minister, has insisted that all members of his party be compelled to vote "pro-choice."[16] After learning what we have so far in this chapter, should it surprise us that two powerful Canadian men are leading the charge to keep abortion the status quo? Like many other men, they are standing up for a set of rights that, though they are sold as women's rights, actually serve their own political, sexual, and economic interests.

I have quoted Florynce Kennedy at the beginning of this chapter: "If men could get pregnant, abortion would be a sacrament." She's right, of course, but with one essential qualification. Abortion is *already* a sacramental right in our culture for many "pro-choice" men precisely because it already serves their economic and social interests.

Does the Choice for Abortion Lead to More Freedom?

So abortion serves the interests of men. But might it also, overall, serve the interests of women? In fact, while there are burdens for our culture to bear any time we make space for choice, the fact that women are now broadly free to make their own reproductive choices is a very good thing, isn't it? In the section that follows, I will join with Sidney Callahan and other "pro-life feminists" in arguing that broad abortion choice actually makes women *less* free. Paradoxically, offering women the choice to have an abortion does not improve or enhance women's reproductive freedom. On the contrary, it coerces and limits it.

This position is obviously heretical within the secular religion of Americanism. Want more freedom? Our secular faith tells us that the answer is "more choice." The idea that *restraining* choice could actually lead to more freedom is another claim that seems so counterintuitive as to be absurd. But forget abortion for a moment. Let's begin by focusing on other examples that illustrate this relationship between choice and freedom.

First, consider an easy example: the alcoholic. In what does his freedom consist? Increasing and protecting his choices about whether and what kinds of beverages to consume? Hardly. His freedom consists precisely in *not* having to make these kinds of choices. Or how about sexual choices? Suppose someone is attempting to resist the desire to hook up with a very attractive person she just met at a bar. Is it in her interest to make a difficult decision at the end of the night whether to go home with that person? Of course not, especially if there is alcohol involved (as there almost always is). I often tell my undergraduate students that if they have to choose at the end of the night whether they are going to go home with someone, it is almost certainly too late. The freedom to avoid the "walk of shame" back to the dorm room or apartment the next morning requires setting boundaries on the choices you are willing to consider. True freedom is often the result of limiting the choices available to us, especially in light of coercive forces pulling us in destructive directions.

And what about our consumer culture? In his book *The Paradox of Choice*, psychologist Barry Schwartz shows that as our consumer choices have expanded, our freedom has actually become limited and even paralyzed.[17] And the Christian ethicist William Cavanaugh has demonstrated that the corporations offering us all these choices have actually spent millions studying the best social science on how human beings react to advertising. Their goal? Carefully crafting the options available so that our choices create "organized dissatisfaction." The remedy for feeling bad ourselves, it turns out, is to buy their products.[18] Yes, in a strict sense we have the "choice" to buy the newest smart phone, weight-loss remedy, video game console, or trendy pair of boots, but that choice takes place within a coercive consumerist social structure. Indeed, these products are designed to satisfy us only for a short time — at which point we'll need the newest version of product X to remedy the latest bad feeling about ourselves. More consumer "choice" certainly does not lead to more freedom.

As we have seen above, women's choices are made in the context of social structures created by powerful and privileged men. To further illustrate the point, the sociologist Lisa Wade asks us to consider the Miley Cyrus phenomenon as a classic example of how giving women more choices within such social structures does not offer more freedom.[19] Yes, women like Cyrus are making their own choices. Yes, she makes the decisions on where and when to appear naked, where and when to twerk, and where and when to do virtually anything she wants. But, notes Wade, all of these choices take place within a system. Cyrus's choices are "what the system rewards. That's not freedom, that's a strategy. In sociological terms, we call this a patriarchal bargain." After all, men have created the social structures that determine how our culture dispenses money and creates fame. For women, this is almost always tied to the sexual exploitation of their bodies — most often to make corporations lots and lots of money. Yes, there are more "choices" available to women to let corporations exploit their bodies and sexuality for financial gain than ever before, but this has not led to greater *freedom*. Indeed, it has led to precisely the opposite: destructive coercion of women's freedom. Miley Cyrus is certainly not the first to be victimized by the system, and she will not be the last.

Given what we have already learned about how an increased focus on abortion choices serves the interests of men, we might be able to guess how this turns out for the freedom of women. As I was thinking about the outline for this chapter, I wrote several female colleagues and asked them what I should be thinking about as I did so. This was one of the responses:

> Women need to ask themselves if access to abortion really has done more to liberate them. If a woman does decide to parent, is she really free to make that decision if she has no partner, limited 12 weeks unpaid maternity leave, hopelessly expensive childcare, and on and on and on? Abortion has made women free not to have children, but it has arguably made it more difficult for women to choose to have children. What else have women gained? A hook-up culture which breeds sexual violence, increasing numbers of STDs, less-committed and even child-like male partners who couldn't identify responsibility if it hit them in the face, and a culture that values them only when they are young and skinny. Is that freedom?

And what about the freedom of women who want to resist our consumerist social structures, for example, by living in a modest home or apartment and staying home to raise multiple children? How has all of this "choice" worked out for the freedom of these women? Nancy Wilson submits that widespread abortion choice, like other choices that are coerced by male-created social structures, has led to social pressure to choose a certain lifestyle in conformity with such structures.[20] Stay-at-home mothers often get reactions that barely conceal outright contempt for their life choices. Women who have more than just one or two children are "regularly met with rude comments from total strangers." Wilson recounts a situation in which her daughter, a stay-at-home mother, walked into a market with her several children. The reaction of a nearby vendor was: "Well, look at that. Here comes the circus."

However, Wilson is making a social argument that does not rely on

anecdotal evidence. Broad access to abortion choice, in a patriarchal social context that claims that one's worth comes primarily from how one
makes one's money, has remade our understanding of what women "are
for." Women, it turns out, are for what privileged, powerful men have decided everyone is for: working forty-plus hours per week to make enough
money to support a consumerist lifestyle. A culture of abortion choice has
created social expectations in which women who resist that kind of patriarchal bargain are shamed — often by other women. Wilson is a true coun-
tercultural radical who, like Sidney Callahan, urges women to confidently
resist male-created consumerist expectations and relish their ability to do
what men cannot. But in a culture where women's reproductive choices
are pressured and even coerced by our social structures, it goes without
saying that she has a tough road ahead.

But here we should pause with an important caution. Though we
should absolutely make space for women to resist our culture and be stay-
at-home mothers, we should also absolutely make space for women who
are not called to this lifestyle. And though this calling takes place in the
context of our consumer culture, it cannot be reduced to mere selfishness.
Women, just like men, should have the freedom to pursue a profession to
which they feel called. But as we saw in Callahan's argument above, asking women to pursue such a profession in the context of a male-created
consumerist culture is fundamentally coercive. Women, often because of
structural issues stemming from the basic fact that they can get pregnant
and bear children, do not get equal pay for equal work. They risk being
fired or demoted if they become pregnant.[21] They are very rarely offered
sufficient maternity leave. They are not provided with child-care. (Women
often can't even find a place to pump breast milk — to say nothing of actually nursing!) But they *are* offered the so-called choice to have an abortion. If you are a woman in pursuit of a career, our American consumerist
culture insists that you do it like a man. But it is not freedom for women
to have the "choice" to pretend they can participate in the workforce as if
they don't sometimes get pregnant. It is the kind of pressure and coercion
that contributes to 1.2 million abortions each year.

But now we are confronted with another caution. The idea that
women are "free" to pursue a career that will lead to their flourishing comes
from a privileged point of view. One must, of course, come from a socioeconomic background in which one has enough resources to "choose" to
work hard in a good school (free from violence, malnutrition, and other
coercive forces) in order to feel confident about getting a good job, afford-

ing child-care, and so on. In light of these considerations, it is perhaps not surprising that those who have a privileged socioeconomic background are more than 20 percent more likely to identify as "pro-choice" than those without such privilege.[22] Furthermore, according to Planned Parenthood, rich people are also more likely to terminate an unplanned pregnancy than are people without these means.[23] One's "choice" takes place within the socioeconomic background into which one is born, something that none of us has any control over whatsoever.

And isn't this really what it's all about? *Control.* Even in the face of overwhelming evidence to the contrary, many of us persist in believing that more choice equals more freedom. Making choices gives us the illusion that we are in control. For instance, some Americans keep guns "for protection" despite the fact that it makes death by a firearm in one's residence *more* rather than less likely. Gun ownership gives us the (false) sense that we are in control over our safety. Or consider football. National Football League head coaches (before it was made illegal) often called timeout right before an opposing team lined up for a game-winning try — despite the fact that doing so made the second field goal attempt more rather than less likely to succeed. It also gave them a (false) sense of control. And even in the face of clear evidence that a medical intervention would make a particular sickness worse rather than better, we often go ahead with the treatment nonetheless, rather than do nothing and let the body heal itself. "Doing something" helps convince us that we have some control in a vulnerable and difficult situation.

This sense of control is often a harmful illusion. And given that it is an illusion from which (privileged) men disproportionately suffer, it is that much more important for women to resist and dispel it. The Catholic ethicist Jana Bennett, for instance, points out that women's experience of pregnancy and parenthood puts them in a better place to understand that *we aren't in control:*

> You can choose to avoid pregnancy with a condom, pill or IUD — but sometimes that baby's there anyway. You can try to get pregnant for months on end, even "choosing" IVF, and it doesn't happen. You can get pregnant and miscarry. And if you get pregnant and your boss decides that you are therefore a liability, you can lose your job unless you make "the right choice"; any resultant poverty is your "choice." In other words, we try to control sex and parenthood under the guise of individual choice, but it really isn't a choice. . . . No — it's a "choice"

made in concert with a whole host of racial, economic, technological, age, and other factors.[24]

The Data of an "Unchoice"

Our social structures force women to choose between (1) honoring their roles as the procreators and sustainers of the earliest stages of human life and (2) having social and economic equality with men. This difficult situation has led some in the "pro-life" movement to call abortion the "unchoice."[25] But don't take their word for it; instead, check out the social science data. For example, here is some of what a study appearing in *Medical Science Monitor* found about those women seeking abortions in the United States:[26]

- Over half said they "needed more time" to make the decision.
- Fewer than 30 percent received counseling.
- Sixty-four percent said they felt pressured by others to have the abortion.
- Twenty-eight percent said they were sure about the decision to have the abortion.
- Over half thought that the abortion was "morally wrong."

Also consider a story in *The New York Times* entitled "What Happens to Women Who Are Denied Abortions?"[27] The article looked at cases of women who sought an abortion but were denied getting one for various reasons. The result? Only *5 percent* were found to have later regretted not getting the abortion. Five percent!

Given these realities, it would not be surprising to find out that having an abortion often dramatically impacts a woman's well-being and happiness. The *Medical Science Monitor* study discovered the following about American women after their abortions:

- Relationship with partner improved: 0.9 percent
- Felt better about myself: 0.9 percent
- Felt more in control of my life: 0.3 percent
- Felt guilt: 77.9 percent
- Felt that "part of me died": 59.5 percent
- Unable to forgive self: 62.2 percent

It even found that one in seven American women who had abortions meet full diagnostic criteria for posttraumatic stress disorder. Those who wish to downplay these numbers mention that there is nothing like "postabortion syndrome," and that is correct in the sense that the American Psychological Association has not formally accepted such a category. But considering the APA's support of "pro-choice" advocacy for four-plus decades, it is not difficult to understand why they are reluctant to support the idea.[28] Undoubtedly, "pro-life" bias also exists for those who wish to speak about something like "postabortion syndrome," but we should really stop arguing about what phrase or category to use and instead focus more on what the data tell us about abortion and women's flourishing.

Can we get beyond the politically motivated bias in attempting to do this?[29] In 2011 the prestigious *British Journal of Psychiatry* published a thoroughly peer-reviewed meta-analysis of studies done on abortion and mental health from 1995 to 2009.[30] Such an analysis is like a "poll of polls" that weighs in on the basis of objective criteria such as sample size and strength of effect. It tries to take the political cherry-picking of a single study out of the picture. What did the meta-analysis find? In a monstrously large sample of 877,297 participants in twenty-two different studies, women who had an abortion were 81 percent more likely to have mental health problems. One common response to these numbers is that anyone with an unplanned pregnancy is likely to have increased mental health problems, whether she gets an abortion or not. But when the (very large) group of women who aborted was compared to another (very large) control group of women who delivered the baby, the study found that women who aborted were still 55 percent more likely to experience mental health problems. This data is from the largest quantitative estimate available in the world, and it is unambiguous.[31]

Let's not forget that abortion is anything but rare: one-third of American women have an abortion in their lifetimes; 50 percent of all abortions are the mother's second or third abortion. Before *Roe v. Wade,* women's self-reported happiness was significantly higher than that of men. Today, not only is women's happiness significantly lower that it was in the early 1970s, but women are now less happy than are men.[32] Correlation is, of course, never proof of causation. And many things have changed for women since the 1970s. But given the huge numbers of women who have had abortions, along with evidence that the "unchoice" of abortion causes significant distress and mental anguish, we should at least consider the possibility that our coercive abortion rights regime has contributed to increasing unhappiness in American women.[33]

Conclusion

In light of what we learned in this chapter, it is perhaps no longer surprising that women are significantly more skeptical of abortion than men are. Despite being told (often by men) that abortion is necessary for their freedom and flourishing, the data and their own experiences tell a very different story. Widely available legal abortion came about largely as a result of the efforts of men, and this "choice" continues to serve male interests, while it often pressures and even coerces women into choices most would prefer not to make. More abortion choice does not lead to more reproductive freedom.

Fortunately, this means that our culture can refuse the false choice between having concern for women and defending their prenatal children. In the overwhelming majority of circumstances, we can love and protect them both. There is no need, as Sidney Callahan says, "to pit women against their own offspring." Instead of trying to force women to fit into the impossible position of pretending that their reproductive concerns can fit into male-created social structures, we should force men (and our whole society) to acknowledge the important differences between men and women. Women can get pregnant and have babies. Men cannot. We should and can change our social structures to respect and make room for this reality.

As I write this chapter, precisely these kinds of considerations are being debated in other countries. Spain, a country with the highest abortion rate in all of Europe, is proposing to limit abortion to circumstances that include only the exceptional cases of rape, fetal malformation, and the life of the mother.[34] The leader of the Socialist Reform Movement, Alfredo Pérez Rubalcaba, opposed the change and, like so many other "pro-choice" men before him, called it an "unacceptable setback for women."[35] But the Spanish Justice minister defended the push to change the law by giving examples of "structural gender violence" that exert "by the mere fact of pregnancy," a "pressure" that causes women to abort. "I think of the fear of losing one's job or not getting a job in the first place as a result of pregnancy," he said. "I think of the pressure for many immigrants, I think of women in these situations with lack of support from public authorities to freely choose an alternative to termination of pregnancy." Ruiz-Gallardón claims that the absence of measures "related to employment, welfare, housing assistance or transport" prevents a woman from "freely" deciding about her pregnancy.[36]

Sound familiar? The United States must also change its public policy on abortion and support genuinely free reproductive choices. There is never a wrong time to push for "equal justice under law," of course. But, as I will show in the next chapter, the time is right for proposing what I call the *Mother and Prenatal Child Protection Act.*

CHAPTER SIX

A Way Forward

"You say that you think slavery is wrong, but you denounce all attempts to restrain it. Is there anything else that you think wrong, that you are not willing to deal with as a wrong?"

Abraham Lincoln

Introduction

In some ways, the book could stop right here. If the arguments and evidence presented so far convince us on a moral level, we should honor these conclusions with how we live our lives. Not only should we obviously refuse to have or coerce birth-control abortions ourselves, but we should resist it in our communities as well. We must make serious and passionate cases in our nuclear and extended families, churches, synagogues, mosques, local bars, country clubs, school boards, Facebook/Twitter feeds, and so forth. And we must make them often.

But what about public policy? Some people, including many Christian thinkers I am proud to call friends, worry that the debate over abortion spends too much time obsessing about what the law should be and not enough time on what happens in the actual lives of real people and communities. For instance, despite the church's strong teaching against abortion, there is evidence that Roman Catholics have abortions at a rate similar to the rest of the population.[1] One could argue that Christians, in particular, should focus their energies on "removing the plank from our own eye" before we start thinking about changing a law to coerce others.

Furthermore, haven't the attempts of the "pro-life" community to change abortion law aligned us in strange ways with political figures who don't otherwise share the philosophy of using government to impose a particular understanding of morality onto others? To be blunt, in hitching their wagons to the Republican political machine to be effective on abortion, it looks like American "pro-lifers" end up sacrificing energetic government concern for other vulnerable populations: undocumented workers, racial minorities, those who cannot afford health care, poor single parents, and so on. Furthermore, a focus on changing public policy can sometimes appear to crowd out concern for making a difference in our local communities. I could not be a more energetic supporter of my church's defense of prenatal life, but it is an utter scandal that local Catholic communities don't do more to support local pregnant women in difficult situations. We should be lining up to adopt babies of various races and health conditions; we should be using our free time to provide free child-care for needy women in our local communities and churches; every parish and church should offer shelter and assistance to pregnant women in difficult situations and offer programs of counseling and healing for women who have had abortions.

And there are some groups doing good work in these and other areas. "Pro-choice" pundits who lazily resort to the tried and true zinger that "pro-lifers" "don't care about babies after birth" are mistaken to paint with such a broad brush. But these groups, as wonderful as they are, are the exceptions that prove the rule. It must be said that the "pro-life" community (over half the population in the United States) has, overall, done an inadequate job of living out our stated values. Even Pope Francis admits that "we have done little to adequately accompany women in very difficult situations."[2]

These are all very serious concerns. Far too often, "pro-lifers" make an idol out of trying to change our public policy on abortion such that they ignore, or even oppose, many other aspects of where our principles lead us. However, we should once against resist making a false choice between these two kinds of goals. The pope's challenge to accompany women in difficult situations in our personal lives is perfectly consistent with also pushing for equal justice under law for both women and their prenatal children. Yes, we must refuse to make an idol of our quest for legal justice, and we should be very careful not to make political bargains that end up undermining the fundamental values we stand for. But in the end, justice must be done. This has been the case made for other vulnerable populations who are denied their basic civil rights, and it should be no different for prenatal children and their mothers. Our communities must recognize their full and unique moral value, and this means equal protection of the law at all levels. This is not only necessary for political equality but also to unleash the power of the law as moral teacher to push for full social equality as well.

An Opening for a New Public Policy on Abortion

Let me return to an insight we explored in the first pages of this book: the time is right to change our public policy to better reflect this political and social equality. Indeed, we are clearly in the midst of not only a new moment in the abortion debate but in our American political culture more generally. Recall from chapter 1 the following breakdown in political affiliation in the United States:[3]

9 percent	Very Conservative
31 percent	Conservative
35 percent	Moderate
16 percent	Liberal
5 percent	Very Liberal
4 percent	No Opinion

Despite the polarized rhetoric that comes from Washington and the corporate media, the American people are hardly a polarized group. Only 14 percent are in the "extremes," and more than a third refuse to say that they lean in one direction or the other. Indeed, a record 40 percent of the electorate now think of themselves as "independent," refusing to put themselves in our simplistic binary political categories.[4] Interestingly — especially when we think of what's coming in the next generation — *half* of Millennials refuse to use the categories of Republican/conservative and Democrat/liberal to describe themselves politically.[5]

As frustration with Washington and our media grows, and as Millennials come into their own, the United States is poised to have a very different kind of political conversation more generally — and about our abortion discourse specifically. As we also saw in chapter 1, the "Costanza strategy," used by each party with respect to abortion, is already beginning to unravel and is not long for this world. We saw that "pro-life/pro-choice binary," the longtime categories forced upon us to think and speak about abortion, is no longer adequate. A strong majority of Americans think of themselves as either "pro-life" or "pro-choice" depending on how the question is asked. We also saw that the demographic future of the United States — Hispanics and Millennials — are significantly more skeptical about abortion than is the rest of the population. While almost no one wants *all* abortions to be illegal, a record low number of people describe themselves as "pro-choice."

Opinions about abortion are also changing with another very important group: doctors. A recent study published in *Obstetrics and Gynecology* found that, while 97 percent of OB-GYN physicians encountered patients seeking abortions, only 14 percent performed them.[6] This number is "lower than estimated in previous research," and it maps onto a growing trend of physicians who are increasingly unwilling to do abortions.[7] This trend was identified by *The New York Times* back in 1998,[8] and groups like Medical Students for Choice have been consistently alarmed by the fact that present-day physicians are refusing to be trained to do abortions at an ever higher rate.[9] The situation is so serious that in some parts of the country there are de facto abortion bans because no physician in the area is willing to provide one. This is at least part of the reason that California recently passed an unprecedented law allowing nonphysicians like midwives and nurse practitioners to perform surgical abortions.[10]

The unwillingness of physicians to do abortions is also one of the major reasons why more than seventy abortion clinics have closed in the United States since 2011.[11] Crackdowns on "unfit providers" also contributed to these closings, as did a huge increase in laws requiring abortion clinics to be regulated as other kinds of surgical medical centers.[12] The previously mentioned California bill was the only one in 2013 that actually increased access to abortion. All other laws curbed access, and here is a reminder of examples we encountered in chapter 1:

- Thirty-three states have passed informed consent laws (twenty-four include an ultrasound requirement).
- Thirty-one states have passed abortion clinic regulations.
- Thirty-eight states have passed parental notification/involvement.
- Thirty-eight states have wrongful-death laws that treat the unborn child as a person, and eleven of these protect the fetus from the time of fertilization. Thirty-seven states have fetal homicide laws, and twenty-five of these extend the protection from the time of fertilization.

- Fourteen states have passed laws banning abortion after twenty weeks.

Again, while there are virtually no serious attempts to make abortion flatly illegal, the "pro-life" trend in our changing abortion policy is unmistakable.

When we consider these factors together, it becomes clear that we now have a unique moment to rethink our national abortion policy and move beyond the intense polarization that has dominated politics for the last four decades. In this penultimate chapter, I lay out the outlines of a proposal for doing precisely this: the *Mother and Prenatal Child Protection Act* (MPCPA). I propose it as a national abortion policy that, I believe, not only reflects the views of a large majority of Americans but also is consistent with both the currently settled doctrine of the Roman Catholic Church and the ongoing shift in U.S. constitutional law, especially with the evolving "undue burden" standard of *Roe*'s successor case, *Planned Parenthood v. Casey.*

I will begin by highlighting the shift in constitutional law on abortion since *Casey,* and suggest that it is a time for a reevaluation of what the "undue burden" standard means a generation after that decision. Second, I will discuss three key aspects of MPCPA:

- Legal recognition of the full moral standing of the prenatal child
- Protection and support of the mother, including self-defense
- Refusing to aid the fetus for a proportionately serious reason

Third, and finally, I will propose the formal details of the MPCPA, and I will show that it is a legally and politically viable public policy for the United States.

Shifting from *Roe*'s "Privacy" to *Casey*'s "Undue Burden"

In reacting to a chapter like this one, which explicitly argues for a new abortion public policy, someone might argue that abortion law is "settled" in the United States. But as we saw in in the previous two chapters, this could not be further from the truth. The shift from "privacy" in *Roe* to "undue burden" in *Casey* is so substantial that it is almost as if *Roe* has already been overturned. But don't take my word for it; listen to "pro-choice" legal scholars who are worried about the shift that has taken place.

In a 2010 article in the *William and Mary Journal of Women and the Law,* Caitlin E. Borgmann says quite directly that *Casey* "established a new, less protective, constitutional standard for abortion restrictions."[13] The undue burden standard it established, she says, "immediately enabled states to invade women's privacy in new ways." She notes that the Roberts court "has interpreted *Casey* expansively," resulting in "erosions of the privacy boundaries" that were once protected by *Roe.* Indeed, she makes the very strong claim that certain privacy rights to abortion were "eviscerated" by *Casey,* especially as interpreted by the all-important swing voter on the Supreme Court, Justice Anthony Kennedy.

Ironically, notes Borgmann, though *Roe* clearly focuses on autonomy and privacy, it contained a few lines that may have planted the seed of its own demise:

> [The mother] cannot be isolated in her privacy. She carries an embryo, and, later, a fetus. . . . The situation therefore is inherently different from marital intimacy. . . . [I]t is reasonable and appropriate for a State to decide that at some point in time another interest, that of the health of the mother or that of potential human life, becomes significantly involved. The woman's privacy is no longer sole and any right of privacy she possesses must be measured accordingly.[14]

Casey builds on this idea when it concludes that a state may regulate abortion in defense of fetal life as long as such regulations do not pose an "undue burden" on the mother in seeking abortion. That we are now asking whether a particular abortion regulation poses an undue burden — rather than about the privacy rights of the woman — is evidence of what Borgmann describes as our "changing standard for abortion."

The Supreme Court, at least as it exists at the time I write these pages, seems to have four clear "pro-choice" interpreters of the law, and four who have clear "pro-life" interpretations. Justice Kennedy appears to be the swing vote, and Borgmann argues that his "quite expansive" interpretation of the undue burden standard paints a "bleak picture" for future of abortion rights. We saw in chapter 1 that the legal scholar Jeffrey Toobin also believes that Kennedy is shifting toward a more "pro-life" interpretation of the undue burden standard. According to Toobin, what counted as an undue burden for Kennedy when he helped decide *Casey* in 1992 looked very different to him fifteen years later, when he upheld the ban on partial-birth abortion. Indeed, in every case decided on the merits since *Casey*

(*Stenberg,* 2000; *Ayotte,* 2006; and *Gonzales,* 2007), Kennedy has upheld the "pro-life" law as not imposing an undue burden.

Thus we can say, no, U.S. abortion law is not "settled." Indeed, given the inherent cultural variability of the undue burden standard, this kind of law will find itself in a near-constant state of flux. Restrictions considered burdensome in one decade are not in another. The burden on pregnant women in the United States has changed since 1992, not least due to the implementation of many different kinds of social programs. Here are just a few:

- Family and Medical Leave Act (1993)
- Mickey Leland Childhood Hunger Relief Act (1993)
- Mental Health Parity Act (1996)
- Newborns' and Mothers' Health Protection Act (1996)
- The State Child Health Insurance Program (1997)
- Unemployment Compensation Act (2010)
- Healthy, Hunger-Free Kids Act (2010)

Perhaps the most important development since 1992, however, was the passage of the Affordable Care Act in 2010. This not only provided for a very important expansion of Medicaid health benefits to poor women (and men) within 133 percent of the federal poverty level, but the law gives even those within 400 percent of the poverty level substantial government assistance in buying health insurance. Furthermore, the Affordable Care Act also includes provisions of the Pregnant Woman Support Act, legislation that has been pushed by "pro-lifers" for many years.[15] Among other things, this part of the Affordable Care Act

- increases the tax credit for adoption and makes it permanent;
- eliminates pregnancy as a "preexisting condition";
- requires the State Child Health Insurance Program to cover pregnant women and their prenatal children;
- requires that prenatal care now be covered by all insurance carriers;
- makes grant money available to states for home visits by nurses, campus child care, pregnancy counseling, ultrasound equipment, campus child care, and so on.

While much more needs to be done to support the social equality of women in our culture (and the Mother and Prenatal Child Protection Act will attempt to address many of these issues), one could scarcely deny that our culture has made significant strides in supporting the needs of mothers of prenatal and postnatal children. The burden of some restrictions on abortion today, therefore, is simply not the same burden that the same restrictions would have imposed in 1992.

There are also at least two other important factors that were not part of the conversation in 1992. In the previous chapter we saw that abortion choice, paradoxically, puts a very severe burden on many women. Some of that burden comes from the lack of social support for making the choice to keep and raise their children, but some of that burden comes merely from the stark fact that women are the sole "choice-makers." If the woman has a "free choice," then we expect her, the choice-maker, to be the one to take the responsibility and bear the burdens that result from making such a choice. As long as women are understood to be "free" to end their pregnancies, our American culture is unlikely to provide women the support they need to be both mothers and the social equals of men.

Another thing that has changed since 1992 is increasing appreciation for the moral standing of the fetus. We've already seen how the percentage of Americans who describe themselves as "pro-choice" is at or near record lows, especially among the young. Scientific and technological advances, in particular, have made it impossible to deny that a prenatal child is a fellow member of the species Homo sapiens. We not only see their human reality via 3-D ultrasound pictures posted on Facebook and Twitter, but we come across incredible stories of fetal surgeries *in utero* that save the lives of babies who otherwise would have died. We now even have constitutional laws that treat the violent killing of prenatal children (by someone other than the mother) as *homicide*. Indeed, in the infamous trial of Scott Peterson, he was sentenced to death for killing his pregnant wife Laci only because the state of California considered what he did to be double murder.[16] And in response to Remee Lee's boyfriend tricking her into taking RU-486 in order to kill the fetus, the state of Florida recently passed the Offenses Against Unborn Children Act.[17]

When deciding whether a particular change in abortion law is an "undue burden" on women in our present situation, all of these new and developing factors must be taken into account.[18] The calculation involved in determining whether a burden is "undue" changes with the increasing value of the fetus. It also changes based on the relative presence or absence of social structures available to support a woman in the keeping and raising of her child. And the X factor — often overlooked — may very well be the most burdensome thing of all: forcing a woman into the so-called free choice to have an abortion when she is, in fact, pressured and even coerced into a decision she would prefer not to make.

Working toward a New Public Policy

So the United States is primed for a new public policy on abortion. This conclusion is supported not only by shifting (and often misunderstood) public opinion, but by the shifting (and also often misunderstood) interpretation of constitutional law. My proposal for a new public policy is supported by the arguments I made in the previous chapters, but — as I intend to show later in the chapter — it has the advantage of also being consistent with public opinion and the direction of legal interpretation of the Constitution by the Supreme Court. In what follows I make a brief case for the three key aspects of the proposed law: legal recognition of the fetus, protection and support of her mother, and circumstances in which one may be justified in refusing to sustain the prenatal child.

Legal Recognition of the Fetus

Currently, American law at least purports to recognize all living human beings as persons with a right to life. If by "living human being" one simply means "member of the species Homo sapiens," then the law should consider prenatal human children as persons with a right to life. The science on this is now unmistakably clear: fetuses are fellow members of our species. There is no longer any serious debate about this. Indeed, there is no consistent way for the law to insist that neonatal children are human persons and then avoid the conclusion that prenatal children are also human persons.

And in some ways, we could simply stop here and move on to the next two aspects of the proposed law. This, after all, is the commonsense way the law should work, at least if it were not all bound up the politics of the abortion debate. (1) All human beings are persons with a right to life; (2) a prenatal child is a human being; therefore, (3) a prenatal child is a person with a right to life. But as we saw in chapter 2, some will claim that until a fetus is "viable" or "capable of independence," she cannot be considered a person with a right to life. But we also saw that this has some strange implications — especially since viability can be at different stages based on one's race, gender, time period, sophistication of technology in one's community, or even the ability of one's parents to travel to another community. Furthermore, American law doesn't consider "radical dependence" to lower moral or legal standing. A newborn infant, a medical patient on a ventilator, and an astronaut on a spacewalk are all "radically dependent"; but this dependence does not lower their moral or legal status. Indeed, one could argue that the law exists precisely to protect radically dependent individuals who rely on others to speak up for them and protect their moral and legal value.

Chapter 2 also considered the view of moral status called "Trait X." This view claims that when a fetus has "Trait X," she becomes a person; before that time she is not a person. This view, however, also has strange and unacceptable implications. If you pick a "low" trait, such as capacity to feel pain, then it looks as if rats and mice count as persons with a right to life; but if you pick a "high" trait, such as self-awareness or capacity to make moral choices, then it looks like newborn infants and severely disabled humans do not count. Neither of these is an acceptable option.

In thinking about the legal status of the fetus, justice requires that we use the legal standards used in other contexts, independent of the baggage of the abortion debate. The law should protect all living members of our species — including our prenatal children — as persons with a right to life. This is required by our understanding of civil rights, our understanding of fundamental justice, and our commitment to inclusivity and consistency when applying our legal principles. Furthermore, it isn't as if this kind of legal standing for the fetus is a brand new thing. In legal contexts other than abortion (as in the double murder of Laci Peterson and her prenatal child), the killing of a human fetus is already understood to be homicide. Indeed, "pro-choice" activists have opposed such laws precisely because they presume legal standing for the fetus.[19]

What happens when we bring the full moral and legal status of prenatal child into the abortion debate? Chapter 3 demonstrated that there are further questions to ask, but we can say a few things before going into those issues. All persons, including prenatal children, have a moral and legal right to life, and this means that we cannot aim at their death except in self-defense or defense of another. Having said that, however, we can see that a legal right to life does not bring with it an absolute legal duty on the part of others to aid. One may legally refuse to aid another person, even if one foresees (but doesn't intend) that the other person will die without such aid. These considerations play large roles in several aspects of the law discussed below.

But let me say the following unequivocally: Basic and fundamental justice requires that our prenatal children be the next group in our human family to receive equal protection of the law and the civil rights of other very young children. Period. It is well past time for justice for this voiceless and vulnerable population whose dignity so many find inconvenient.

Protection and Support for the Mother

A mother and her prenatal child are, in some ways, a dual entity. This makes it not only difficult but often inappropriate to try to change the law with regard to one without considering the other. (This is another example where our disproportionate focus on "the individual" in American law simply doesn't work.) Any law that protects the moral standing and rights of the fetus, insofar as it impacts the life of her mother, should also give due consideration to protecting and supporting her as well.

We saw in chapter 5 that women are already pressured and even co-erced to have abortions, often because our culture has not given them the protection and support they are due. By supporting both, the Mother and Prenatal Child Protection Act will refuse to prioritize one over the other. As the right to life of the fetus is fully recognized by the law, we must admit that this brings special responsibilities and burdens on the part of her mother. If we do not make significant changes to our social structures, these responsibilities and burdens risk turning women into second-class citizens. We should, therefore, take the necessary steps to support the ability of women to be both mothers and full participants in our broader culture. Obviously, the specifics of the MPCPA in this regard would have to be carefully crafted in great detail (detail that goes beyond the scope of what I'm doing in this book). In what follows below, however, I merely outline the pillars of the proposed law.

The MPCPA will protect and support the basic civil rights of women by passing, at the federal level, several provisions from New York's failed "Women's Equity Act."[20] This would include the following:

- *Ensure equal pay for equal work.* The MPCPA would eliminate the ability of employers to use "any factor other than sex" to justify pay disparities and instead require that their pay decisions be based on legitimate reasons. In addition, it would protect an employee's right to share wage information with other employees without being retaliated against, and increase damages to successful plaintiffs in pay-equity discrimination cases. Finally, it would extend the length of time that women would have to file lawsuits for violations of these provisions.

- *Remove barriers to remedying gender and "family-status" discrimination in hiring and firing.* The MPCPA would allow successful plaintiffs to recover attorney's fees in employment- or credit-discrimination cases based on sex. This will enable victims, most of whom are women, to have the opportunity to vindicate their rights and be made whole in cases where they prevail. Currently, plaintiffs are not allowed to recover attorney fees at trial for employment-discrimination cases, making it costly to bring a case. The bill would also prohibit employers from denying work or promotions to workers simply because they have children.

- *Protect victims of domestic violence.*Eighty-five percent are women, and this law would protect such women from being discriminated against in housing. In addition, it would strengthen "order of protection" laws by enabling women to file such an order electronically rather than having to appear at the court in person.

- *End pregnancy and "new mother" discrimination in the workplace.* The legislation would create a specific protection that requires employers to provide accommodations for pregnant employees. The current protections for working pregnant women are confusing and have been misinterpreted. The MPCPA would also insist that employers make provision for new mothers as well — including designating places to breast pump.

The MPCPA would go well beyond the proposed New York law, however, and would enact the following additional provisions:

- *Reform of parental leave.* United States federal law would guarantee parents twenty-one weeks (for both mothers and fathers) of paid maternity and paternity leave for each child, with the mandate that all businesses return the parent to the job they left.

- *Universal prekindergarten and subsidized child-care.* All states would receive federal grants to develop and run mandated, universal pre-K programs. There would also be substantial tax relief and other benefits for companies and colleges/universities that provide child-care for their employees and students.

- *Removal of adoption from the for-profit private sector and support for campaigns to remove the adoption stigma.* Babies should not be bought and sold, and the MPCPA would move adoption processes to the state-based model that we currently use for foster care. This will drive down costs to families, thus increasing the number of people who can afford to adopt children. Furthermore, the MPCPA will coordinate a major public and private campaign to resist and ultimately end the bias and stigma that currently exist against adoption, with a particular focus on both interracial adoption and the (false) idea that choosing adoption is somehow an irresponsible choice for the biological mother. The law would also nationalize "safe haven" laws, where biological mothers could leave their infant children at the hospital without fear of being charged with child abandonment.
- *Coordinated, systematic attempts to collect child support.* A new law-enforcement database would be established that allows all levels of government (federal, state, county, city) to communicate with each other and access each other's data in order to track down fathers who refuse to pay child support. In addition, "best practices" would be shared across the country, including amnesty programs for parents with warrants out for their arrest if they come into court to commit to a reasonable payment plan.
- *Protection of and support for women at risk for coerced abortions and other violence.* The MPCPA would make it a federal crime, punishable under homicide statutes, to coerce a woman to have an abortion. It would give special protection to girls and women in abusive families and relationships, and would make federal grant money available to public and private entities for the creation of shelters to protect girls and women in these situations. This law would also fund awareness campaigns concerning sexual violence in a culture of nonconsensual sex, and would dramatically increase prosecution of rape that involves alcohol and structural violence.

One thing I hear fairly often — from both "pro-choice" and "pro-life" advocates — is that we should make abortion "unthinkable" rather than making it illegal. The above provisions are quite powerful, and they are exactly the kinds of structural changes that those who make such statements have called for. Isn't this the time to ask, then, Why wouldn't these public-policy changes be enough? Why do anything to limit the legality of abortion? Wouldn't these changes in our social structures make abortion unthinkable?

The data do not bear that out. Consider that many other rich Western countries have social structures already in place similar to the ones mentioned above. And while their abortion rates were once substantially lower than those in the United States, this is often not the case today. Sweden, for instance, offers sixteen months of leave — at 80 percent pay — to be split between either parent.[21] The United Kingdom offers an astonishing fifty-two weeks of maternity leave, thirty-nine of which is paid, for British women. Given these and other social supports for women, studies in the mid-1990s found what we might expect: abortion rates were substantially higher in the United States than in these countries. The teenage abortion rate in the United States was 29 per 1,000 women, for instance, but it was 22 in the UK and 18 in Sweden.[22] But while today the United States still has an abortion rate higher than that of other comparable countries among women twenty to twenty-five years of age, the rates among American women older than thirty were *lower* than those in many developed countries. And the teenage abortion rate in the United States (now 22 per 1,000 women) has become comparable to that of England (23 per 1,000) and *lower* than that of Sweden (25 per 1,000).[23]

So we absolutely should support women in the ways that the MPCPA proposes. It is the right thing to do. Period. And in a situation where abortion is broadly legal, it is likely that this support would help many women choose something other than abortion. But as the abortion numbers in places like Sweden and the UK demonstrate, serious protection of the civil rights of our prenatal children will require more than this. Indeed, even if the United States adopted the social supports of most of Western Europe, we would still have about 700,000 abortions every year.[24]

I give more details of the proposed law in this regard later in the chapter; however, at a very basic level, the MPCPA will obviously give the human fetus the same legal standing as other kinds of human beings. But some extremist "pro-lifers" want to give prenatal children *more* legal protection than other human persons. As we discussed in chapter 3, suppose a six-year-old child or insane adult poses a material mortal threat to his mother or another person. That child or insane adult has a right to life, of course, but the people whose lives the child endangers (even if through no moral or legal fault of their own) may nevertheless defend themselves with deadly force. This insight has a long history in the legal tradition of "justifiable homicide" as long as there is a "clear and present" mortal threat. This legal tradition not only permits self-defense, but also defense of another.

But "pro-life" extremists who argue for a legal ban on all direct abortions — including even abortion to save a mother's life — create a legal right for a prenatal child that no other human person has. Namely, they suppose a fetus has the right not to be killed even when (again, through no fault of their own) they pose a clear and present mortal threat. In horrifically tragic cases where the mother's life is threatened by her own prenatal child, the MPCPA would protect women the same way that all others are protected when their lives are threatened. It would protect the right of women to use direct and deadly force to defend themselves when their life is clearly in danger. In saying this, we should not forget, however, that the percentage of abortions that are necessary to save the mother's life is very small, and we saw in chapter 3 that the percentage that require direct abortion to save the mother's life is flat-out *tiny*. Given that the use of deadly force must be the absolute last resort, a direct abortion would be permitted under the MPCPA only in the extremely rare cases when indirect abortion could not save the mother's life. Nevertheless, even if it is rarely invoked, adequate legal protection of women means that we must be absolutely clear that they have the right to self-defense in the face of a deadly threat.

But is "life of the mother" the only reason for which one could legitimately get a direct abortion? What about the health of the mother — would that be an acceptable reason? Not in a tradition of ethics and law in which the use of deadly force against another person must be "proportionate." That is, in order to use deadly force against another individual, the harm to be avoided must be proportionate with the harm caused. The harm caused is the death of a human being, so that kind of value ("life," not just "health") is what must be at stake in the case of the direct killing of a prenatal child.

But what if a fetus has a serious malformation or disease, such as Potter's, Trisomy 13 or 18, or anencephaly? These babies often do not survive much past birth, and some people will even claim that their lives are not worth living. Are these tragic cases ones in which we should permit the direct killing of prenatal children? I think not. Each of these children has a disability, and we should treat them like we would treat other disabled people with a terminal illness. We need not take extraordinary measures to save their lives if such treatment would cause them an undue burden, but we should *never* aim at their deaths — either by an action or by refusal to aid. Especially given the goals of this book, it is worth pointing out that this point of view is held not only by "pro-lifers" but by important "pro-choice" thinkers as well.[25]

All humans, no matter how long they have to live, no matter their level of ability or cognition, no matter how vulnerable and needy they are, are equal in moral value. The law exists, in large part, to protect vulnerable populations from those who find this inconvenient. Indeed, we have rightly installed special respect and protections in the law for the disabled and other groups who are traditionally subjected to wrongful discrimination. This should be the case before birth as well as after. Fortunately, the perinatal hospice movement offers mothers and other family members the opportunity to treat their very sick children with precisely this kind of special respect.[26] At the time this book goes to press, over 250 health-care institutions offer this kind of care, and the numbers keep rising. Perinatal hospice also protects against an event that happens far too often when the patient is in utero: misdiagnosis. Instead of having an abortion on the basis of incomplete and often misleading data, those who go with perinatal hospice can bring their child to birth and have a much more confident diagnosis and prognosis.

Perhaps you think that we don't really need this kind of special protection for particularly vulnerable populations when it comes to abortion decisions. In chapter 1 we saw that over 90 percent of fetuses diagnosed with Down syndrome are killed via abortion, despite people with Down syndrome reporting happiness levels greater than those who are "healthy." But the discrimination doesn't stop there; a huge percentage of babies diagnosed with spina bifida are killed via abortion, despite the fact that in 2013 a woman born with this disease completed "an unprecedented Grand Slam sweep of the Boston, London, Chicago, and New York marathons in a single year."[27] Some say babies born with the horrific-looking skin disease called *harlequin ichthyosis* do not have a life worth living, especially because they are so susceptible to infections and other problems. But one child born with this disease managed to compete in a triathlon.[28]

Nor is this kind of discrimination limited to disability. It is well known that abortion/infanticide has been explicitly used for decades to attack girls. Though we've been told for decades about these practices in places like China and India, it is now becoming a problem in the developed West. In certain places in the UK, for instance, the second child born is 20 percent more likely to be a boy than a girl.[29] With growing evidence that sex-selection abortion is taking place in the United States, Congress attempted to ban that kind of abortion with the Prenatal Nondiscrimination Act. Remarkably, the bill failed.[30] Both Sweden and the UK also recently affirmed the right to abort a fetus based on its gender.[31] The MPCPA would explicitly ban these kinds of abortions, and because they clearly involve malice directed against a vulnerable population with special legal protection from discrimination, it would treat them as federal hate crimes.

Refusal to Aid for a Proportionately Serious Reason

Recall that in chapter 3 we discussed not only the (very rare) circumstances in which it might be legitimate to do a direct abortion to save the life of the mother, but also to do an indirect abortion understood as "refusing to aid" a fetus. We found that various kinds of indirect abortions (C-sections, hysterectomies, and even RU-486) could, in fact, be better described as refusing to aid rather than killing. Therefore, such indirect abortions, while perhaps morally wrong, would not be aiming at the death of an innocent person, an intrinsically evil act. Even from the perspective of traditional Catholic moral theology, if a pregnant woman has a proportionately serious reason she could refuse to sustain even a fetus before it is viable, as long as she merely foresaw (and did not intend) that the fetus would die. Importantly for our purposes in this chapter, this kind of proportionate reasoning has overlap with the "undue burden" model currently used in American abortion law. If a woman has a proportionately serious reason for choosing not to aid the prenatal child, then we could also say that the pregnancy places an "undue burden" on her. A law banning such abortions, therefore, would put an "undue burden" on the woman and would be unconstitutional.

But how would the "undue burden" calculation work out if the MPCPA were to be passed? Perhaps most importantly, because the fetus is a person with a right to life, our American tradition of family law would immediately require substantial support from both her mother and father. This tradition insists that parents have incredibly strong and often burdensome legal responsibilities for their children — indeed, as we saw in chapter 3, one could argue that many of these responsibilities (e.g., 30 percent of one's salary paid in child support for two decades) could be considered at least as burdensome as most pregnancies.[32] So when the law considers a prenatal child to be the legal son or daughter of the mother, what counts as an "undue" burden on that child's parent changes dramatically.

And don't forget the increased support for women and mothers. We have already seen the increases in such support since the undue burden standard was first invoked by the Supreme Court in 1992 (Children's Health Insurance Program, the Affordable Care Act, Pregnant Women Support

Act, etc.), but the support that would come with the MPCPA is even more significant. Among other things, it would mandate equal pay for equal work, universal pre-K, paid maternity leave for more than three months (with total job protection), and ending discrimination against women and new mothers in the workplace. These new and powerful supports for women would *dramatically* shift our sense of what kind of pregnancies count as an "undue burden" on women. Indeed, some would be tempted to say that with the passage of the MPCPA, beyond the mother's life being in danger, no such unduly burdensome pregnancy exists.

But is this really the case? What about when pregnancy threatens the mother's health? Current law does not permit *direct* taking of life in such situations, but could this be a proportionately serious reason for an *indirect* abortion? Recall, once again from chapter 3, the discussion that all parents have their physical and/or psychological health dramatically affected by their children. If there is going to be a health exception that allows for indirect abortion, it must rise above the substantial health risks that many parents of older children are subject to each day. As far as the MPCPA is concerned, for a health exception to count as a proportionately serious reason, the risk would have to be such that the mother is in danger of death — which is already covered with the life of the mother exception.[33]

But what about the prenatal child we considered who was diagnosed with Potter's? The fetus had no kidneys, an insufficient amount of amniotic fluid, underdeveloped lungs, and no ability to breathe on his own at birth. There is no cure, and the child was either going to die in utero or shortly after birth. Recall that the parents induced labor so that they could see, cuddle, and baptize their son. This seemed like a proportionately serious reason to induce labor, even preterm, and the MPCPA would indeed protect the right of parents to do this. If there is (1) a clear and unambiguous terminal diagnosis, confirmed by more than one OB-GYN, and agreed to by the attending neonatologist, and (2) a situation in which there is a significant chance the baby will die in utero, labor could be induced prematurely.

Readers will no doubt recall a final candidate for a proportionately serious reason to refuse to aid the fetus: when the pregnancy comes as a result of rape. Two things dramatically change the calculus in these kinds of pregnancies. First, the pregnancy is often burdensome on the woman in ways that few of us can begin to understand. For many women it may be horrific to carry the child of the person who assaulted you in one of the most devastating ways possible. Furthermore, both the law and common morality insist that we do not have the same kinds of obligations to our biologically related children when they did not come from our consensual choice to have sex. (A man who is raped by a woman should not be forced to pay child support, for instance.) With such an increased burden, and a decreased sense of what is owed the child, I believe the law should respect a mother's choice to refuse to aid a child via indirect abortion in the case of rape. While it is always wrong to aim at the death of an innocent person (the MPCPA would not permit direct abortion in the case of rape), it is not always wrong to refuse to aid such a person.[34]

Attempts by some to discount the burden, not only of the pregnancy, but also the lingering effects of the sexual assault (of which the prenatal child can serve as a near constant reminder), are part of a long and sorry history of our culture not taking sexual violence against women seriously. And if we do take it seriously, we must ask even more difficult questions. For instance, if rape is defined as "nonconsensual sex," then rape occurs far more often than in the explicitly violent situations just considered. If a woman's sexual partner has a significant amount of power over her (e.g., if he is her boss, teacher, abusive boyfriend or husband, etc.), then her "consent" to have sex with him is certainly pressured — even coerced. In such situations, especially when she or her children are financially dependent on the man, a woman is not necessarily free to decline his sexual advances. Furthermore, the law is becoming more and more aware of the fact that everyone's ability to consent to or refuse sex after having consumed a substantial amount of alcohol is seriously impaired. Indeed, it is likely that a large number of women get pregnant as a result of having sex when they were unable to discern consent or refusal due to their consumption of alcohol. Are these pregnancies the result of rape?

These difficult and intensely personal judgments should be made by the pregnant woman rather than the law. Even when there is a violent rape, the case can be difficult to prove legally due to lack of evidence. When it involves the matters raised above, it becomes more difficult, even impossible, for the law to determine answers to the questions that must be asked. This being the case, it thus falls to the mother to decide whether the sex was consensual and, if not, whether the pregnancy imposes an undue burden on her. Since the law is incapable of making these kinds of determinations, the MPCPA would permit indirect abortion until the eighth week of pregnancy via RU-486 (available by prescription with the presentation of a signed affidavit claiming that the pregnancy is a result of nonconsensual sex and of certification of a German-style counseling requirement during a three-day waiting period),[35] and leave the above determinations to the mother of the prenatal child.[36]

Some "pro-lifers" I know will be seriously dismayed by this proposed compromise. They will say that this simply gives abortion on demand a green light, given that large numbers of women will lie about being raped to get abortions they want for other reasons. Though I think this may be true of fewer women than these critics suspect — especially in light of the massive supports for women in the MPCPA — I agree that deceit would be a serious problem.[37] That very real evil, however, must be balanced against the evil of a powerful federal government inserting itself into the kinds of decisions just described. For example, can our federal government, without unduly violating the rights of women (and usurping our American understanding of limited government), really be expected to make judgments about whether a woman has had enough alcohol such that she would have sex without consenting to it? Or whether her relationship was sufficiently abusive such that she could not freely refuse to have sex with her boyfriend? Given that what is at stake are the lives of babies, this is an exceedingly difficult call — no question about it. But I ultimately think that the answer is, "No, the government should not do those things," especially in light of women's history of being forced to cede control of their bodies to the state.

What about beyond week eight of a pregnancy? In a considerable number of cases, women do not even find out that they are pregnant until well after this time, to say nothing of allowing these new mothers enough time to come to terms with the fact that their pregnancy has been the result of nonconsensual sex. In these situations, the MPCPA would also permit indirect abortion (C-section, early labor induction, etc.), but only if the mother can legally demonstrate (with the help of legal counsel, if she cannot afford it) by the preponderance of the evidence that the sex that produced the child was nonconsensual. Some "pro-choice" people I know will be outraged by this aspect of the proposed compromise. They will say that this displays a shocking disregard for the horrific trauma of a rape victim, and that it simply heaps more burdens onto an already terribly burdensome situation for the woman. While I'm sensitive to this critique, at a certain point justice concerns for the prenatal child must again be the trump card. These vulnerable prenatal children will still be aborted in huge numbers if nothing is done to stop the abortions, and having "indirect abortion on demand" is simply too large a loophole to leave open. Yes, this aspect of the compromise will be burdensome on some women, but it is required in order to do justice to the equal dignity of the fetus.

The Mother and Prenatal Child Protection Act

It cannot be stated often enough: the mother and her prenatal child are, at least in some sense, a dual entity and should not be considered isolated individuals. Most laws about abortion should think about and address mother and child together. Let's recap how this proposed federal law defends the basic civil rights of both mother and child:[38]

EQUAL PROTECTION OF THE LAW FOR THE PRENATAL CHILD

Prenatal children, like all other human children, are provided equal protection of the laws of the United States.

Direct or indirect surgical abortion procured to end the life of a fetus based on her mental disability, physical disability, gender, or race is banned. Testing for these traits will also be banned until after week eight (see below). Physicians performing such abortions will be charged with a "Class A" felony under a federal fetal homicide law, and also charged with a federal hate crime, given that there is specific malice being directed at a vulnerable and protected class.

Direct surgical abortions of other kinds are also banned except to save the life of the mother (see below). Physicians performing such abortions will be charged with the "Class A" felony mentioned above, without special circumstances.

EQUAL PROTECTION OF THE LAW
FOR WOMEN DURING PREGNANCY

As in all other aspects of her life, a pregnant woman has the legal right to defend herself with deadly force against a clear and present mortal threat.

Unless the situation is emergent, direct abortion to save the mother's life is permitted only when an independent team of physicians and community members confirms that (1) the pregnancy poses a "clear and present" threat to her life and (2) indirect abortion will not be effective.[39]

SUPPORT OF MOTHERS AND THEIR CHILDREN
DURING AND AFTER PREGNANCY

The civil rights and social equality of women require that they be given a genuine opportunity to be both mothers and full and equal members of our economic and political society. Toward that end, the following measures will be enacted:

— Equal pay for equal work, regardless of gender

— Increased protection for women and mothers when it comes to hiring and firing. Employers who fire or refuse to hire a person on the basis of real or perceived family responsibilities shall be presumed to have violated Title VII of the Civil Rights Act.

— Universal access to postpartum maternal health care

— Dramatically increased paid pregnancy leave with complete job protection

— Two years of universally available prekindergarten and more widely available and affordable child care at work and school

— Through appropriate legislation and public campaigns, attempts to resist and reform both the huge cost of adoption and the stigma that still surrounds adoption in our culture

— Systematic attempts to be both smarter and more aggressive in collecting child support, along with systematic campaigns to prosecute boyfriends, husbands, and parents who pressure women or girls into having an abortion[40]

REFUSAL TO AID FOR A PROPORTIONATELY SERIOUS REASON

The established tradition of family law insists that parents in general, even in the face of very great burdens, have a legal requirement to aid their children — including a duty to make substantial sacrifices to their own mental and physical health. The same strong legal requirement also exists for parents to support their child during pregnancy. Indirect abortion is therefore banned, and it is treated as a Class B felony — except to save the mother's life and in the cases below.

A woman may choose to get an indirect abortion up to week eight of pregnancy via the prescription drug RU-486. Given the gravity of the decision to refuse to aid a child who will die without such aid, a signed affidavit will be required claiming that the pregnancy is the result of non-consensual sex, along with certification of counseling during a three-day waiting period.

Beyond week eight, an indirect abortion (C-section, early pregnancy induction, hysterectomy, etc.) may be procured, but in such a case — again, given the gravity of the decision to refuse to aid a child who will die without such aid — nonconsensual sex must be demonstrated in court by a preponderance of the evidence.

Indirect abortion is also permitted in the case of a clear and unambiguous terminal diagnosis (made by more than one physician) and the likelihood that the baby will die in utero, so that the mother and other family may baptize, cuddle, or otherwise bond with the child. In addition, significant incentives will be offered to physicians and hospitals (like better reimbursement rates) for providing perinatal hospice care.

What the Law Does Not Do

So, in very broad strokes (again, closely watched policy-makers will have to fill in more specifics), that is what the MPCPA will do. Some readers may note that some important abortion-related issues do not appear in the above description, and they would be right. There is nothing in this proposed law, for instance, that addresses the complicated question of the moral status of the early embryo. Some argue that, because of the early embryo's ability to "twin" and "recombine," the embryo cannot be an individual person or even an individual member of the species Homo sapiens. Others argue that the early embryo constitutes a transition stage between gametes and human beings — kind of like the "dusk" between "day" and "night." We have seen early on that the Catholic Church, though it insists that the early embryo should be treated as a person, has refused to come down one way or another on the actual arguments. The MPCPA does not come down one way or the other on the moral status of the early embryo, though individual states could make their own laws about this question. But this proposed federal law says nothing about the embryo, nor about procedures and drugs that affect the embryo. The MPCPA says nothing, for instance, about stem-cell research or embryo experimentation. It says nothing about possible abortifacients such as Ella or the morning-after pill. Nothing at all in this law has implications for the legality or availability of contraception.[41]

Legal and Political Viability

We have already seen much to indicate that the MPCPA is legally viable. American constitutional law on abortion is in a state of flux, especially as it tries to figure out what the "undue burden" standard means as our culture shifts in various ways. Justice Kennedy is the swing vote on the Supreme Court, and he has signaled not only a willingness to revise his interpretation of the undue burden standard, but has also implied that this should be done in light of changes in the moral standing of the prenatal child. In *Steinberg v. Carhart,* for instance, Kennedy explicitly claimed that the Supreme Court has self-consciously refused to create an "exhaustive list" of the reasons that a state may have an interest in the life of the fetus.[42]

This is an opening through which one could drive a legislative Mack truck. Indeed, much has changed with respect to our culture's understanding of the value of the fetus since 1992. The debate on abortion has been further engaged, and the percentage of Americans who now think of themselves as "pro-choice" is at a record low. A clear majority of Americans would prefer that abortion be restricted far more than it is today, and individual states continue to pass bill after bill that accomplish precisely that. Dozens of states even have explicitly named "fetal homicide" laws. Consistent with the history of many pushes for civil rights, the push to recognize that our prenatal children have the same moral and legal standing as other children is gaining momentum. And the Supreme Court has left the door wide open to consider the growing interest our culture has taken in the moral value of the fetus.

The MPCPA also explicitly imagines itself working within the "undue burden" framework, refusing to exclude the equal value of the mother in thinking about these matters. In fact, in giving women the support necessary to participate as both mothers and the political and economic equals of men, this law concerns itself with something that our abortion laws have never done: it offers women the social support necessary to choose to gestate and keep their child. Indeed, previous abortion jurisprudence has effectively trapped women by forcing them to play the political and economic game by the rules designed for people who could not have children. On that understanding, abortion is not a "choice"; rather, it is a necessary component of women's equal participation in our patriarchal culture. But it should go without saying that forcing women to have abortions in order to have equality with men is anything but authentic equality.

Furthermore, we have already seen that other Western industrial countries have dramatically and effectively limited abortion rights. Ireland and Poland (and perhaps Spain) are obvious examples. And even countries that allow for abortion more broadly put significant and even dramatic limits on the procedure. Most European countries, for instance, allow abortion only until week twelve of pregnancy — and some go even lower.[43] The policy proposed by the MPCPA would be solidly within the spectrum of European abortion policies.

So this law would be legally viable. But would it be *politically* viable? In chapter 1 we explored a number of important and telling polls, but at this point recall the CBS/*New York Times* poll that found that 55 percent of Americans either wanted abortion "banned" (20 percent) or "available under stricter limits" (35 percent). A CNN poll found that 62 percent want abortion legal either in "no" circumstances (20 percent) or "few" circumstances (42 percent). The numbers say that a clear majority of Americans want abortion widely restricted, but what restrictions do they want? Even according to Gallup's own interpretation of its numbers, there is quite a bit of common ground when it comes to this question.[44] Check out these numbers on the percentage of those on "both sides" who support the following:

Policy	"Pro-Choice"	"Pro-Life"
Abortion Legal to Save the Life of the Mother	97%	69%
Abortion Legal in the Case of Nonconsensual Sex	91%	68%
Abortion Illegal in the Third Trimester	79%	94%
Abortion Illegal in the Second Trimester	52%	92%

These numbers are quite telling. They are not only more evidence of the incoherence of our lazy "pro-life"/"pro-choice" binary way of thinking about abortion, but they also line up very well with the conclusions of the MPCPA, which allows abortion to save the life of the mother, allows indirect abortion in the case of rape early in a pregnancy, and restricts it more substantially later in a pregnancy. Recall also another CBS/*New York Times* poll (quoted in chapter 1) that confirms these numbers: 52 percent of Americans either wanted abortion "illegal without exception" (10 percent) or "illegal except in cases of rape, incest, or life of the mother" (42 percent).

Though our corporate/media/political-industrial complex makes it difficult to see (I will explore this further in the conclusion to this book), the American people are already explicitly in favor of the abortion restrictions and permissions proposed by the MPCPA. If a truly democratic process were permitted to lead directly to our abortion policy, something like this law would already exist. But the majority's advantage is not huge: based on the numbers cited above, I suspect that somewhere around 55-60 percent of the American public would support the law. What about the substantial number of people who disagree? Does this proposal simply leave them out in the cold? Let me directly address four groups who, I imagine, might disagree most strongly with this proposal.

The first group I call to mind understands the value of the fetus as existing on a continuum. I have already explained in chapter 2 why I think the arguments for this position don't work, but let's leave that aside for the moment. This group believes that while all prenatal children have some value, the later-term fetus has very significant value (and perhaps even the value of a human person); on the other hand, the early-term prenatal child "has a claim on us, but not a full one." In this view, abortion in the cases of rape and a threat to the mother's life is a less difficult call: if the fetus does not have a full claim, then a woman would not have a strong duty to aid her. But especially in light of the social supports proposed by the MPCPA, are abortions simply procured as birth control morally acceptable? What about getting an abortion because of relationship problems? Or how about a baby with Down syndrome not fitting into one's life plan? Even with a view that the fetus has "moderate" moral status, this prenatal child still makes a moral claim on us such that we could call these kinds of abortion into question. I think many in this group could actually support the basic thrust of the MPCPA.

A second group who would likely disagree with the MPCPA one might call the "hardcore pro-choicers." Unlike the continuum group above, they don't see the fetus as having any moral value worthy of consideration unless the mother decides that she does. For this group, the sacrosanct value of individual women deciding what they will do with their bodies is unassailable. I've already responded to these arguments at several points in this book, so let's also put those aside for the moment. To this group I ask the following: How much of your deeply held "pro-choice" stance comes from your view of women as structurally disadvantaged in our culture? If we had a culture in which pregnancy was not penalized, and in which pregnancy and childbirth were supported economically, socially, and culturally — such that women's life plans need not be jeopardized by pregnancy, and such that every child would be born into a world with guaranteed health care, child-care, and economic support — wouldn't it be easier to accept stronger limits on abortion?

Without minimizing our common ground, let me be clear with the "hardcore pro-choice" advocates about something else. The handwriting is on the wall with regard to our current abortion laws. Much like those who oppose gay marriage, the tide has turned dramatically against your position, especially among the demographic groups who will lead the way in the coming years. The MPCPA may seem like something you want to oppose, but the examples of Ireland, Poland, and Spain show that our law could be even more restrictive. Especially given some of the trends we saw earlier in this chapter (Hispanics and Millennials being more skeptical of abortion than the rest of the population, more and more physicians refusing to do abortions, etc.), your prudential judgment about current and future American political realities may mean supporting something like this proposal. And given the ways in which abortion restrictions have been used mainly to restrict women's options without a complementary focus on protecting, celebrating, and promoting women's rights and women's bodies as those of equal political people, this law is actually quite positive and powerful. To conflate it with other attempts to restrict abortion is to miss a major opportunity for true progress.

Third, what about small-government conservatives? Won't they be loath to support something like the MPCPA? For "pro-lifers" who fall into this group, I would note that it is highly unlikely that Justice Kennedy or other future swing justices will reinterpret the "undue burden" standard in a way that broadly protects the fetus from abortion unless something like the supports for women offered by the MPCPA are enacted. Furthermore, Catholics (and all those of good will) in this group are invited by Pope John Paul II to embrace the following from his encyclical *Laborem Exercens:*

> In this context it should be emphasized that, on a more general level, the whole labor process must be organized and adapted in such a way

as to respect the requirements of the person and his or her forms of life, above all life in the home, taking into account the individual's age and sex. It is a fact that in many societies women work in nearly every sector of life. But it is fitting that they should be able to fulfil their tasks *in accordance with their own nature* — without being discriminated against and without being excluded from jobs for which they are capable, but also without lack of respect for their family aspirations and for their specific role in contributing, together with men, to the good of society. The *true advancement of women* requires that labor should be structured in such a way that women do not have to pay for their advancement by abandoning what is specific to them and at the expense of the family, in which women as mothers have an irreplaceable role.[45]

Catholic social doctrine insists that labor be structured to allow women to be both mothers and professionals, and the MPCPA goes a long way toward doing this.

Finally, what about the hardcore "pro-lifers" who want to ban all abortions? First, let me say something directly to the Catholics who fall into this group. You may not think that the MPCPA perfectly reflects your view of abortion, but you really should support something like it nevertheless. You should support it because the church explicitly teaches that faithful Catholics may support incremental legislative change if the political realities give you a proportionately serious reason to do so. And if you don't think our current discourse on abortion in the United States gives you such a reason, frankly, you need a dose of political reality. (And now I'm also speaking to all those who hold the "hardcore" view, not just Catholics.) Though the tide is turning against abortion on demand, it is absolutely *not* turning in the direction of banning all abortion. There is overwhelming support for abortion choice in the cases of rape and life of the mother. Indeed, over 90 percent of "pro-choicers" support these exceptions, *as do almost 70 percent of "pro-lifers."*

The position in favor of banning all abortion is a political nonstarter. Those who have pushed this position aggressively in the public sphere have done tremendous damage to the "pro-life" cause. As "pro-lifers," we achieve our goals when we help focus the public debate on the overwhelming majority of abortions, most of which the public does not support. But the "ban all abortion" strategy has allowed "pro-choicers" to shift our debate away from the reality of our abortion culture by focusing public attention on the 2 percent of abortions taking place in the cases of rape and when the mother's life is in danger. Instead of discussing the millions of killings of the most helpless children imaginable for reasons the public rejects, "pro-lifers" are painted as people who are in favor of "forcing women to die" and "ignoring the victims of rape." If you want to put actual justice for babies and women ahead of abortion policy purity tests, then you should support something like the MPCPA.

Conclusion

Given the legal, social, and demographic trends, the question we should be asking is not "Will there be a new abortion policy in the United States?" Rather, it should be "What will the coming U.S. abortion policy look like?" The Mother and Prenatal Child Protection Act is consistently and authentically "pro-life" in that it refuses to choose between the dignity, rights, and social equality of women and their prenatal children. It also happens to reflect the views of a substantial majority of Americans, works within the framework of our shifting constitutional law, and is even consistent with currently defined Catholic doctrine.

The passage of a law like this, however, could be derailed by U.S. political, media, and corporate interests and structures. These entities, after all, are responsible for telling our ridiculously simple binary story about two polarized extreme points of view warring against one another. They will likely continue to strongly resist attempts to tell the complex and *nonpolarized* story of what Americans actually believe about abortion. In concluding this book, I offer some thoughts about how to move beyond our polarized abortion discourse.

Beyond Polarization

If what I have claimed in this book is correct, some questions present themselves. Why hasn't something like the MPCPA been passed already? Wouldn't one of the two major parties put it forward in an attempt to gain votes and otherwise take advantage of this political opening? Wouldn't the media be pouncing all over this important and exciting story in an attempt to scoop their rivals? In a first attempt to answer these important questions, let's return to a claim I made in the introduction: One of my central themes is that confusion and polarization — which feed and build on each other, especially via media sound bites — have created the *illusion* that the abortion debate is at a hopeless stalemate. The received wisdom is that the debate is hopelessly deadlocked, and the best we can do is yell at each other about the big stuff, and maybe make a tiny amount of progress by nibbling around the edges of the small stuff. As I've shown in these pages, however, this could not be further from the truth. There is a very important opening — in terms of both public opinion and the interpretation of constitutional law — to take giant steps forward in the abortion debate.

The Media/Corporate/Political-Industrial Complex

Should we think the reason we have failed to take these steps is *merely* because of confusion? No, our media/corporate/political-industrial complex is responsible for the structures and language our culture uses to have the abortion debate in, and they have a strong interest in keeping this debate right in the familiar place it currently resides. Consider, for instance, that the corporations that run our major media organizations make a ton of money off our polarized discourse in general and our polarized abortion discourse in particular. Ruled by television and Internet advertising revenue, these corporations know that, above all, their content must get ratings and "hits." What *doesn't* get high ratings and lots of Internet hits is a nuanced, complex argument about how a clear majority of Americans agree about the basic outlines of an abortion policy. Do you know what *does* get high ratings and lots of Internet hits? Activist hacks with polarized, extreme positions on abortion going all CNN *Crossfire* on each other. In that kind of spectacle, a viewer is entertained and tantalized by the verbal violence and, in the process, she is fed an overly simplistic and easy-to-follow story about the "two sides" of a particular issue: the "good side" they are for and, perhaps more important, the "bad side" they are rooting against.

Anyone who has ever taken a journalism class is familiar with the newsroom principle that "if it bleeds, it leads." In the context of political debate, this means that aggressive, antagonistic arguments are what get ratings and hits — and ultimately make money for the shareholders of Turner Broadcasting, Newscorp, and NBC Universal. Making these shareholders money is what these companies exist to do, even in the face of severe scrutiny. In response to public shaming led by Jon Stewart, for instance, CNN decided to cancel its *Crossfire* show. But this attempt to drag our political discourse from the polarized gutter was hurt by low ratings. Many people simply didn't watch the more nuanced and honest approach to politics. Unsurprisingly, CNN brought the show back.[1]

It is also important to note that most media have a blind spot when it comes to abortion.[2] Remarkably — and despite the fact that the issues themselves, and public opinion about them, are so different — we often hear "abortion and gay marriage" lumped together in a news story as if they are virtually the same issue. Furthermore, the national media admit that they lean left, and when you consider that journalism is still generally dominated by men of considerable power and privilege, one can understand (especially in light of the discussion in chapter 5) why they generally refuse to challenge the "pro-choice" status quo.[3] It serves both their political and social interests to view the issue through the old lens.

And while the media deserve considerable blame for how they frame the public debate on abortion, we should not let the political parties off the hook. Indeed, in many cases it is becoming difficult to distinguish between the corporate media and the political parties with which they increasingly align themselves. While there are some exceptions that prove the rule (like regular appearances by conservative Joe Scarborough or liberal Kirsten Powers), the interests of MSNBC and Fox News are connected with the interests of the Democratic and Republican parties. And these parties also have a strong interest in keeping the abortion status quo. Consider Juan Williams's important insight in his *Muzzled: The Assault on Honest Debate*:

> Their strategy is all about a desire to keep the conversation locked in failure. Abortion is a premium "wedge" issue for producing money and votes. . . . Political strategists used these debates to excite their base voters, pro or con, but also as a form of negative advertising to attack the character of opposing candidates. . . . [Abortion] fits into the same fixed pattern of debate with the same prescribed divisions being held in place by the gravity of big money and power to excite voters.[4]

The Costanza strategy continues — despite its incoherency — *because it works.* It keeps the current arrangements of political power safe for those who benefit from them.

So this is the answer to the question I started with above. The corporate/media/political-industrial complex that frames the abortion debate in the United States has every reason to keep the debate in its current safe and familiar place. If we are to move beyond the polarized discourse that is so firmly entrenched in our culture, we need to challenge this framework and begin to use new ways of thinking and speaking about abortion. Only then will we be able to resist the lazy, false, and harmful idea that there are "two sides" to the abortion debate. Only then will we be able to resist the idea that we must choose between Republicans if we want to protect babies and Democrats if we want to protect their mothers.

Can We Shift Our Framework?

What are the prospects for such a shift? Again, when we think about what real people actually believe about abortion (recall that two-thirds of Americans identify with both "pro-life" and "pro-choice" labels, record numbers identify as independents, etc.), the prospects seem quite good. Could this ever really break into our public discourse in a meaningful way? I think that the answer is yes — even a confident yes. Especially at a time when women, Millennials, and Hispanics are coming into the power structures of American culture, our media and politics will be all but forced to look at how these groups think about abortion differently. Especially in the age of Facebook, Twitter, and the blogosphere — as we have recently seen with issues related to the rights of gays and lesbians — a new way of thinking can replace the old one very quickly. When major media are forced to cover our culture's shifting abortion politics, that will create an opening to have a more authentic and honest public discussion.

Furthermore, and even beyond the Costanza strategy, there are signs that our political categories are unstable in a deeper sense. The coalitions cobbled together in the 1970s no longer work and do not appear to be long for this world. The idea that we can divide the political world neatly between those who are "either for small or big government," or between those who are "either for traditional or progressive values," does not do justice to the complexity of what real people actually believe. As this becomes more and more obvious, the uneasy alliances made forty years ago are beginning to fall apart. Does anyone really believe that Republican leaders like Rand Paul and Ted Cruz have the stomach to use a big government to enact the views of religious conservatives or of neoconservative hawks? And who thinks that Democratic leaders like Hillary Clinton or Barack Obama are capable of truly standing up for the marginalized as they are forced to reward the Wall Street and other corporate paymasters who made their campaigns possible? The unstable coalitions of diverse constituencies that we call "Democrats" and "Republicans" were artificial even when they were created four decades ago. But today, despite the life-support they receive from a national media largely still using 1970s ideas to frame their stories, they are simply on the verge of becoming irrelevant. We see now that, led by Millennials, record numbers of Americans identify as neither Republican nor Democrat. And this trend shows no signs of slowing down.

So I believe that there is reason to be hopeful and even confident. The political shift necessary to finally have an honest discussion of abortion (and many other issues) in this country is already underway. Furthermore, this shift provides a wonderful opportunity for Christian churches to participate more authentically in the public sphere. Most Christians have imagined that bringing about gospel-inspired social change meant (1) aligning with the Democratic coalition, (2) aligning with the Republican coalition, or (3) condemning the secular political process altogether and focusing entirely on other means of bringing about social change. But these are three deeply unattractive options. The secular political process is responsible for so much injustice that it is difficult to imagine how Christians could authentically live the gospel without trying to resist and change it. But what people in their right mind believe that a tradition that began with a Jewish carpenter in the ancient Middle East, and that has been deeply impacted by each of the twenty centuries (and by numerous, diverse cultures) since that time, could somehow be made to fit into political coalitions created in the United States of the 1970s? The Christian tradition can be found in neither the Democratic Party nor the Republican Party, and Christians who sit comfortably with either party risk idolatry.

Fortunately, our shifting political culture presents the Christian churches with an absolutely golden opportunity to avoid this problem. For the first two-thirds of the twentieth century, for instance, the American Catholic Church was basically aligned with the Democratic Party. And for the last four decades it has been basically aligned with the Republican Party. But now we find ourselves in the happy position of being able to engage a new kind of public political discussion as the unstable coalitions begin to collapse and new ways of imagining our most important debates have a real opportunity to take hold. American Christian churches have a golden opportunity to put aside our idolatrous ties to Republicans and Democrats and think more critically and creatively about how the gospel relates to our new and emerging political culture.

When it comes to abortion as a particular issue within such a culture, Christians should lead by example. Again, while it is true that some churches resist the false choice presented by our secular political culture by serving the interests of both mother and child, they are the exceptions that prove the rule. Every church that has a "pro-life" ministry with regard to abortion should have a similar ministry to aid pregnant women and needy mothers and their children. Period. No excuses. Furthermore, a Christian political stance on abortion should come from a consistently lived, gospel-centered presumption against violence more generally — whether that is a stance against war, the death penalty, euthanasia, torture, or abortion. And we should be prepared to support political candidates and initiatives that reflect our commitments to nonviolence, regardless of the party involved.

New Ways to Think and Speak about Abortion

What happens if we manage to pull off a national conversation about abortion that resists the frameworks and ideas from the 1970s? For starters, in resisting polarized binaries (liberal/conservative, life/choice, etc.) we open up new ways to engage with those who think differently about abortion. Instead of thinking of them as the "enemy" on "the other side" of the debate (where engagement most often looks something like "war"), we can think of our engagement as a positive thing. If we engage in the spirit of "intellectual solidarity," we should expect the encounter to involve an attempt to convince and persuade, but also a readiness to listen, to learn something new, and perhaps even the rare opportunity to change our minds in light of what we have learned. The mere willingness to treat those with whom we strongly disagree as persons worthy of respect and even love — manifested in authentically listening to them — would be a huge upgrade from our current discourse. It is the kind of practice that can replace confusion with understanding and polarization with authentic relationship. It is the anti-Costanza strategy.

It is also the kind of thing that could lead to new ways of envisioning the debate, and even to the formation of new alliances. Is a self-identified "pro-life" conservative who claims that "abortion hurts women" really that far apart from a self-identified "pro-choice" liberal who claims that "abortion restriction hurts women"? They are both after the same thing: the flourishing of women. Instead of getting lost in the simplistic and unhelpful pro-life/pro-choice, liberal/conservative battles, they could direct their energy toward taking an honest and open-minded look at what the social sciences have to say about this question. They could also likely agree about many social policies that would give women the genuine freedom to choose to parent their children. Such a fundamental shift in attitude and framework allows us to imagine the kind of cooperation that would have seemed impossible when viewed through the binary either/or lens of 1970s American politics. To propose just one example: a woman who prays in front of an abortion clinic each morning and voted for Sarah Palin as a write-in candidate for president in 2012 could actually be allied with a reproductive justice activist who is reluctant to support Hillary Clinton because "she's just too conservative." How? Through their mutual attempts to aggressively prosecute and eradicate workplace discrimination against women, to reform adoption polices, to give parents a sufficient amount of maternal and paternal leave from work, and much more.

And this is only a beginning. Many other kinds of alliances could also emerge. What about disability-rights activists collaborating with their "pro-life" counterparts in resisting abortions done on the basis of gender, disability, and (perhaps in the not-too-distant future) sexual orientation? What about animal rights activists collaborating with their "pro-life" counterparts in resisting abortion beyond the point where the fetus can feel pain? What about "pro-lifers" collaborating with those fighting to pay single mothers a living wage and have subsidized child-care? What about "pro-lifers" engaging in broad-based attempts to protect women from physical violence and other kinds of pressure and coercion?

Before leaving the section on new ways to think and speak about abortion, let me highlight two general moral principles that I think can help illuminate the way toward discovering and solidifying these new kinds of alliances. I've argued elsewhere that the principle of "consistent nonviolence" could be helpful in reimagining our abortion discourse.[5] Focusing on a principle like this transcends our old and tired polarized divides, takes us out of our comfortable categories, and forces a hard look at our positions and how they relate to violence. If consistently nonviolent, many "pro-life" activists would be forced to examine both their rhetoric and tactics and see the extent to which they contribute to both physical and structural violence. Many would also need to take more seriously the important worry that women will undergo unacceptable violence if abortion is legally banned. "Pro-lifers" should never forget the violent history of men controlling women's bodies and reproductive capacities; but "pro-choice" advocates, looking through the same nonviolent lens, should also see that this kind of violence is still present in a culture with broad access to abortion. Such violence is allowed to flourish, at least in part, because appeals to autonomy and choice ignore our social structures. Furthermore, a nonviolent lens would compel "pro-choicers" to consider the violence present in the act of abortion itself and the effect that such violence has not only on our prenatal children but on abortion providers and on women. The principle of "consistent nonviolence" challenges the rhetoric, ideas, and tactics of everyone playing by the 1970s rules, and it provides one way to unite those who previously imagined themselves to be opposed.

Another principle that can do this is what Catholic moral theology calls a "preferential option" for the vulnerable and marginalized. It focuses our attention on identifying those who are without power in our political arrangements; on the missing voices from the conversation; on those whose dignity is inconvenient. It also invites skepticism of mere appeals to autonomy and choice — which simply reinforce the injustice by asking those without power to choose within a system that has been stacked against them. Having a preferential option for the vulnerable and marginalized means resisting the ideas and social structures that keep them without power and outside the central concern of the community. Notice

BEYOND THE ABORTION WARS

that this concern applies very well to both women and their prenatal children. We've been more aware over the past century of how women fit this description; and despite the many gains our culture has made for women's rights, chapter 5 demonstrated that far more work needs to be done. But prenatal children are an absolutely classic example of a vulnerable and marginalized population, and having this kind of preferential option means giving them a voice and protecting them from those who find their dignity inconvenient. Like the principle of consistent nonviolence, a preferential option for the vulnerable challenges us to move beyond the false and dangerous 1970s view that we are forced to choose between protecting either the fetus or her mother.

A Sense of Confidence and Urgency

It is no secret that academics often say and write things that aren't grounded in reality. To some of you, what I've called for in this book may seem like the pie-in-the-sky ramblings of someone who spends too much time in an ivory tower. In many other contexts, I'm very sympathetic to this critique. However, if you have this reaction, I politely challenge you to consider the possibility that you are looking at my arguments with a political lens created more than two generations ago. That lens is long past its sell-by date. Shifting public opinion, shifting demographics, and shifting interpretations of constitutional law all favor something like what I have proposed in this book. Far from skepticism or hesitation, these trends should give us a sense of confidence that something like the Mother and Prenatal Child Protection Act is a realistic goal. In fact, what I have called for is already well underway.[6]

But in addition to a sense of confidence, I also ask you to have a sense of urgency. And for two reasons. First, the political realignment currently underway — as women, Hispanics, and Millennials assert themselves in our culture's power structures — will not come again. This is a unique moment in American political culture and history, and one that provides a unique opportunity to enact fundamental social change. Second, one important reason why abortion has persisted as a monstrously important topic after all these decades is because the stakes are just so high: 1.2 million prenatal children aborted each year in the United States, often simply because they are inconvenient. But it is also difficult to imagine a more serious concern than the authentic flourishing, reproductive and social

166

freedom, and bodily integrity of tens of millions of women and girls. If we have a genuine opportunity to shift the abortion conversation such that we are able to address both sets of these huge concerns, how can we be anything other than "all in"?

This becomes an even more powerful point when we consider that the specter of our abortion politics haunts many other kinds of issues as well — from stem-cell research, to end-of-life issues, to health-care reform. If we managed to turn abortion into something other than a polarized disaster, the positive effects would be felt well beyond the issue of abortion itself. Indeed, we would take one of the major reasons for our current general political gridlock out of play and create an opening for government to function once again as a tool for the common good.

In the introduction to this book I cited Dan Henninger's claim that abortion is America's second civil war. This is certainly a fair description of our abortion discourse during the past two generations, and our media/corporate/political-industrial complex has an interest in continuing to make money off the many battles of this war. But a combination of legal, political, and demographic trends now signals not only the general possibility of having this debate in a very different way but also some very specific ways that we can move forward. An alternative path, away from the abortion wars, has presented itself and is now there for the taking. Here's hoping that a sense of confidence and urgency provides us with the courage to take it.

Notes

Notes to the Introduction

1. Daniel Henninger, "America's Second Civil War: The Gosnell Verdict Means that the Abortion Status Quo Must Change," *The Wall Street Journal* (2013): http://online.wsj .com/news/articles/SB10001424127887324767004578485283789264450?mg=reno64-wsj &url=http://online.wsj.com/article/SB10001424127887324767004578485283789264450 .html (accessed June 20, 2013).

2. Jessica Chasmar, "Pro-life Group at Johns Hopkins Denied Official Club Status," *The Washington Times* (2013): http://www.washingtontimes.com/news/2013/apr/1/pro-life -group-johns-hopkins-denied-official-club-/ (accessed June 20, 2013).

3. http://www.politico.com/news/stories/0310/34782.html (accessed June 9, 2014).

4. Caitlin Moran, "Feminism for a New Generation of Women," *The Cycle,* Web: http://video.msnbc.msn.com/the-cycle/48200177 (accessed June 20, 2013).

5. Daniel Jenky, "Daniel Jenky, Peoria Catholic Bishop: President Obama Follow- ing 'A Similar Path' As Hitler, Stalin." Web: http://www.huffingtonpost.com/2012/04/19/ daniel-jenky-peoria-catho_n_1438393.html (accessed June 20, 2013).

6. Lizzie Parry, "Oxford Student Found Hanged after Splitting Up with Her Boyfriend Endured a 'Campaign of Harrassment' by College Lecturer as well as Abortion Heartache," *The Daily Mail* (2014): http://www.dailymail.co.uk/news/article-2568586/Oxford-student -hanged-splitting-boyfriend.html (accessed Apr. 8, 2014).

7. Meaghan Winter, "My Abortion," *New York* (2013): http://nymag.com/news/ features/abortion-stories-2013-11/ (accessed Apr. 8, 2014).

8. "U.S. Catholics: Key Data from Pew Research," *Pew Research Center* (2013): http://www.pewresearch.org/key-data-points/u-s-catholics-key-data-from-pew-research/ #abortion (accessed Mar. 25, 2014); see also "The Facts Tell the Story: Catholics and Choice," *Catholics for Choice* (2006): http://www.catholicsforchoice.org/topics/reform/ documents/2006catholicsandchoice.pdf (accessed June 2, 2014).

9. Alan Greenblatt, "Why Partisans Can't Kick The Hypocrisy Habit," *Political News from NPR* (2013): http://www.npr.org/blogs/itsallpolitics/2013/06/14/191601623/why -partisans-cant-kick-the-hypocrisy-habit (accessed June 20, 2013).

10. "How Mitt Romney Has Positioned Himself on Abortion and Immigration," *The New York Times* (2012): http://www.nytimes.com/interactive/2012/10/11/us/politics/20121011-romney.html?_r=1& (accessed Dec. 1, 2012). And while it is true that Republicans generally attempt to pass anti-abortion bills and Democrats attempt to pass bills that favor abortion choice, neither party seems willing to fight for big ideas in the debate. Republicans seem content to nibble around the edges, and they come nowhere close to sweeping restrictions. Democrats seem content to keep the status quo, with no interest in, say, getting federal funding for abortion for poor women.

11. Sen. Lindsey Graham, interview by Anderson Cooper, "What's Next for President Obama?" *CNN Transcript Providers,* Podcast Video, Nov. 7, 2012: http://transcripts.cnn.com/TRANSCRIPTS/1211/07/acd.02.html (accessed Dec. 1, 2012).

12. Connor Simpson, "McCain Wants to Leave Abortion Alone," *The Atlantic Wire* (2012): http://news.yahoo.com/mccain-wants-leave-abortion-alone-republicans-move-away-200053520.html (accessed Dec. 1, 2012).

13. Victoria Toensing, "Pro-choice Republicans Go Public," *Washington Post* (2012): http://www.washingtonpost.com/opinions/pro-choice-republicans-have-a-place-in-the-party/2012/11/29/4ab72106-332e-11e2-bfd5-e202b6d7b501_story.html?wpisrc=emailtoafriend (accessed Dec. 1, 2012).

14. Steven Ertelt, "Nevada Republican Party Strips Pro-Life Language on Abortion from Its Platform," *Life News* (2014): http://www.lifenews.com/2014/04/14/nevada-republican-party-strips-pro-life-language-on-abortion-from-its-platform/ (accessed Apr. 27, 2014).

15. "About RM4C," *Republican Majority for Choice:* http://www.gopchoice.org/about/ (accessed Dec. 1, 2012).

16. William Saletan, *Bearing Right: How Conservatives Won the Abortion War* (Berkeley: University of California Press, 2004).

17. Lydia Saad, "Americans Still Split along 'Pro-Choice,' 'Pro-Life' Lines," Gallup (2011): http://www.gallup.com/poll/147734/americans-split-along-pro-choice-pro-life-lines.aspx (accessed June 21, 2013).

18. "Open Hearts, Open Minds, and Fair Minded Words: A Conference on Life and Choice in the Abortion Debate," *Princeton UCHV:* http://uchv.princeton.edu/Life_Choice/ (accessed June 21, 2013).

19. Charles Camosy, "Is Disagreement between Peter Singer and Catholic Teaching on Abortion 'Narrow'? A Response to Critics," *Catholic Moral Theology* (2013): http://catholicmoraltheology.com/is-disagreement-between-peter-singer-and-catholic-teaching-on-abortion-narrow-a-response-to-critics/ (accessed June 21, 2013).

20. That woman, Juana Villegas, ended up winning a settlement. Julia Preston, "Settlement for a Shackled Pregnant Woman," *The New York Times* (2013): http://www.nytimes.com/2013/10/18/us/settlement-for-a-shackled-pregnant-woman.html?_r=0 (accessed June 2, 2014).

21. Stephanie Slifer, "NYC Victoria's Secret Shoplifting Suspect Found with Dead Fetus in Bag, Police Say," *Crimesider* (2013): http://www.cbsnews.com/news/nyc-victorias-secret-shoplifting-suspect-found-with-dead-fetus-in-bag-police-say/ (accessed Dec. 17, 2013).

22. "Remains of Fetus Found at Illinois Laundry," United Press International (2010):

http://www.upi.com/Top_News/US/2010/03/18/Remains-of-fetus-found-at-Illinois -laundry/UPI-26471268928788/ (accessed Dec. 17, 2013).

23. "Survey: Committed to Availability, Conflicted about Morality: What the Millennial Generation Tells Us about the Future of the Abortion Debate and the Culture Wars," Public Religion Research Institute (2011): http://publicreligion.org/research/2011/06/ committed-to-availability-conflicted-about-morality-what-the-millennial-generation-tells -us-about-the-future-of-the-abortion-debate-and-the-culture-wars/ (accessed June 21, 2013).

24. In some cases, what has been defined as Catholic doctrine in these areas — even from the perspective of "pro-life," orthodox theologians and philosophers — is contested and often quite murky. Especially if you are interested in these kinds of "inside baseball" Catholic concerns, be sure to follow footnotes with regard to what you consider controversial claims. Let me also be clear that if the institutional church at some future time declares that something I write in this book is inconsistent with defined Catholic doctrine, I urge my Catholic readers to use the teaching of the church — and not the claims of this book — to form their conscientious views.

Notes to Chapter 1

1. Many readers will be familiar with the popular TV show *Seinfeld,* which dominated American situation comedy ratings during the 1990s. In one of the most hilarious episodes in the series, George Costanza, one of the main characters, decides to take on a new strategy and do the opposite of every instinct he's ever had. It works out quite well for him.

2. Kathryn Kost and Stanley Henshaw, "Trends in the Characteristics of Women Obtaining Abortions, 1974 to 2004," Guttmacher Institute (2008): http://www.guttmacher .org/pubs/2008/09/18/Report_Trends_Women_Obtaining_Abortions.pdf (accessed June 24, 2013).

3. R. K. Jones and K. Kooistra, "Abortion Incidence and Access to Services in the United States 2008," *Perspectives on Sexual and Reproductive Health* 43, no. 1 (2011): 41-50: http://www.guttmacher.org/pubs/psrh/full/4304111.pdf (accessed June 24, 2013).

4. "Vital Statistics," The New York City Department of Health and Mental Hygiene (2012): http://www.nyc.gov/html/doh/html/data/vs-summary.shtml (accessed June 24, 2013).

5. Barack Obama, "Address to Notre Dame's Class of 2009" (speech, Notre Dame, IN, May 17, 2009), NPR: http://www.npr.org/templates/story/story.php?storyId=104226887 (accessed June 24, 2013).

6. The 1 in 3 Campaign, "The 1 in 3 Campaign — These are OUR Stories": http://www .1in3campaign.org/about (accessed June 24, 2013).

7. Olivia Fleming, " 'Got a Quickie Aborsh': Comedienne Sarah Silverman Supports Pro-Choice Debate, Tweeting 'Before-and-After Abortion' Photos," *The Daily Mail* (2012): http://www.dailymail.co.uk/femail/article-2129490/Sarah-Silverman-posts-quicky -abortion-photo-Twitter-support-pro-choice-debate.html (accessed June 2, 2014).

8. Heather Wood Rudulph, "Why I Filmed My Abortion," *Cosmopolitan* (2014): http://www.cosmopolitan.com/advice/health/why-i-filmed-my-abortion (accessed May 7, 2014).

9. Lawrence B. Finer et al., "Reasons U.S. Women Have Abortions: Quantitative and Qualitative Perspectives," Guttmacher Institute (2005): http://www.guttmacher.org/pubs/journals/3711005.pdf (accessed June 24, 2013).

10. Caroline Mansfield, Suellen Hopfer, and Theresa Marteau, "Termination Rates after Prenatal Diagnosis of Down Syndrome, Spina Bifida, Anencephaly, and Turner and Klinefelter Syndromes: A Systematic Literature Review," *Prenatal Diagnosis* 19, no. 9 (1999): 808-12: http://onlinelibrary.wiley.com/doi/10.1002/(SICI)1097-0223(199909)19:9<808::AID-PD637>3.0.CO;2-B/abstract (accessed June 24, 2013).

11. Brian Skotko, Susan Levine, and Richard Goldstein, "Self-perceptions from People with Down Syndrome," *American Journal of Medical Genetics* 155, no. 10 (2011): 2360-69: http://onlinelibrary.wiley.com/doi/10.1002/ajmg.a.34235/full (accessed June 24, 2013).

12. John Bingham, "MPs: Abortions Being Carried Out for Cleft Palates," *The Telegraph* (2013): http://www.telegraph.co.uk/news/politics/10183668/MPs-Abortions-being-carried-out-for-cleft-palates.html (accessed Dec. 17, 2013).

13. Ruth Padawer, "The Two-Minus-One Pregnancy," *The New York Times* (2011): http://www.nytimes.com/2011/08/14/magazine/the-two-minus-one-pregnancy.html?ref=magazine (accessed June 24, 2014).

14. "An Overview of Abortion in the United States," Guttmacher Institute (2014): http://www.guttmacher.org/presentations/abort_slides.pdf (accessed June 24, 2013).

15. Rachel K. Jones, Lawrence B. Finer, and Susheela Singh, "Characteristics of U.S. Abortion Patients, 2009," Guttmacher Institute (2010): http://www.guttmacher.org/pubs/US-Abortion-Patients.pdf (accessed June 24, 2013).

16. Though I will make no explicit arguments about contraception in this book, it is worth noting that both the UK and Sweden have sweeping and publicly supported use of contraception, and they still have a very high abortion rate.

17. "Fact Sheet: Induced Abortion in the United States," Guttmacher Institute (2014): http://www.guttmacher.org/pubs/fb_induced_abortion.html (accessed June 24, 2013).

18. Though a new blood test can be used to try to screen for Down syndrome in the first trimester, it would need to be confirmed by tests (usually by amniocentesis) in the second trimester.

19. Josh Voorhees, "Abortion Provider Kermit Gosnell Found Guilty on Three Counts of First-Degree Murder," *Slate* (2013): http://www.slate.com/blogs/the_slatest/2013/05/13/kermit_gosnell_jury_reaches_verdict_in_case_of_pa_abortion_doctor_accused.html (accessed June 24, 2013).

20. Melinda Henneberger, "Are There More Abortion Doctors like Kermit Gosnell? And Do We Want to Know?" *The Washington Post* (2013): http://www.washingtonpost.com/blogs/she-the-people/wp/2013/04/28/are-there-more-abortion-doctors-like-kermit-gosnell-do-we-want-to-know/ (accessed June 24, 2013).

21. Lawrence B. Finer et al., "Reasons U.S. Women Have Abortions: Quantitative and Qualitative Perspectives," Guttmacher Institute (2005): http://www.guttmacher.org/pubs/journals/3711005.pdf (accessed June 24, 2013).

22. Landrum Shettles and David Rorvik, *Rites of Life* (Grand Rapids: Zondervan, 1983), p. 129.

23. "Herstory Worth Repeating," *Feminists for Life:* http://www.feministsforlife.org/herstory/ (accessed June 28, 2013).

24. Kristen Day, *Democrats for Life: Pro-Life Politics and the Silenced Majority* (Green Forest, AR: New Leaf Press, 2006), pp. 71-145.

25. Some now argue that Blackmun was convinced by other "pro-choice" colleagues (and their clerks) on the Court, and that he originally had a much more restrictive vision for *Roe.* See David Garrow, "How *Roe v. Wade* Was Written," *Washington and Lee Law Review* (2014): http://scholarlycommons.law.wlu.edu/cgi/viewcontent.cgi?article=4393&context =wlulr (accessed June 2, 2014).

26. Though many in the movement are totally sincere today, there is some evidence that the religious right of the late 1970s self-consciously used abortion as an ad hoc way of creating a broader political coalition within the Republican Party. See Randall Balmer, *Thy Kingdom Come: An Evangelical's Lament* (New York: Basic Books, 2006), p. 16.

27. Day, *Democrats for Life,* p. 96.

28. Lydia Saad, " 'Conservatives' Are Single-Largest Ideological Group," Gallup (2009): http://www.gallup.com/poll/120857/conservatives-single-largest-ideological -group.aspx (accessed June 30, 2013).

29. Neil King Jr. and Allison Prang, "More Voters Turn on Obama," *The Wall Street Journal* (2013): http://online.wsj.com/news/articles/SB10001424052702304527504579167 853049782242 (accessed Feb. 7, 2014).

30. "End of the Party?" *The Economist* (2014): http://www.economist.com/blogs/ democracyinamerica/2014/01/american-politics (accessed Feb. 7, 2014).

31. "Survey: A Generation in Transition: Religion, Values, and Politics among College-Age Millennials," Public Religion Research Institute (2012): http://publicreligion.org/ research/2012/04/millennial-values-survey-2012/ (accessed June 30, 2014).

32. "Abortion and Birth Control," CBS News Poll: http://www.pollingreport.com/ abortion.htm (last modified July 31, 2013; accessed Aug. 1, 2013).

33. Lydia Saad, "Majority of Americans Still Support *Roe v. Wade* Decision," Gallup (2013): http://www.gallup.com/poll/160058/majority-americans-support-roe-wade -decision.aspx (accessed June 30, 2013).

34. U.S. House of Representatives, "Final Vote Results for Roll Call 884," United States Congress (2009): http://clerk.house.gov/evs/2009/roll884.xml. That such a large number of "pro-life" Democrats could vote for such a "pro-life" bill was the first sign that something was different this time around.

35. J. Peter Nixon, "A Pro-Life Victory?" *Commonweal* (2010): http://www.common wealmagazine.org/blog/?p=7442 (accessed June 30, 2013).

36. See chap. 6 for a more detailed discussion of these provisions.

37. Jodi Jacobson, "Nelson Restrictions Most Likely Outcome of Reconciliation Process," *RH Reality Check* (2010): http://rhrealitycheck.org/article/2010/03/03/nelson -restrictions-most-likely-outcome-reconciliation-process/ (accessed June 30, 2013); "White House Crafting Deal with Stupak on Executive Order," *RH Reality Check* (2010): http:// www.rhrealitycheck.org/blog/2010/03/21/update-correction-white-house-crafting-deal -stupak-executive-order (accessed June 30, 2013).

38. In 2013, for instance, "pro-life" Democrats were essential in defeating New York Gov. Andrew Cuomo's attempt to expand late-term abortion (Charles Camosy, "Late-Term Abortion Expansion Defeated in New York State . . . Thanks to Pro-Life Democrats," *Catholic Moral Theology* [2013]: http://catholicmoraltheology.com/late-term-abortion-expansion -defeated-in-new-york-state-thanks-to-pro-life-democrats/ [accessed June 30, 2013]).

39. Some, including many legal scholars, may simply deny that *Roe* is still the law of the land, especially given its successor cases, such as *Planned Parenthood v. Casey,* which have substantially modified the decision. I explore this in some detail in later chapters.

40. Pew Research Religion and Public Life Project, "*Roe v. Wade* at 40: Most Oppose Overturning Abortion Decision": http://www.pewforum.org/2013/01/16/roe-v-wade-at -40/ (last modified Jan. 16, 2013; accessed June 30, 2013).

41. Raymond J. Ademak, "A Review: Public Opinion and *Roe v. Wade*: Measurement Difficulties," *The Public Opinion Quarterly* 58, no. 3 (1994): 409-18: http://www.jstor.org/ stable/2749730 (accessed June 30, 2013).

42. Linda Greenhouse, "Misconceptions About Roe v. Wade," *The New York Times* (2013): http://opinionator.blogs.nytimes.com/2013/01/23/misconceptions/?_r=0 (accessed June 30, 2013).

43. Jason Keyser, "Ginsburg: Roe Gave Abortion Opponents a Target," *ABC News* (2013): http://abcnews.go.com/m/story?id=19160673 (accessed June 30, 2013).

44. Princeton UCHV, "Open Hearts, Open Minds, and Fair Minded Words: A Conference on Life and Choice in the Abortion Debate": http://uchv.princeton.edu/Life_Choice/ (accessed June 21, 2013).

45. http://www.washingtonpost.com/blogs/she-the-people/wp/2013/06/26/wendy -davis-beats-the-clock-with-an-assist-from-the-gallery/ (accessed June 9, 2014).

46. "Europe's Abortion Rules," BBC News: http://news.bbc.co.uk/2/hi/europe/6235557 .stm (last modified Feb. 12, 2007; accessed July 1, 2013).

47. Tobias Buck, "Spain's Mariano Rajoy in Fight to Reverse Liberalized Abortion Law," *Financial Times* (2013): http://www.ft.com/cms/s/0/376f6bf0-c477-11e2-bc94 -00144feab7de.html.

48. "Gallardón: I Think the Fear of Losing Their Jobs because of Pregnancy," *El País Sociedad* (2012): http://translate.google.com/translate?act=url&depth=1&hl=en&ie= UTF8&prev=_t&rurl=translate.google.com&sl=auto&tl=en&u=http://sociedad.elpais .com/sociedad/2012/03/08/actualidad/1331177681_396483.html (accessed July 1, 2013).

49. This fact is the fulfillment of the hope and argument first made more than twenty-five years ago by Mary Ann Glendon in her *Abortion and Divorce in Western Law: American Failures, European Challenges* (Cambridge, MA: Harvard University Press, 1989).

50. Clarke D. Forsythe, "Progress after Casey," *National Review Online* (2012), http://www.nationalreview.com/corner/304416/progress-after-icaseyi-clarke-d -forsythe (accessed July 1, 2013).

51. Sarah Kliff, "The Abortion Ban Texas Is Debating? It Already Exists in 12 Other States," *The Washington Post* (2013): http://www.washingtonpost.com/blogs/wonkblog/ wp/2013/07/01/the-20-week-abortion-ban-texas-is-debating-already-exists-in-12-states/ (accessed July 1, 2013).

52. Paul Bedard, "70 New Anti-abortion Laws OK'd in 22 States, Second-most Ever," *The Washington Examiner* (2014): http://washingtonexaminer.com/70-new-anti-abortion -laws-okd-in-22-states-second-most-ever/article/2541498 (accessed Feb. 7, 2014).

53. Guttmacher Institute, "2012 Saw Second-Highest Number of Abortion Restrictions Ever": http://www.guttmacher.org/media/inthenews/2013/01/02/ (last modified Jan. 2, 2013; accessed July 1, 2013).

54. Linda Feldmann, "Nine States Charging Hard against Abortion," *The Christian Science Monitor* (2013): http://www.csmonitor.com/USA/Politics/2013/0614/Nine-states

-charging-hard-against-abortion/Arkansas-Legislature-overrides-governor-bans-abortion -after-12-weeks (accessed May 11, 2014).

55. Liz Benjamin, "Klein Offers Hostile Abortion Amendment, Fails," *State of Politics* (2013): http://www.nystateofpolitics.com/2013/06/klein-offers-hostile-abortion -amendment-fails/ (accessed July 1, 2013).

56. Victoria M. DeFrancesco Soto, "Opinion: Can the Republicans Connect with Latinos on Abortion?" *NBC Latino* (2012): http://nbclatino.com/2012/08/24/opinion-can -the-republicans-connect-with-latinos-on-abortion/ (accessed July 1, 2013).

57. Damla Ergun, "Majority Supports Legal Abortion, But Details Indicate Ambivalence," *ABC News* (2013): http://abcnews.go.com/blogs/politics/2013/07/majority-sup ports-legal-abortion-but-details-indicate-ambivalence/ (accessed Mar. 29, 2014).

58. Anna Simonton, "The Future of the Pro-Choice Movement," *The Nation* (2013): http://www.thenation.com/article/172713/future-pro-choice (accessed July 3, 2013).

59. Elizabeth Hayt, "Surprise, Mom: I'm Against Abortion," *The New York Times* (2003): http://www.nytimes.com/2003/03/30/style/surprise-mom-i-m-against-abortion .html?pagewanted=all&src=pm (accessed July 3, 2013).

60. Chris McComb, "Teens Lean Conservative on Abortion," Gallup (2003): http:// www.gallup.com/poll/9715/Teens-Lean-Conservative-Abortion.aspx (accessed Mar. 29, 2014).

61. Lydia Saad, "Generational Differences on Abortion Narrow," Gallup (2010): http://www.gallup.com/poll/126581/generational-differences-abortion-narrow.aspx (accessed July 3, 2013).

62. "Survey: A Generation in Transition; Religion, Values, and Politics among College-Age Millennials," Public Religion Research Institute (2012): http://publicreligion.org/ research/2012/04/millennial-values-survey-2012/ (accessed July 3, 2014).

63. Sarah Kliff, "The Abortion Ban Texas Is Debating? It Already Exists in 12 Other States," *The Washington Post* (2013): http://www.washingtonpost.com/blogs/wonkblog/ wp/2013/07/01/the-20-week-abortion-ban-texas-is-debating-already-exists-in-12-states/ (accessed July 3, 2013).

64. "Americans on the Catholic Church," *The New York Times* and *CBS News* (2013): http://www.nytimes.com/interactive/2013/03/05/us/catholics-poll-graphic.html?ref=us &_r=0 (accessed Feb. 24, 2013).

65. Sarah Kliff, "Exclusive: NARAL President Nancy Keenan to Step Down," http:// www.washingtonpost.com/blogs/wonkblog/post/exclusive-naral-president-nancy-keenan -to-step-down/2012/05/10/gIQAn85PGU_blog.html (accessed Dec. 3, 2014).

66. Pew Research Religion and Public Life Project, "Roe v. Wade at 40: Most Oppose Overturning Abortion Decision": http://www.pewforum.org/2013/01/16/roe-v-wade-at -40/ (last modified Jan. 16, 2013; accessed July 3, 2013).

67. Jeffrey Toobin, "The Abortion Issue Returns," *The New Yorker* (2013): http:// www.newyorker.com/online/blogs/comment/2013/05/abortion-returns-to-the-supreme -court.html (accessed July 3, 2013).

68. Frances Kissling, "Abortion Rights Are Under Attack, and Pro-choice Advocates Are Caught in a Time Warp," *The Washington Post* (2011): http://www.washingtonpost.com/ wp-dyn/content/article/2011/02/18/AR2011021802434.html (accessed July 3, 2013).

Notes to Chapter 2

1. Peter Singer, *Practical Ethics* (Cambridge, UK: Cambridge University Press, 2011), p. 151.

2. "89, 90, or 93? Expert Sheds Light on Tycoon's Age," *The Star Online* (2007): http://www.thestar.com.my/story.aspx/?file=/2007/10/25/nation/19269368 (accessed July 20, 2013).

3. Some colleagues whom I respect would not be convinced by this point; they would reject the idea that moral status or value matters at all. Especially those having a Christian theological perspective see the idea of a "person" as a foreign import into the discussion, mostly coming from the secular Enlightenment, which thought of all "good" in terms of either utilitarian or economic/capitalistic reasoning. They argue that moral status comes not from the abstract arguments like those I express in this chapter, but from stories we tell about the relationships within a particular community. It is beyond the scope of this chapter to get into this complex debate, but this view, in my opinion, fails to account for even basic intuitions that seem to rely on a concept like moral status. For instance, why should we think of the prenatal child inside her mother as different from a tapeworm inside her mother? Perhaps my opponent would make the relational point that the fetus is the mother's daughter and the tapeworm is not. I agree with this conclusion, but I don't see how you get there without also making a claim about the personhood of the child outside of the context of the relationship. As I will argue below, the prenatal child is a substance of a rational nature, like her mother, and the tapeworm is not. This is what is actually setting the table for us to describe the fetus as the daughter of her mother. It is difficult to see how invoking "community" helps without first establishing moral status — and this is the goal of the current chapter.

4. Meeri Kim, "Newborn Babies in Study Recognized Songs Played to Them While in the Womb," *The Washington Post* (2013): http://www.washingtonpost.com/national/health-science/newborn-babies-in-study-recognized-songs-played-to-them-while-in-the-womb/2013/11/02/294fc458-433d-11e3-a624-41d661b0bb78_story.html (accessed Dec. 17, 2013).

5. Brandon Keim, "Babies Want to Be Social, Even Before They're Born," *Wired* (2010): http://www.wired.com/wiredscience/2010/10/social-babies/ (accessed July 20, 2013).

6. Vivian, "Bellabeat Tracking System — Lets Moms Listen to Their Baby's Heartbeat and Track Their Pregnancy," *Natural Mama* (2014): http://www.naturalbabygoods.com/bellabeat/ (accessed Mar. 25, 2014).

7. Steven B. Morse et al., "Racial and Gender Differences in the Viability of Extremely Low Birth Weight Infants: A Population-Based Study," *Pediatrics* 117, no. 1 (Jan. 2006). Available on-line at http://familydata.health.ufl.edu/files/2010/10/morse_racial_gender_differences_in_viability.pdf.

8. Julian Savulescu, "Abortion, Infanticide and Allowing Babies to Die, Forty Years On," *Journal of Medical Ethics* 39, no. 5 (2013): http://jme.bmj.com/content/39/5.toc (accessed July 21, 2013).

9. I will say, however, that I think mice and rats, though not persons, have a high moral status that is worthy of significant moral respect. As this book goes to press, I'm finishing an article (co-authored with Susan Kopp) in the *Journal of Moral Theology* on the

ethics of using such animals in medical experiments. I think that such experiments should be bound by serious respect for the meaningful and even beautiful lives of mice and rats.

10. Jha Alok, "Pope's Astronomer Says He Would Baptise an Alien If It Asked Him," *The Guardian* (2010): http://www.theguardian.com/science/2010/sep/17/ pope-astronomer-baptise-aliens (accessed July 21, 2013).

11. Antonia Blumberg, "Pope Francis Says He Would Baptize Martians, Asks 'Who Are We to Close Doors?'" *The Huffington Post* (2014): http://www.huffingtonpost.com/2014/05/12/ pope-francis-aliens_n_5310935.html?1399919226&ncid=tweetlnkushpmg00000067 (accessed May 12, 2014).

12. Charles Camosy, *Peter Singer and Christian Ethics* (Cambridge, UK: Cambridge University Press, 2012), chap. 1. For a similar argument in favor of moral status based on natural kinds, see also the work of Robert George and Patrick Lee, including their "The Wrong of Abortion" in Andrew I. Cohen and Christopher Health Wellman, eds., *Contemporary Debates in Applied Ethics* (Hoboken, NJ: Wiley-Blackwell, 2014), pp. 37-43.

13. For the most recent confirmation of this position, see §5 of *Dignitatis Personae*: http://www.vatican.va/roman_curia/congregations/cfaith/documents/rc_con_cfaith_doc _20081208_dignitas-personae_en.html (accessed Mar. 29, 2014).

14. Margaret Olivia Little, "Abortion at the Margins of Personhood," *Rutgers Law Journal* 39, no. 331 (2008): 3339-40.

15. When I use the phrase "equal protection of the law," I want to make it clear that I am not making a specific claim about the complex jurisprudential history about how the 14th and 15th Amendments have been interpreted. Rather, I'm making the broad, general point that all vulnerable persons have their basic rights (like the right to life) protected equally, without discrimination (in this case) on the basis of age or condition of dependency.

Notes to Chapter 3

1. For those readers concerned with orthodox Catholic moral theology, it is important not to confuse "proportionate reasoning" with "proportionalism." The former is an indispensable part of the Catholic moral tradition, but the latter has been condemned for rejecting the idea that certain acts are, of their very nature, intrinsically evil. My argument in this book often relies on proportionate reasoning, but rejects proportionalism — not least because I insist that aiming at the death of an innocent person is intrinsically evil.

2. I think that killing animals like pigs merely because they taste good, for instance, is morally problematic. See Charles Camosy. *For Love of Animals: Christian Ethics, Consistent Action* (Cincinnati: Franciscan Media, 2013).

3. Anthony Levatino, "Testimony of Anthony Levatino, M.D., before the Subcommittee on the Constitution and Civil Justice," U.S. House of Representatives (2013): http:// judiciary.house.gov/hearings/113th/05232013/Levatino%2005232013.pdf (accessed Aug. 8, 2013).

4. At least in the abstract. Especially from the perspective of Catholic teaching, an action can be intrinsically evil without much (if any) blame attaching to the person who committed the act. For instance, a woman who is coerced into abortion may not be guilty of anything at all. Other circumstances (like someone's state of mind) might also mitigate guilt.

5. See Benedict M. Ashley, Jean deBlois, and Kevin D. O'Rourke, *Health Care Ethics:*

A Catholic Theological Analysis, 5th ed. (Washington, DC: Georgetown University Press, 2006), p. 82; William E. May, *Catholic Bioethics and the Gift of Life,* 2nd ed. (Huntington, IN: Our Sunday Visitor, 2008), pp. 199-202; Kaczor, "The Ethics of Ectopic Pregnancy: A Critical Reconsideration of Salpingostomy and Methotrexate," *Linacre Quarterly* 76, no. 3 (August 2009): 265-82.

6. Germain Grisez, *The Way of the Lord Jesus,* chap. 8: "Life, Health, and Bodily Inviolability: Question D: Is Abortion Always the Wrongful Killing of a Person?" (Chicago: Franciscan Herald Press, 1983).

7. The fact that merely knowing that the peasant/baby is alive or dead can change the object of the act is evidence that the view for which I'm arguing here is not purely physicalist.

8. Some would say that there is actually a third option. In the case of "Vital Conflicts," when both mother and child will otherwise die, pro-life Catholics such as Martin Rohnheimer (*Vital Conflicts* [Washington, DC: Catholic University of America Press, 2009]) have suggested that directly killing the fetus to save her mother's life is morally acceptable. Or, perhaps better, if the prenatal child is going to die anyway, then it is not wrong to kill her to save her mother's life. But it is difficult for me to see why justice (in the form of respecting the principle "it is always wrong to aim at the death of an innocent person") would not apply to the fetus. In other contexts (after birth) in which an innocent person is almost certainly going to die in the future, this does not change the fact that we may not kill her, even to produce a very good outcome.

Regardless of one's views of these matters, it is worth noting that even after making this argument, Rohnheimer has maintained impeccable "pro-life" credentials and has not been censured by any Catholic authority. As I note toward the end of this chapter, this really goes to show how badly the institutional church wants to find a solution to the tension between defending the innocent and allowing mothers a right to self-defense.

9. Another way to approach this problem is to use the thought of Thomas Aquinas on "double effect" to try to show that use of deadly force in defense of self or another is not really aiming at death. This would be true in all circumstances: whether using deadly force against a mortal threat with a noninnocent will or a mortal threat with an innocent will. For an excellent discussion of this approach, see Thomas Cavanaugh, *Double-Effect Reasoning: Doing Good and Avoiding Evil* (Oxford: Oxford University Press, 2006).

10. Online Etymology Dictionary, "innocent (adj.)": http://www.etymonline.com/ index.php?term=innocent&allowed_in_frame=0 (accessed Sept. 5, 2013).

11. *Casti Cannubii,* §64: http://www.vatican.va/holy_father/pius_xi/encyclicals/ documents/hf_p-xi_enc_31121930_casti-connubii_en.html; see also *Evangelium Vitae,* §58: http://www.vatican.va/holy_father/john_paul_ii/encyclicals/documents/hf_jp-ii_enc _25031995_evangelium-vitae_en.html#-1M.

12. James Gustafson, an important Protestant moral theologian, helpfully discusses the moral sense of tragedy in such situations. See his "A Protestant Ethical Approach," in John T. Noonan Jr., ed., *The Morality of Abortion: Legal and Historical Perspectives* (Cambridge, MA: Harvard University Press, 1970), pp. 101-22.

13. John Connery, SJ, has a wonderful history of Catholic thought on this question: he identifies just how many orthodox Catholic voices thought that deadly force was morally acceptable to defend the life of the pregnant mother in these situations. See Connery, *Abortion: The Development of the Roman Catholic Perspective* (Chicago: Loyola University Press, 1977), pp. 126, 135-37, 159, 185, 193, 201, 214-19, 231, 239, 255-59, 267-69.

14. Some might worry that this understanding of innocence could be used by the powerful against the marginalized in nefarious ways. For instance, couldn't powerful healthy people argue that very, very sick people disproportionately drain our community's health-care resources, and that this constitutes a "material mortal threat" to others? The key response to this kind of worry is to return to the idea of a "clear and present" material mortal threat standard, which obviously wouldn't apply in this case. Indeed, this is the standard already in place in just war and just policing theories.

15. For more detail on a similar version of this argument, see Terrence W. Tilley, "The Principle of Innocents' Immunity," *Horizons* 15, no. 1 (1988): 43-63. Christine Gudorf makes a similar point in her "To Make a Seamless Garment, Use a Single Piece of Cloth," *Conscience* 17, no. 3 (1996). Notice that this conclusion also follows from the view of Thomas Aquinas on double effect and defensive use of deadly force cited above.

16. Some resist the very idea of using analogy in arguments about abortion, pointing out that "pregnancy is a unique situation," unlike any other kind of relationship. But this response misunderstands how arguments from analogy function. Instead of denying the uniqueness of cases, arguments from analogy attempt to show morally relevant similarities between different and even unique cases, and then reason consistently with respect to those similarities. Yes, pregnancy is different overall from other kinds of relationships, but it shares certain *morally relevant features in common* with other kinds of relationships, and these features create an opening to use arguments from analogy. For a good discussion of these considerations, see Lisa Cahill, "Abortion and Argument by Analogy," *Horizons* 9, no. 27 (1982).

17. Just-war theorists know that while many wars have been waged when other options clearly existed, there are gray areas where it is less clear that no other options exist. Similarly, it can be less than clear in clinical practice when we cross a line and should conclude that abortion is the last resort to save a mother's life. That these gray areas exist, however, is not a reason for abandoning the principle. Furthermore, the relationship between mother and child is different from the relationship between, say, an adult soldier and the child soldier, or a police officer and the insane shooter. As we will see below, since parents have special duties to protect their children, this means that the standard for having an abortion to save the life of the mother should be even more strict when we find ourselves in that gray area.

18. Anthony Levatino, "Testimony of Anthony Levatino, M.D., before the Subcommittee on the Constitution and Civil Justice," U.S. House of Representatives (2013): http://judiciary.house.gov/hearings/113th/05232013/Levatino%2005232013.pdf (accessed Sept. 5, 2013).

19. "Medical Symposium: Abortion Is Never Medically Necessary," *Zenit* (2012): http://www.zenit.org/en/articles/medical-symposium-abortion-is-never-medically-necessary (accessed Sept. 5, 2013).

20. *National Catholic Bioethics Quarterly* (Autumn 2011): 455-56.

21. *Evangelium Vitae,* §58.

22. *Ethical and Religious Directives for Catholic Health Care Services,* United States Conference of Catholic Bishops (2009): http://www.usccb.org/issues-and-action/human-life-and-dignity/health-care/upload/Ethical-Religious-Directives-Catholic-Health-Care-Services-fifth-edition-2009.pdf, #47 (accessed Dec. 17, 2013).

23. I discuss the last criterion in Charles Camosy, *Too Expensive to Treat? Finitude, Tragedy, and the Neonatal ICU* (Grand Rapids: Eerdmans, 2010).

24. John J. Hardt, "Birth Plan: Chronicle of a Brief Life Foretold," *America: The National Catholic Review* (2009): http://americamagazine.org/issue/715/faith-focus/birth-plan (accessed Sept. 6, 2013).

25. And it is interesting that this procedure is often approved (even at Catholic hospitals) even when there is mere *risk* to the mother's life. The threat does not have to be imminent.

26. Judith Jarvis Thomson, "A Defense of Abortion," *Philosophy and Public Affairs* 1, no. 1 (1971): http://spot.colorado.edu/~heathwoo/Phil160,Fall02/thomson.htm (accessed Sept. 6, 2013).

27. Francis J. Beckwith, *Defending Life* (Cambridge, UK: Cambridge University Press, 2007), pp. 179-81; Gilbert Meilaender, "The Fetus as Parasite and Mushroom," in Stephen Lammers and Allen Verhey, eds., *On Moral Medicine,* 2nd ed. (Grand Rapids: Eerdmans, 1998).

28. Charles Camosy, "Is Sex of Any Kind Consent to Child Support?" *Catholic Moral Theology* (2011): http://catholicmoraltheology.com/is-consent-to-oral-sex-consent-to-800month-in-child-support/ (accessed Sept. 16, 2013).

29. But how far does this duty go? Some, like Patricia Beattie Jung, argue that we should think about gestating a child and organ donation as similar acts. See Jung, "Abortion and Organ Donation: Christian Reflections on Bodily Life Support," *Journal of Religious Ethics* 16, no. 2 (1988): 273-305. If mothers have a natural duty to give of their body for their child, might this imply that fathers (and presumably mothers) should be forced to give up their kidney or other organ to aid their child? It is possible that a parent does have an obligation to donate, but two differences between the cases indicate that the duty might not be as strong. First, and most important, in most cases of pregnancy the need of the child comes about as a result of something the parents did, something philosophers call a "proximate cause." But in the case of the kidney donor parent, the child's predicament is not caused by the parent's act. Second, the pregnant woman's physiological structure is ordered toward the nurturing and development of her child's good, while the same cannot be said of the parent's capacity to donate a kidney.

30. There are very rare occasions where pregnancy causes mental anguish to the point that it threatens the life of the mother. Such cases must be handled delicately, but there does not appear to be a principled reason why the "life of the mother" exception wouldn't apply in these cases as well — at least if the "clear and present danger" of death criteria were met.

31. Some might be tempted to say that there is no moral duty to aid in such situations. After all, no choice to have sex was made, so how could there be an obligation to aid? But for most of us, especially if we claim the name Christian, we accept plenty of moral obligations that are not chosen. Obligations ranging from "give to the poor" to "honor your father and mother" are not the result of our choice. Having said that, we must acknowledge that even if there is an obligation present here, it is not clear how strong the obligation is, and the proportional analysis must be done.

32. *Catechism of the Catholic Church,* §2269.

33. Recall, once again, the fact that abortions in the cases of rape represent a very small percentage of all abortions. This will become an important point when we begin to look at public policy.

34. Some Catholics may worry that interventions like C-sections and hysterectomies may constitute mutilation. However, though at times it was considered an intrinsically evil act, various kinds of interventions that at least appear to count as mutilation are now permitted by Catholic teaching. See, in particular, the shift surrounding mutilation and organ donation: Albert R. Johnson, "From Mutilation to Donation: The Evolution of Catholic Moral Theology regarding Organ Transplantation," Lane Center for Catholic Studies and Social Thought (2005): http://www.usfca.edu/uploadedFiles/Destinations/Institutes_and_Centers/Lane/Publications/Mutilation-to-Donation_sp06.pdf (accessed May 7, 2014).

35. Connecticut Catholic Bishops, "Statement by Connecticut Bishops Regarding Plan B," *CatholicCulture.org* (2007): http://www.catholicculture.org/culture/library/view.cfm?recnum=7836 (accessed Sept. 22, 2013).

36. Daniel P. Sulmasy, "Emergency Contraception for Women Who Have Been Raped: Must Catholics Test for Ovulation, or Is Testing for Pregnancy Morally Sufficient?" *Kennedy Institute of Ethics Journal* 16, no. 4 (2006): 305-51: http://muse.jhu.edu/login?auth=0&type=summary&url=/journals/kennedy_institute_of_ethics_journal/v016/16.4sulmasy.pdf (accessed Sept. 22, 2013).

37. Thomas J. Davis Jr., "Plan B Agnostics: Doubt, Debate, and Denial," National Catholic Bioethics Center (2010): http://www.holyapostles.edu/sites/default/files/bioethics/Plan_B_Agonistics_%28NCBC%29.pdf (accessed June 24, 2013).

38. Indeed, this seems to directly follow from the kind of reasoning used by many "pro-lifers" when it comes to the use of methotrexate. If taking a drug to remove a prenatal child in that situation is not intrinsically evil, then it is not clear why it would be different in this situation. Of course, one would still need a proportionately serious reason for doing so — and the number of such reasons is very, very small.

39. Sarah Terzo, "Raped Women Who Had Their Babies Defy Pro-Choice Stereotypes," *Life Site News* (2013): http://www.lifesitenews.com/news/raped-women-who-had-their-babies-defy-pro-choice-stereotypes (accessed Apr. 12, 2014).

40. There are rare times, however, when RU-486 fails and a direct abortion would be needed. I will discuss this situation in more detail in chap. 6 below.

41. For evidence of this, see the preface of Martin Rhonheimer's *Vital Conflicts,* which explains how his book was written at the request of the Congregation for the Doctrine of the Faith (CDF) and published with its encouragement, so Catholic ethicists could debate the life-of-the-mother exception. See also the *National Catholic Bioethics Quarterly* (Spring 2012): 11-12, where Prof. Rhonheimer discusses a letter sent to him in March 2012 by then Prefect Levada of the CDF, at the request of then Pope Benedict XVI, thanking him for his writings and stating the freedom of moralists to write on these issues. I owe these insights to Bill Murphy, who graciously commented on a post of mine at the Catholic Moral Theology website: http://catholicmoraltheology.com/from-the-honest-question-file-could-a-prenatal-child-be-a-innocent-aggressor/ (accessed Sept. 28, 2013).

42. Even from a strict perspective of defined Catholic doctrine, there are many open questions to explore in this regard. Oxford's David Albert Jones takes just such a strict orthodox Catholic perspective and concludes that (among other things) what constitutes direct killing of an innocent prenatal child, along with the permissibility of indirect abortion priority to viability, remain open questions. Rather than appeals to authority, he claims that arguments about these open questions should be made "on the basis of appeal to philosophical or theological argument." See his "Magisterial Teaching on Vital Conflicts: A Reply to

Rev. Kevin Flannery, SJ," *National Catholic Bioethics Quarterly* (Spring 2014). In addition to the journal *National Catholic Bioethics Quarterly* in the United States, these issues are being debated in the *Catholic Medical Quarterly* in the UK. See especially the May 2014 issue: http://www.cmq.org.uk/CMQ/2014/Contents_May_2014.html. Even for orthodox Catholics, these matters remain open questions with which theologians, philosophers, and others must continue to struggle. However, let me reiterate what I said previously: If the church were to define its doctrine against a position for which I argue in this book, I urge Catholics to form their consciences in light of the church's position rather than the one I offer here.

Notes to Chapter 4

1. Congregation for the Doctrine of the Faith, *Declaration on Procured Abortion* (Libreria Editrice Vaticana, 1974), §14.

2. Michael Tooley, Celia Wolf-Devine, Philip E. Devine, and Alison M. Jagger, *Abortion: Three Perspectives* (Oxford: Oxford University Press, 2010), p. 6.

3. Tooley et al., *Abortion*, p. 15.

4. See esp. the following works: Alasdair MacIntyre, *After Virtue* (Notre Dame, IN: University of Notre Dame Press, 1981); MacIntyre, *Whose Justice? Which Rationality?* (Notre Dame, IN: University of Notre Dame Press, 1988); Michael Sandal, *Liberalism and the Limits of Justice* (Cambridge, UK: Cambridge University Press, 1982); Jeffrey Stout, *The Flight from Authority* (Notre Dame, IN: University of Notre Dame Press, 1981); Stout, *Ethics After Babel* (Boston: Beacon Press, 1988).

5. Paul Simmons, "Religious Liberty and Abortion Policy: *Casey* as 'Catch 22,' " *Journal of Church and State* 42 (2000): 69.

6. Simmons, "Religious Liberty," p. 71.

7. Simmons, "Religious Liberty," p. 73.

8. The slave trade in this case was also abolished on the basis of theological principle.

9. *The Parliamentary History of England from the Earliest Period to the Year 1803* (London: T. C. Hansard, 1817), p. 278.

10. While this may in fact take place via rational argument, it may more often happen by presenting one's views, or living a life informed by one's views, in a way that is beautiful or attractive. Also, if we are honest, it may happen via raw imposition of power.

11. M. Cathleen Kaveny, "Toward a Thomistic Perspective on Abortion and the Law in Contemporary America," *The Thomist* 55, no. 33 (July 1991): 345. Hereafter, page references to this essay appear in parentheses in the text.

12. See, esp., *Summa Theologica*, I-II: 96, 2, and II-II: 10, 11.

13. Simmons, "Religious Liberty," p. 82.

14. Indeed, one important consideration appears to mirror Thomas's concern about changing a law that has been settled when the court reminds us that "an entire generation has come of age free to assume Roe's concept of liberty in defining the capacity of women to act in society, and to make reproductive decisions; no erosion of principle going to liberty or personal autonomy has left Roe's central holding a doctrinal remnant." *Planned Parenthoods of Southeastern PA v. Casey* (91-744), 505 U.S. 833, Supreme Court of the United States (1992): http://www.law.cornell.edu/supct/html/91-744.ZO.html. But given Americans'

complex attitudes about abortion that we have seen above, at least as many people have "come of age" rejecting the essential holding of *Roe*.

15. Julie Rovner, "Restrictions on Abortion Multiply This Year," *Shots: Health News from NPR* (2011): http://www.npr.org/blogs/health/2011/07/14/137848984/restrictions-on -abortions-multiply-this-year (accessed Oct. 4, 2011).

16. Many of these situations will be the focus of the compromise proposed in the final chapter of this book. No criminalization of abortion can take place, I argue, without substantial social support for women — and especially women in difficult situations.

17. Cristina Page, *How the Pro-Choice Movement Saved America* (New York: Basic Books, 2006), p. 147.

18. Daniel Callahan, *Abortion Law, Choice and Morality* (New York: Macmillan, 1970), p. 132.

19. Callahan, *Abortion Law,* p. 133.

20. R. K. Jones and K. Kooistra, "Abortion Incidence and Access to Services in the United States, 2008," *Perspectives on Sexual and Reproductive Health* 43, no. 1 (2011): 41-50.

21. R. K. Jones et al., "Repeal Abortion in the United States," *Occasional Report* no. 29 (New York: Guttmacher Institute, 2006).

22. Callahan, *Abortion Law,* pp. 132-33.

23. Steven D. Levitt and Stephen J. Dubner, *Freakanomics Intl.: A Rogue Economist Explores the Hidden Side of Everything* (New York: Harper, 2011), p. 138.

24. Kaveny, "Toward a Thomistic Perspective," pp. 363-64.

25. Here it is worth mentioning that, in her *Casey* opinion, Justice O'Connor seems to assume this relationship between the law and public opinion when, as mentioned above, she noted that an entire generation came of age free assuming *Roe*'s concept of liberty in defining the capacity of women in society today (505 U.S. at 860, from Findlaw.com).

26. Callahan, *Abortion Law,* p. 134.

27. Mary S. Calderone, "Illegal Abortion as a Public Health Problem," *American Journal of Public Health* 50, no. 7 (July 1960): 949.

28. In my proposed shift in public policy, OB-GYNs will still need to do abortions to save a mother's life.

29. Bernard Nathanson, *Aborting America* (New York: Doubleday, 1979), p. 193.

30. Gilda Sedgh et al., "Induced Abortion: Incidence and Trends Worldwide from 1995 to 2008," *The Lancet* (2012): http://www.thelancet.com/journals/lancet/article/PIIS0140-6736%2811%2961786-8/fulltext#article_upsell.

31. Rohini Boddu, "A Review of Abortion in Ireland," *Royal College of Surgeons in Ireland Student Medical Journal* 4, no. 1 (2011): 78-81: http://www.rcsismj.com/4th-edition/abortion/ (accessed Oct. 27, 2011).

32. "Case of A, B, and C v. Ireland," European Court of Human Rights (2010): http://cmiskp.echr.coe.int/tkp197/view.asp?action=html&documentId=878721&portal=hbkm &source=externalbydocnumber&table=F69A27FD8FB86142BF01C1166DEA398649 (accessed Oct. 27, 2011).

33. Stanley K. Henshaw, Susheela Singh, and Taylor Haas, "The Incidence of Abortion Worldwide," *Family Planning Perspectives* 25 (1999): http://www.guttmacher.org/pubs/journals/25s3099.html (accessed Oct. 27, 2011).

34. Some might say that it is simply Ireland's Catholicism that is responsible for the

low incidence of abortion, but other very Catholic countries have a high incidence of abortion, such as Italy, which has a rate of 11.4.

35. "Fewer Irish Women Opt for Abortion," *BBC News* (2009): http://news.bbc.co.uk/2/hi/europe/8160806.stm (accessed Oct. 27, 2011).

36. Charles Camosy, "Catholic Church in Ireland Faces Abortion Question," *The Washington Post: On Faith* (2013). Similarly, a recent study shows that after Chile made abortion broadly illegal there in 1989 morality and morbidity rates due to abortion actually went down. See E. Koch, "Epidemiología del aborto y su prevención en Chile" [Epidemiology of abortion and its prevention in Chile], *Rev Chil Obstet Ginecol* 7, no. 5 (2014): 351-60.

37. "Highlights on Health in Poland," World Health Organization Europe (2005): http://www.euro.who.int/__data/assets/pdf_file/0020/103565/E88745.pdf (accessed Oct. 27, 2011).

38. Central Intelligence Agency, "The World Factbook: Maternal Mortality Rate": http://www.cia.gov/library/publications/the-world-factbook/rankorder/2223rank.html (accessed Oct. 26, 2013).

39. Though, as we will see in chap. 6, the law need not choose between protecting either population.

40. We even have an ancient papyrus letter from a migrant worker named Hilarion writing a loving letter to his pregnant wife, Alis, in which he casually remarks that she should keep their child if it is a boy but commit infanticide if it is a girl: http://www.stoa.org/diotima/anthology/wlgr/wlgr-privatelife249.shtml (accessed May 13, 2014).

41. Aaron Lewis, "Bill Clinton Responds to Anti-Abortion Rights Activists," *CBS News* (2008): http://www.cbsnews.com/news/bill-clinton-responds-to-anti-abortion-rights-activists/ (accessed June 2, 2014).

42. George Dennis O'Brien, *The Church and Abortion: A Catholic Dissent* (Lanham, MD: Rowman and Littlefield, 2010). Hereafter, page references to this work appear in parentheses within the text.

43. Cathleen Kaveny, "Can We Talk about Abortion? An Exchange," *Commonweal* (2011): http://www.commonwealmagazine.org/can-we-talk-about-abortion (accessed Oct. 29, 2011).

44. Information on this ministry is available in English, Spanish, French, and German here: http://www.rachelsvineyard.org/ (accessed May 7, 2014).

45. Pope John Paul II, "Letter of Pope John Paul II to Women," The Vatican (1995): http://www.vatican.va/holy_father/john_paul_ii/letters/documents/hf_jp-ii_let_29061995_women_en.html, 5.

46. "The Emperor's New Clothes and Other Myths: Cardinal Sean O'Malley at Vigil for Life," *Salt and Light Media* (2014): http://saltandlighttv.org/blog/general/the-emperors-new-clothes-and-other-myths-cardinal-sean-omalley-at-vigil-for-life (accessed Feb. 7, 2014).

47. O'Brien, *The Church and Abortion*, p. 28.

48. Lauren Sandler, "The Mother Majority," *Slate* (2011): http://www.slate.com/articles/double_x/doublex/2011/10/most_surprising_abortion_statistic_the_majority_of_women_who_ter.html (accessed Oct. 29, 2011).

Notes to Chapter 5

1. Some might argue that the key point about referring to women's experience in the abortion debate has less to do with their ability to be pregnant and more to do with

their distinct perspective as embodied females. Experiences of abortion are not just about childbirth; they are entangled with the larger picture of experiences that women have with respect to gender, power, violence, etc. Stay tuned for more on this perspective from "pro-life" feminist Sidney Callahan.

2. Sidney Callahan, "Abortion and the Sexual Agenda: A Case for Pro-Life Feminism," in Therese Lysaught et al., eds., *On Moral Medicine,* 3rd ed. (Grand Rapids: Eerdmans, 2013), pp. 938-44.

3. Interestingly, a minority of feminists who do not identify as "pro-life" — such as Andrea Dworkin and Catharine MacKinnon — have made points similar to those Callahan makes below. See esp. Catharine MacKinnon, "Roe v. Wade: A Study in Male Ideology," *Abortion: Moral and Legal Perspectives* 45 (1984): 52-53.

4. Wil S. Hylton, "What I've Learned: Hugh Hefner," *Esquire* (2002): http://www .esquire.com/features/what-ive-learned/ESQ0602-JUN_WIL (accessed June 2, 2014).

5. Linda Greenhouse, "Misconceptions about Roe v. Wade," *The New York Times* (2013): http://opinionator.blogs.nytimes.com/2013/01/23/misconceptions/?_r=0 (accessed Nov. 16, 2013).

6. Jason Keyser, "Ginsburg: Roe Gave Abortion Opponents a Target," *ABC News* (2013): http://abcnews.go.com/m/story?id=19160673 (accessed Dec. 17, 2013).

7. Helen M. Alvare, "Constitutional Abortion and Culture," *Christian Bioethics* 19, no. 2 (2013): http://cb.oxfordjournals.org/content/19/2/133.full.pdf+html (accessed Dec. 17, 2013).

8. *Planned Parenthood of Southeastern PA v. Casey,* 505 U.S. 833 (1992)," U.S. Supreme Court (1992): http://caselaw.lp.findlaw.com/scripts/getcase.pl?court=us&vol=505&invol =833.

9. Meghan Clark, "Equity for Women? A Case for Prolife Feminism," *Catholic Moral Theology* (2013): http://catholicmoraltheology.com/equity-for-women-a-case-for-prolife -feminism/ (accessed Nov. 19, 2013).

10. Megan Hall et al., "Associations between Intimate Partner Violence and Ter-mination of Pregnancy: A Systematic Review and Meta-Analysis," *PLOS Medicine* (2014): http://www.plosmedicine.org/article/info%3Adoi%2F10.1371%2Fjournal.pmed.1001581 (accessed May 1, 2014).

11. Ron Dicker, "J. J. Redick Allegedly Had 'Abortion Contract' with Ex-Girlfriend; NBA Player Denies Getting Her Pregnant," *The Huffington Post* (2013): http://www.huff ingtonpost.com/2013/07/25/jj-redick-abortion_n_3652293.html (accessed Nov. 19, 2013).

12. Lawrence B. Finer et al., "Reasons U.S. Women Have Abortions: Quantitative and Qualitative Perspectives," Guttmacher Institute (2005): http://www.guttmacher.org/ pubs/journals/3711005.pdf (accessed June 24, 2013).

13. "Texas Teen Sues Parents to Stop Them from Forcing Her Abortion," *Fox News* (2013): http://www.foxnews.com/us/2013/02/13/texas-teen-sues-parents-to-stop-them -from-forcing-her-abortion/.

14. Anna O'Loughlin, "Boyfriend Challenges 'Forced' Abortion," *Irish Examiner* (2013): http://www.irishexaminer.com/archives/2013/0718/world/boyfriend-challenges -aposforcedapos-abortion-237188.html (accessed Nov. 19, 2013).

15. "Harper to Oppose Any Attempt to Create New Abortion Law," *CTV News* (2010): http://www.ctvnews.ca/harper-to-oppose-any-attempt-to-create-new-abortion-law-1.514832.

16. Daniel Proussalidis, "Liberal Candidates Must Be Pro-Choice: Trudeau," *Sun*

News Network (2014): http://www.sunnewsnetwork.ca/sunnews/politics/archives/
2014/05/20140507-154734.html (accessed Mar. 17, 2014).

17. Barry Schwartz, *The Paradox of Choice* (New York: HarperCollins, 2005): http://
books.google.com/books?id=zutxr7rGc_QC&vq=barry+schwartz+paradox+contents
(accessed Nov. 23, 2013).

18. William T. Cavanaugh, *Being Consumed: Economics and Christian Desire* (Grand
Rapids: Eerdmans, 2008): http://www.amazon.com/Being-Consumed-Economics-Christian
-Desire/dp/0802845614 (accessed Nov. 23, 2013).

19. Lisa Wade, "My Two Cents on Feminism and Miley Cyrus," *Sociological Images; Inspiring Sociological Imaginations Everywhere* (2013): http://thesocietypages.org/
socimages/2013/12/28/my-two-cents-on-feminism-and-miley-cyrus/ (accessed Dec. 29,
2013).

20. Nancy A. Wilson, "War on Woman," *Christian Bioethics* 19, no. 2 (2013): 242-45:
http://cb.oxfordjournals.org/content/19/2/242.full.pdf+html (accessed Nov. 23, 2013).

21. Rachel L. Swarns, "Placed on Unpaid Leave: A Pregnant Employee Finds Hope in
a New Law," *The New York Times* (2014): http://www.nytimes.com/2014/02/03/nyregion/
suspended-for-being-pregnant-an-employee-finds-hope-in-a-new-law.html?smid=tw-share
&_r=1 (accessed Feb. 7, 2014).

22. Lydia Saad, "In U.S., Nonreligious Postgrads Are Highly Pro-Choice," Gallup
Politics (2012): http://www.gallup.com/poll/154946/non-christians-postgrads-highly
-pro-choice.aspx (accessed Apr. 30, 2014).

23. "Unintended Pregnancy in the United States," Guttmacher Institute (2013):
http://www.guttmacher.org/pubs/FB-Unintended-Pregnancy-US.pdf (accessed Apr. 30,
2014).

24. Jana Bennett, "A Tale of Two Choices . . . ," *Catholic Moral Theology* (2013):
http://catholicmoraltheology.com/a-tale-of-two-choices/?utm_source=rss&utm_medium
=rss&utm_campaign=a-tale-of-two-choices (accessed Nov. 23, 2013).

25. The Elliot Institute (2010): http://www.theunchoice.com/ (accessed Nov. 23,
2013).

26. Vincent Rue, Priscilla Coleman, James Rue, and David Reardon, "Induced Abortion and Traumatic Stress: A Preliminary Comparison of American and Russian Women,"
Medical Science Monitor 10, no. 10 (2004): 5-16.

27. Joshua Lang, "What Happens to Women Who Are Denied Abortions?" *The New
York Times* (2013): http://www.nytimes.com/2013/06/16/magazine/study-women-denied
-abortions.html?_r=1&adxnnl=1&smid=fb-share&pagewanted=5&adxnnlx=1385208844-zE
tlwu9V8oxGn+Xz5WxShw (accessed Nov. 23, 2013).

28. Priscilla K. Coleman, "Author's reply," *British Journal of Psychiatry* (2012): http://
bjp.rcpsych.org/content/200/1/79.full.

29. I must admit that, while I'm hopeful that we can move in this direction, I have
my doubts about how quickly it will happen. At one point, for instance, I thought about
having had an extended discussion in this chapter of a Chinese meta-analysis showing that
induced abortion was "significantly associated with an increased risk of breast cancer":
http://link.springer.com/article/10.1007%2Fs10552-013-0325-7. I ultimately decided against
having such a discussion, however, given the risk that it would be so politically "hot" (even
though the Chinese are hardly invested in the abortion debate in the way Americans are)
that it would distract from the overall argument of the chapter. This is a sad state of affairs.

30. Priscilla K. Coleman. "Abortion and Mental Health: A Quantitative Synthesis and Analysis of Research Published, 1995-2009," *British Journal of Psychiatry* (2011).

31. Despite the fact that the piece was thoroughly peer-reviewed and published in the top journal in the field, some critics of the meta-analysis claim that it did not follow accepted standards of reporting. The author responds to those critics here: http://bjp.rcpsych.org/content/200/1/79.full Even if these critics are correct (and my admittedly nonspecialist reading is that they are not), the *best* they can say is that women who have abortions do not have better mental health outcomes than those in similar situations who keep their babies. Even with the best "pro-choice" spin possible, there is no evidence that broad access to abortion is necessary for women's mental health.

32. Betsey Stevenson and Justin Wolfers, "The Paradox of Declining Female Happiness," National Bureau of Economic Research (2009): http://www.nber.org/papers/w14969.pdf (accessed Nov. 23, 2013).

33. Indeed, the meta-analysis cited above found that a remarkable 10 percent of *all* mental health problems were shown to be directly attributable to abortion.

34. "Spain Grapples with Abortion Revision," *Euronews* (2013): http://www.euronews.com/2013/11/15/spain-grapples-with-abortion-revision/ (accessed Nov. 23, 2013).

35. "Rubalcaba: The Reform of Abortion Is an Unacceptable Setback for Women," *El Pais: Sociedad* (2012): http://translate.google.com/translate?act=url&depth=1&hl=en&ie=UTF8&prev=_t&rurl=translate.google.com&sl=auto&tl=en&u=http://sociedad.elpais.com/sociedad/2012/01/25/actualidad/1327505385_935304.html (accessed Nov. 23, 2013).

36. "Gallardón: I Think of the Fear of Losing Their Jobs because of Pregnancy," *El Pais Sociedad* (2012): http://translate.google.com/translate?act=url&depth=1&hl=en&ie=UTF8&prev=_t&rurl=translate.google.com&sl=auto&tl=en&u=http://sociedad.elpais.com/sociedad/2012/03/08/actualidad/1331177681_396483.html (accessed Nov. 23, 2013).

Notes to Chapter 6

1. Alissa J. Rubin, "The Catholic Abortion Paradox," *Beliefnet* (2001): http://www.beliefnet.com/Faiths/Catholic/2001/01/The-Catholic-Abortion-Paradox.aspx?p=1 (accessed Dec. 1, 2013).

2. Pope Francis, *Evangelii Gaudium* §214: http://www.vatican.va/holy_father/francesco/apost_exhortations/documents/papa-francesco_esortazione-ap_20131124_evangelii-gaudium_en.pdf (accessed Dec. 1, 2013).

3. Lydia Saad, " 'Conservatives' Are Single-Largest Ideological Group," Gallup (2009): http://www.gallup.com/poll/120857/conservatives-single-largest-ideological-group.aspx (accessed June 30, 2013).

4. Jeffrey M. Jones, "Record-High 40% of Americans Identify as Independents in '11," Gallup (2012): http://www.gallup.com/poll/151943/record-high-americans-identify-independents.aspx (accessed June 30, 2013).

5. "Survey | A Generation in Transition: Religion, Values, and Politics among College-Age Millennials," Public Religion Research Institute (2012): http://publicreligion.org/research/2012/04/millennial-values-survey-2012/ (accessed July 3, 2014).

6. D. B. Stulberg, A. M. Dude, I. Dahlquist, and F. A. Curlin, "Abortion Provision

among Practicing Obstetrician-Gynecologists," *Obstetrics and Gynecology* 118, no. 3 (2011): 609-14: http://www.ncbi.nlm.nih.gov/pubmed/21860290 (accessed Nov. 23, 2013).

7. Lawrence B. Finer and S. K. Henshaw, "The Accessibility of Abortion Services in the United States, 2001," *Perspectives on Sexual and Reproductive Health* 35, no. 1 (2003): 16-24.

8. Jack Hitt, "Who Will Do Abortions Here?" *The New York Times* (1998): http://www.nytimes.com/1998/01/18/magazine/who-will-do-abortions-here.html (accessed Nov. 23, 2013).

9. "Training of Abortion Providers/Medical Students for Choice," Abortion Rights Coalition of Canada (2005): http://www.arcc-cdac.ca/postionpapers/06-Training-Abortion-Providers-MSFC.PDF (accessed June 2, 2014).

10. Josh Richman, "Bills Increasing Abortion Access Signed by Gov. Jerry Brown," *Mercury News* (2013): http://www.mercurynews.com/politics-government/ci_24274908/ (accessed Dec. 1, 2013).

11. Esme E. Deprez, "The Vanishing Abortion Clinic," *Bloomberg Buisnessweek* (2013): http://www.businessweek.com/articles/2013-11-27/abortion-clinics-face-shutdown-spiral-as-republicans-push-restrictions (accessed Dec. 1, 2013).

12. Ironically, "pro-choice" advocacy calls for abortion to be treated like "any other medical procedure," which opens it up to the kind of very serious regulations to which all medical procedures are subject.

13. Caitlin E. Borgmann, "Abortion, The Undue Burden Standard, and the Eviscera-tion of Women's Privacy," *William and Mary Journal of Women and the Law* (2010): http://scholarship.law.wm.edu/cgi/viewcontent.cgi?article=1055&context=wmjowl.

14. *Roe,* 410 U.S. at 159.

15. Democrats for Life of America, "Pregnant Women Support Act (95-10)": http://www.democratsforlife.org/index.php?option=com_content&task=view&id=48 (accessed Dec. 3, 2013).

16. CNN, "Scott Peterson Trial Fast Facts": http://www.cnn.com/2013/10/15/us/scott-peterson-trial-fast-facts/ (accessed Dec. 3, 2013).

17. Terri LaPoint, "Bill to Protect Women from Being Tricked or Forced into Taking Abortion Pills Called Senseless by Democratic Party Chair," *Inquisitor* (2014): http://www.inquisitor.com/1253139/bill-to-protect-women-from-being-tricked-or-forced-into-taking-abortion-pills-called-senseless-by-democratic-party-chair/ (accessed May 17, 2014).

18. Some may claim that these factors should not be taken into consideration pre-cisely because abortion law protects the sacred zone of reproductive autonomy and choice. However, in addition to ignoring the concerns raised about the mythic character of such choices that I explored in chap. 5, this point of view misunderstands the shift in constitu-tional law since *Casey.* Autonomy and choice can trump an abortion law only if the law poses an "undue burden" on the woman.

19. Imani Gandy, "Feticide Laws Advance 'Personhood,' Punish Pregnant Women," *RH Reality Check* (2014): http://rhrealitycheck.org/article/2014/01/09/feticide-laws-advance-personhood-punish-pregnant-women/ (accessed Mar. 7, 2014).

20. Governor's Press Office, "Governor Cuomo Introduces Women's Equality Act Leg-islation": http://www.governor.ny.gov/press/06042013Womens-Equality-Act-Legislation. Last modified, June 4, 2013 (accessed Dec. 9, 2013).

21. "U.S. Stands Apart from Other Nations on Maternity Leave," *USA Today*

(2005): http://usatoday30.usatoday.com/news/health/2005-07-26-maternity-leave_x
.htm (accessed Nov. 26, 2011).

22. Gilda Sedgh et al., "Legal Abortion Worldwide: Incidence and Recent Trends,"
International Family Planning Perspectives 33, no. 3 (2007): http://www.guttmacher.org/
pubs/journals/3310607.html (accessed Nov. 30, 2013). Some may argue that other factors
influencing these numbers are better public access to contraception, sex education, and
universal health care; but as we will see below, there is even more to these numbers than
meets the uncritical eye.

23. Sedgh et al., "Legal Abortion Worldwide."

24. David Cloutier, "Abortion, Poverty, Contraception, and Promiscuity," *Commonweal* (2014): https://www.commonwealmagazine.org/blog/abortion-poverty-contra
ception-and-promiscuity (accessed Feb. 7, 2014).

25. See esp. the acclaimed "pro-choice" bioethics scholar Andrienne Asch, who consistently and forcefully resisted abortion on the basis of disability (Asch, *Prenatal Testing
and Disability Rights* [Washington, DC: Georgetown University Press, 2000], pp. 234-59).

26. Perinatal Hospice, "Frequently Asked Questions about Perinatal Hospice and
Palliative Care": http://www.perinatalhospice.org/FAQs.html (accessed Dec. 10, 2013).

27. Kelly Whiteside, "Tatyana McFadden Chases Marathon Grand Slam," *USA Today Sports* (2013): http://www.usatoday.com/story/sports/olympics/2013/10/31/tatyana
-mcfadden-new-york-marathon-grand-slam/3332109/ (accessed Dec. 10, 2013).

28. Don Norcross, "It's All About the Bike," *Union-Tribune* (2004): http://www
.utsandiego.com/uniontrib/20040716/news_lz1s16bike.html (accessed June 2, 2014).

29. Sue Reid, "Slaughtered in the Thousands: The British Babies Killed in the Womb
Just for Being Girls," *The Daily Mail* (2014): http://www.dailymail.co.uk/femail/article
-2548349/Slaughtered-thousands-British-babies-killed-womb-just-girls.html (accessed
Feb. 7, 2014).

30. Alan Silverleib, "House Rejects Abortion Ban Based on Sex of Fetus," *CNN Politics* (2012): http://www.cnn.com/2012/05/31/politics/house-abortion-gender/index.html
(accessed Dec. 10, 2013).

31. "Sweden Rules 'Gender-Based' Abortion Legal," *The Local: Sweden's News in
English* (2009): http://www.thelocal.se/20090512/19392 (accessed Dec. 10, 2013); see also
Holly Watt and Claire Newell, "Law 'Does Not Prohibit' Sex-Selection Abortions, DPP
Warns," *The Telegraph* (2013): http://www.telegraph.co.uk/health/healthnews/10360386/
Law-does-not-prohibit-sex-selection-abortions-DPP-warns.html (accessed Dec. 12, 2013).

32. This becomes clear when we consider that many women become surrogate mothers for far less money than this.

33. There is an important gray area that exists between (1) a health concern that obviously threatens the mother's life and (2) a significant health concern that obviously does
not. Certain health risks from pregnancy carry with them a significant (but not obvious) risk
of death. In such gray areas, both moral and legal claims are made on the basis of prudential
judgment. Bias will be resisted by requiring the decision of the mother and medical team to
be confirmed by an independent team of health-care providers and community members
that a mother's pregnancy poses a "significant," "clear," and "present" risk to her life.

34. The Supreme Court made this distinction clear for the end of life (see esp. *Washington v. Glucksberg* and *Vacco v. Quill*), and it could use a similar distinction at the beginning
of life.

35. For the details of this very effective policy (Germany, e.g., has half the abortion rate of the UK), see section 219 of their criminal code: http://www.iuscomp.org/gla/ statutes/StGB.htm#219 (accessed Mar. 7, 2014).

36. In rare cases, RU-486 doesn't work, and a direct abortion becomes required to save the mother's life. Recall that this situation is already accounted for under the MPCPA.

37. The federal government — and some state governments — have a "rape exception" to prohibition of public funds going to pay for abortions. A 2010 study of abortion-providers seeking Medicaid reimbursement in these exceptional cases found, among other things, that they did sometimes question patient reports that they had been raped. See Kacanek et al., "Medicaid Funding for Abortion: Providers' Experiences with Cases Involving Rape, Incest and Life Endangerment," *Perspectives on Sexual and Reproductive Health* 42, no. 2 (2010): 82.

38. One might think that this proposal doesn't really belong as a federal law because it doesn't involve powers given to the federal government under the Constitution. But I disagree — and for two reasons. First, the MPCPA deals with questions about basic civil rights and equal protection of the law; so the 14th Amendment is in play. Furthermore, many of the provisions deal with regulations that clearly involve interstate commerce.

39. Some may wonder about the need for "community members" here. Wouldn't an independent team of physicians be enough? I think not. While physicians are (generally) good making judgment calls about medicine, they have no special expertise in weighing different values and risks. In fact, their privileged role as physicians sometimes skews their perspective, and it should thus be balanced out by community members from different socioeconomic backgrounds.

40. Other than this consideration, the MPCPA leaves the issue of "parental consent" laws to the several states.

41. Some may find the omission of the contraception debate curious, especially because it is commonly assumed that the use of contraceptives reduces abortion. This may well be true of a certain number of abortions. But because widespread use of contraception also helps form attitudes about sex that lead to riskier choices and habits — and has served to ingrain the idea that consent to sex is not the same as consent to be a parent — its net effect on abortion rates overall is not clear. David Cloutier breaks down the complexity in this piece: https://www.commonwealmagazine.org/blog/abortion-poverty-contraception -and-promiscuity (accessed June 2, 2014).

42. *Stenberg v. Carhart*, 530 U.S. 914 (2000).

43. "Europe's Abortion Rules," BBC News: http://news.bbc.co.uk/2/hi/europe/ 6235557.stm (accessed Dec. 12, 2013).

44. Lydia Saad, "Plenty of Common Ground Found in Abortion Debate," Gallup (2011): http://www.gallup.com/poll/148880/Plenty-Common-Ground-Found-Abortion -Debate.aspx (accessed Dec. 12, 2013).

45. Pope John Paul II, *Laborem Exercens* §19: http://www.vatican.va/holy_father/ john_paul_ii/encyclicals/documents/hf_jp-ii_enc_14091981_laborem-exercens_en.html.

Notes to the Conclusion

1. Bill Carter, "CNN Will Cancel 'Crossfire' and Cut Ties to Commentator," *The New York Times* (2005): http://www.nytimes.com/2005/01/06/business/media/06crossfire

.html?_r=0 (accessed May 9, 2014); Dominic Patten, "CNN's 'Crossfire' Back In June; Cancelled In 2005," CNN (2013): https://tv.yahoo.com/news/cnn-crossfire-back-june -cancelled-2005-224421441.html (accessed May 9, 2014). As this book goes to press, CNN has apparently decided to cancel *Crossfire* yet again.

2. It is also worth mentioning that the schools at which journalists train also have a blind spot when it comes to abortion. Something like a broadly "pro-choice" position is simply the accepted orthodoxy at most major colleges and universities.

3. Dylan Byers, "Journalist Consensus: Media Lean Left," *Politico* (2013): http:// www.politico.com/blogs/media/2013/12/journalist-consensus-media-leans-left-179852 .html (accessed May 9, 2014).

4. Juan Williams, *Muzzled: The Assault on Honest Debate* (New York: Crown Publishing, 2011), pp. 204-5.

5. Charles Camosy, "Nonviolence in Our Abortion Discourse? A Post-Election Opening," *Horizons* (June 2013).

6. More than 150 years ago, the debate over slavery produced new political orientations and coalitions that led to the formation of the Republican Party, and I wonder if the new debate over abortion might produce something similar. Especially if national Republicans continue to pay lip service claiming to be for big-government solutions for protecting our prenatal children, it is likely that "pro-lifers" will look elsewhere for a political home in growing numbers. The new kind of coalition proposed in this book would certainly be a formidable power on the national political stage.

Bibliography

The 1 in 3 Campaign. "The 1 in 3 Campaign — These Are OUR Stories." http://www
.1in3campaign.org/about. Accessed June 24, 2013.

"89, 90, or 93? Expert Sheds Light on Tycoon's Age." *The Star Online.* 2007. http://www
.thestar.com.my/story.aspx/?file=/2007/10/25/nation/19269368. Accessed July
20, 2013.

"Abortion and Birth Control." CBS News Poll. Last modified July 31, 2013. http://www
.pollingreport.com/abortion.htm. Accessed Aug. 1, 2013.

Ademak, Raymond J. "A Review: Public Opinion and *Roe v. Wade:* Measurement Difficulties." *The Public Opinion Quarterly* 3 (1994): 409-18. http://www.jstor.org/
stable/2749730. Accessed June 30, 2013.

Alok, Jha. "Pope's Astronomer Says He Would Baptise an Alien If It Asked Him." *The
Guardian*. 2010. http://www.theguardian.com/science/2010/sep/17/pope
-astronomer-baptise-aliens. Accessed July 21, 2013.

Alvare, Helen M. "Constitutional Abortion and Culture." *Christian Bioethics* 2 (2013).
http://cb.oxfordjournals.org/content/19/2/133.full.pdf+html. Accessed Dec.
17, 2013.

Beckwith, Francis J. *Defending Life.* Cambridge, UK: Cambridge University Press,
2007.

Bedard, Paul. "70 New Anti-abortion Laws OK'd in 22 States, Second-most Ever."
Washington Examiner, Jan. 2, 2014.

"Bellabeat Tracking System — Lets Moms Listen to Their Baby's Heartbeat and Track
Their Pregnancy." http://www.naturalbabygoods.com/bellabeat/. Accessed
Mar. 25, 2014.

Benjamin, Liz. "Klein Offers Hostile Abortion Amendment, Fails." *State of Politics.*
2013. http://www.nystateofpolitics.com/2013/06/klein-offers-hostile-abortion
-amendment-fails/. Accessed July 1, 2013.

Bennett, Jana. "A Tale of Two Choices. . . ." *Catholic Moral Theology.* 2013. http://
catholicmoraltheology.com/a-tale-of-two-choices/?utm_source=rss&utm
_medium=rss&utm_campaign=a-tale-of-two-choices. Accessed Nov. 23, 2013.

Bingham, John. "MPs: Abortions Being Carried Out for Cleft Palates." *The Telegraph.* 2013. http://www.telegraph.co.uk/news/politics/10183668/MPs-Abortions -being-carried-out-for-cleft-palates.html. Accessed Dec. 17, 2013.

Blumberg, Antonia. "Pope Francis Says He Would Baptize Martians, Asks 'Who Are We To Close Doors?'" http://www.huffingtonpost.com/2014/05/12/pope-francis-aliens _n_5310935.html?1399919226&ncid=tweetlnkushpmg00000067. Accessed May 12, 2014.

Boddu, Rohini. "A Review of Abortion in Ireland." *Royal College of Surgeons in Ireland Student Medical Journal* 1 (2011): 78-81. http://www.rcsismj.com/4th-edition/ abortion/. Accessed Oct. 27, 2011.

Borgmann, Caitlin E. "Abortion, the Undue Burden Standard, and the Evisceration of Women's Privacy." *William and Mary Journal of Women and the Law* 16 (2010): 291-325.

Buck, Tobias. "Spain's Mariano Rajoy in Fight to Reverse Liberalized Abortion Law." *Financial Times.* 2013. http://www.ft.com/cms/s/0/376f6bf0-c477-11e2-bc94 -00144feab7de.html.

Byers, Dylan. "Journalist Consensus: Media Lean Left." http://www.politico.com/blogs/ media/2013/12/journalist-consensus-media-leans-left-179852.html. Accessed May 9, 2014.

Cahill, Lisa. "Abortion and Argument by Analogy." *Horizons* 9, no. 27 (1982).

Calderone, Mary S. "Illegal Abortion as a Public Health Problem." *American Journal of Public Health* 50, no. 7 (July 1960): 949.

Callahan, Daniel. *Abortion: Law, Choice and Morality.* New York: Macmillan, 1970.

Callahan, Sidney. "Abortion and the Sexual Agenda: A Case for Prolife Feminism." In *On Moral Medicine.* 3rd ed. Edited by M. Therese Lysaught et al. Grand Rapids: Eerdmans, 2012.

Camosy, Charles. "Catholic Church in Ireland Faces Abortion Question." *The Washington Post: On Faith.* 2013. http://www.faithstreet.com/onfaith/2013/05/09/ abortion-in-ireland. Accessed Oct. 26, 2013.

———. *For Love of Animals: Christian Ethics, Consistent Action.* Cincinnati: Franciscan Media, 2013.

———. "Is Disagreement between Peter Singer and Catholic Teaching on Abortion 'Narrow'? — A Response to Critics." *Catholic Moral Theology.* 2013. http:// catholicmoraltheology.com/is-disagreement-between-peter-singer-and-catho lic-teaching-on-abortion-narrow-a-response-to-critics/. Accessed June 21, 2013.

———. "Is Sex of Any Kind Consent to Child Support?" *Catholic Moral Theology.* 2011. http://catholicmoraltheology.com/is-consent-to-oral-sex-consent-to -800month-in-child-support/. Accessed Sept. 16, 2013.

———. "Late-Term Abortion Expansion Defeated in New York State . . . Thanks to Pro-Life Democrats." *Catholic Moral Theology.* 2013. http://catholicmoraltheology .com/late-term-abortion-expansion-defeated-in-new-york-state-thanks-to-pro -life-democrats/. Accessed June 30, 2013.

———. *Peter Singer and Christian Ethics.* Cambridge, UK: Cambridge University Press, 2012.

Bibliography

Carter, Bill. "CNN Will Cancel 'Crossfire' and Cut Ties to Commentator." *The New York Times,* Jan. 6, 2005.

Catholics for Choice. "The Facts Tell the Story: Catholics and Choice." http://www .catholicsforchoice.org/topics/reform/documents/2006catholicsandchoice .pdf. Accessed June 2, 2014.

Cavanaugh, Thomas A. *Double-Effect Reasoning: Doing Good and Avoiding Evil.* Oxford: Clarendon Press, 2006.

Cavanaugh, William T. *Being Consumed: Economics and Christian Desire.* Grand Rapids: Eerdmans, 2008. http://www.amazon.com/Being-Consumed-Economics -Christian-Desire/dp/0802845614. Accessed Nov. 23, 2013.

Central Intelligence Agency. "The World Factbook: Maternal Mortality Rate." http:// www.cia.gov/library/publications/the-world-factbook/rankorder/2223rank .html. Accessed Oct. 26, 2013.

Chasmar, Jessica. "Pro-life Group at Johns Hopkins Denied Official Club Status." *The Washington Times.* 2013. http://www.washingtontimes.com/news/2013/apr/1/ pro-life-group-johns-hopkins-denied-official-club-/. Accessed June 20, 2013.

Clancy, Michael. "Nun Excommunicated for Allowing Abortion." *National Catholic Reporter.* 2010. http://ncronline.org/news/peace-justice/nun-excommunicated -allowing-abortion. Accessed June 21, 2013.

Clark, Meghan. "Equity for Women? A Case for Prolife Feminism." *Catholic Moral Theology.* 2013. http://catholicmoraltheology.com/equity-for-women-a-case -for-prolife-feminism/. Accessed Nov. 19, 2013.

Cloutier, David. "Abortion, Poverty, Contraception, and Promiscuity." *Commonweal,* Feb. 5, 2014.

CNN. "Scott Peterson Trial Fast Facts." Last modified Oct. 15, 2013. http://www.cnn .com/2013/10/15/us/scott-peterson-trial-fast-facts/. Accessed Dec. 3, 2013.

Coleman, Priscilla K. "Author's Reply." *British Journal of Psychiatry.* http://bjp.rcpsych .org/content/200/1/79.full (2012).

———. "Abortion and Mental Health: A Quantitative Synthesis and Analysis of Research Published from 1995-2009." *British Journal of Psychiatry.* 2011.

Congregation for the Doctrine of the Faith. *Declaration on Procured Abortion.* Libreria Editrice Vaticana, 1974.

———. *Dignitas Personae.* Instruction on Certain Bioethical Questions. Sept. 8, 2008.

Connecticut Catholic Bishops. "Statement by Connecticut Bishops Regarding Plan B." *CatholicCulture.org.* 2007. http://www.catholicculture.org/culture/library/ view.cfm?recnum=7836. Accessed Sept. 22, 2013.

Connery, John R. *Abortion: The Development of the Roman Catholic Perspective.* Chicago: Loyola University Press, 1977.

Craine, Patrick B. "EXCLUSIVE: Poland to Vote on Historic Bill Banning All Abortions after Massive Grassroots Campaign." *LifeSiteNews.com: Life, Family and Culture News.* 2011. http://www.lifesitenews.com/news/breaking-poland-to -vote-on-historic-bill-banning-all-abortions-after-massiv. Accessed Oct. 27, 2011.

Davis, Thomas J., Jr. "Plan B Agnostics: Doubt, Debate, Denial." *The National Catholic Bioethics Quarterly* 10 (June 2013): 741-72.

Day, Kristen. *Democrats for Life: Pro-Life Politics and the Silenced Majority.* Green Forest, AR: New Leaf Press, 2006.

DeFrancesco Soto, Victoria M. "Opinion: Can the Republicans Connect with Latinos on Abortion?" *NBC Latino.* 2012. http://nbclatino.com/2012/08/24/opinion-can-the-republicans-connect-with-latinos-on-abortion/. Accessed July 1, 2013.

Democrats for Life of America. "Pregnant Women Support Act (95-10)." http://www.democratsforlife.org/index.php?option=com_content&task=view&id=48. Accessed Dec. 3, 2013.

Deprez, Esme E. "The Vanishing Abortion Clinic." *Bloomberg Businessweek.* 2013. http://www.businessweek.com/articles/2013-11-27/abortion-clinics-face-shut down-spiral-as-republicans-push-restrictions. Accessed Dec. 1, 2013.

Dicker, Ron. "J. J. Redick Allegedly Had 'Abortion Contract' With Ex-Girlfriend; NBA Player Denies Getting Her Pregnant." *The Huffington Post.* 2013. http://www.huffingtonpost.com/2013/07/25/jj-redick-abortion_n_3652293.html. Accessed Nov. 19, 2013.

"End of the Party?" *The Economist.* http://www.economist.com/blogs/democracy inamerica/2014/01/american-politics. Accessed Feb. 7, 2014.

Ergun, Damla. "Majority Supports Legal Abortion, But Details Indicate Ambivalence." *ABC News,* July 25, 2013.

Ertelt, Steven. "Nevada Republican Party Strips Pro-Life Language on Abortion From its Platform." http://www.lifenews.com/2014/04/14/nevada-republican-party-strips-pro-life-language-on-abortion-from-its-platform/. Accessed Apr. 27, 2014.

European Court of Human Rights. "Case of A, B, and C v. Ireland." http://cmiskp.echr.coe.int/tkp197/view.asp?action=html&documentId=878721&portal=hbkm&source=externalbydocnumber&table=F69A27FD8FB86142BF01C116 6DEA398649. Accessed Oct. 27, 2011.

"Europe's Abortion Rules." BBC News. Last modified Feb. 12, 2007. http://news.bbc.co.uk/2/hi/europe/6235557.stm. Accessed July 1, 2013.

Feldmann, Linda. "Nine States Charging Hard against Abortion." http://www.cs monitor.com/USA/Politics/2013/0614/Nine-states-charging-hard-against-abortion/Arkansas-Legislature-overrides-governor-bans-abortion-after-12-weeks. Accessed May 11, 2014.

Feminists for Life. "Herstory Worth Repeating." http://www.feministsforlife.org/herstory/. Accessed June 28, 2013.

"Fewer Irish Women Opt for Abortion." *BBC News.* 2009. http://news.bbc.co.uk/2/hi/europe/8160806.stm. Accessed Oct. 27, 2011.

Finer, Lawrence B., and S. K. Henshaw. "The Accessibility of Abortion Services in the United States, 2001." *Perspectives on Sexual and Reproductive Health* 35, no. 1 (2003): 16-24.

Finer, Lawrence B., et al. "Reasons U.S. Women Have Abortions: Quantitative and Qualitative Perspectives." *Perspectives on Sexual and Reproductive Health* 3 (2005): 110-18. http://www.guttmacher.org/pubs/journals/3711005.pdf. Accessed June 24, 2013.

Fleming, Olivia. " 'Got a Quickie Aborsh': Comedienne Sarah Silverman Supports Pro-Choice Debate, Tweeting 'Before-and-After Abortion' Photos." Mail Online. http://www.dailymail.co.uk/femail/article-2129490/Sarah-Silverman-posts -quicky-abortion-photo-Twitter-support-pro-choice-debate.html. Accessed June 2, 2014.

Forsythe, Clarke D. "Progress after Casey." *National Review Online.* 2012. http://www .nationalreview.com/corner/304416/progress-after-icaseyi-clarke-d-forsythe. Accessed July 1, 2013.

Francis. *Evangelii Gaudium: Apostolic Exhortation on the Proclamation of the Gospel in Today's World.* Nov. 24, 2013.

Gallagher, James. "Down's Pregnancy Blood Test on Trial." *BBC News.* 2013. http:// www.bbc.co.uk/news/health-24755589. Accessed Dec. 10, 2013.

"Gallardón: Pienso en el miedo a perder el empleo por un embarazo." *El Pais Sociedad.* 2012. http://translate.google.com/translate?act=url&depth=1&hl=en& ie=UTF8&prev=_t&rurl=translate.google.com&sl=auto&tl=en&u=http:// sociedad.elpais.com/sociedad/2012/03/08/actualidad/1331177681_396483.html. Accessed July 1, 2013.

Gandy, Imani. "Feticide Laws Advance 'Personhood,' Punish Pregnant Women." http:// rhrealitycheck.org/article/2014/01/09/feticide-laws-advance-personhood -punish-pregnant-women/. Accessed Mar. 7, 2014.

Garrow, David J. "How Roe v. Wade Was Written." *Washington and Lee Law Review* 71. Accessed June 2, 2014.

Glendon, Mary Ann. *Abortion and Divorce in Western Law.* Cambridge, MA: Harvard University Press, 1987.

Governor's Press Office, "Governor Cuomo Introduces Women's Equality Act Legislation." Last modified June 4, 2013. http://www.governor.ny.gov/press/06042 013Womens-Equality-Act-Legislation. Accessed Dec. 9, 2013.

Graham, Lindsey. "What's Next for President Obama?" *CNN Transcript Providers,* http://transcripts.cnn.com/TRANSCRIPTS/1211/07/acd.02.html. Accessed Nov. 7, 2012; Dec. 1, 2012.

Greenblatt, Alan. "Why Partisans Can't Kick the Hypocrisy Habit." *It's All Politics: Political News from NPR* (2013). http://www.npr.org/blogs/itsallpolitics /2013/06/14/191601623/why-partisans-cant-kick-the-hypocrisy-habit. Accessed June 20, 2013.

Greenhouse, Linda. "Misconceptions About Roe v. Wade." *The New York Times.* 2013. http://opinionator.blogs.nytimes.com/2013/01/23/misconceptions/?_r=0. Accessed June 30, 2013.

Grisez, Germain. Chapter 8: "Life, Health, and Bodily Inviolability: Question D: Is Abortion Always the Wrongful Killing of a Person?" In *The Way of the Lord Jesus.* Chicago: Franciscan Herald Press, 1983.

Gudorf, Christine. "To Make a Seamless Garment, Use a Single Piece of Cloth." *Conscience* 17, no. 3 (1996).

Gustafson, James F. "A Protestant Ethical Approach." In *The Morality of Abortion: Legal and Historical Perspectives,* ed. John Thomas Noonan. Cambridge, MA: Harvard University Press, 1970.

Guttmacher Institute. "2012 Saw Second-Highest Number of Abortion Restrictions Ever." Last modified Jan. 2, 2013. http://www.guttmacher.org/media/inthenews/2013/01/02/. Accessed July 1, 2013.

―――. "Fact Sheet: Induced Abortion in the United States." http://www.guttmacher.org/pubs/fb_induced_abortion.html. Accessed June 24, 2013.

―――. "Unintended Pregnancy in the United States." http://www.guttmacher.org/pubs/fb-Unintended-Pregnancy-US.pdf. Accessed Apr. 30, 2014.

Hall, Megan, et al. "Associations between Intimate Partner Violence and Termination of Pregnancy: A Systematic Review and Meta-Analysis." *PLOS Medicine.* 2014. http://www.plosmedicine.org/article/info%3Adoi%2F10.1371%2Fjournal.pmed.1001581.

Hardt, John J. "Birth Plan: Chronicle of a Brief Life Foretold." *America: The National Catholic Review.* 2009. http://americamagazine.org/issue/715/faith-focus/birth-plan. Accessed Sept. 6, 2013.

"Harper to Oppose Any Attempt to Create New Abortion Law." http://www.ctvnews.ca/harper-to-oppose-any-attempt-to-create-new-abortion-law-1.514832

Hayt, Elizabeth. "Surprise, Mom: I'm Against Abortion." *The New York Times.* 2003. http://www.nytimes.com/2003/03/30/style/surprise-mom-i-m-against-abortion.html?pagewanted=all&src=pm. Accessed July 3, 2013.

Henneberger, Melinda. "Are There More Abortion Doctors like Kermit Gosnell? And Do We Want to Know?" *The Washington Post.* 2013. http://www.washingtonpost.com/blogs/she-the-people/wp/2013/04/28/are-there-more-abortion-doctors-like-kermit-gosnell-do-we-want-to-know/. Accessed June 24, 2013.

Henninger, Daniel. "America's Second Civil War: The Gosnell Verdict Means that the Abortion Status Quo Must Change." *The Wall Street Journal.* 2013. http://online.wsj.com/news/articles/SB10001424127887324767004578485283789264450?mg=reno64-wsj&url=http://online.wsj.com/article/SB10001424127887324767004578485283789264450.html. Accessed June 20, 2013.

Henshaw, Stanley K., Susheela Singh, and Taylor Haas. "The Incidence of Abortion Worldwide." *Family Planning Perspectives.* 1999. http://www.guttmacher.org/pubs/journals/25s3099.html. Accessed Oct. 27, 2011.

Hitt, Jack. "Who Will Do Abortions Here?" *The New York Times.* 1998. http://www.nytimes.com/1998/01/18/magazine/who-will-do-abortions-here.html. Accessed Nov. 23, 2013.

"How Mitt Romney Has Positioned Himself on Abortion and Immigration." *The New York Times.* 2012. http://www.nytimes.com/interactive/2012/10/11/us/politics/20121011-romney.html?_r=1&. Accessed Dec. 1, 2012.

Hylton, Wil S. "What I've Learned: Hugh Hefner." http://www.esquire.com/features/what-ive-learned/ESQ0602-JUN_WIL. Accessed June 2, 2014.

Jacobson, Jodi. "Nelson Restrictions Most Likely Outcome of Reconciliation Process." *RH Reality Check.* 2010. http://rhrealitycheck.org/article/2010/03/03/nelson

-restrictions-most-likely-outcome-reconciliation-process/. Accessed June 30, 2013.

———. "White House Crafting Deal with Stupak on Executive Order." *RH Reality Check*. 2010. http://www.rhrealitycheck.org/blog/2010/03/21/update -correction-white-house-crafting-deal-stupak-executive-order. Accessed June 30, 2013.

Jenky, Daniel. "Daniel Jenky, Peoria Catholic Bishop: President Obama Following 'A Similar Path' As Hitler, Stalin." Recorded April 19, 2012. *The Huffington Post*, Apr. 19, 2012. http://www.huffingtonpost.com/2012/04/19/daniel-jenky-peoria -catho_n_1438393.html. Accessed June 20, 2013.

John Paul II. *Laborem Exercens*. Encyclical letter on Human Work on the Ninetieth Anniversary of *Rerum Novarum*. Sept. 14, 1981.

———. *Letter of Pope John Paul II to Women*. The Vatican, 1995.

Johnson, Albert R. "From Mutilation to Donation: The Evolution of Catholic Moral Theology Regarding Organ Transplantation." Lecture at Lane Center for Catholic Studies and Social Thought, Mar. 1, 2005.

Johnston, Robert. "Historical Abortion Statistics, Poland." *Johnston's Archive*. 2013. http://www.johnstonsarchive.net/policy/abortion/ab-poland.html. Accessed Oct. 27, 2013.

Jones, Jeffrey M. "Record-High 40% of Americans Identify as Independents in '11." Gallup. 2012. http://www.gallup.com/poll/151943/record-high-americans-identify -independents.aspx. Accessed June 30, 2013.

Jones, R. K., and K. Kooistra. "Abortion Incidence and Access to Services in the United States 2008." *Perspectives on Sexual and Reproductive Health* 43, no. 1 (2011): 41-50.

Jones, Rachel K., Lawrence B. Finer, and Susheela Singh. "Characteristics of US Abortion Patients, 2008." http://www.guttmacher.org/pubs/US-Abortion-Patients .pdf. Accessed June 24, 2013.

Jones, R. K., et al. "Repeat Abortion in the United States." *Occasional Report* 29 (2006).

Jung, Patricia Beattie. "Abortion and Organ Donation: Christian Reflections on Bodily Life Support." *Journal of Religious Ethics* 16, no. 2 (1988): 273-305.

Kaveny, Cathleen. "Can We Talk about Abortion? An Exchange." *Commonweal*. 2011. https://www.commonwealmagazine.org/can-we-talk-about-abortion. Accessed Oct. 29, 2011.

———. "Toward a Thomistic Perspective on Abortion and the Law in Contemporary America." *The Thomist* 55, no. 33 (July 1991): 344-76.

Keim, Brandon. "Babies Want to Be Social, Even Before They're Born." *Wired*. 2010. http://www.wired.com/wiredscience/2010/10/social-babies/. Accessed July 20, 2013.

Keyser, Jason. "Ginsburg: Roe Gave Abortion Opponents a Target." *ABC News*. 2013. http://abcnews.go.com/m/story?id=19160673. Accessed June 30, 2013.

Kim, Meeri. "Newborn babies in study recognized songs played to them while in the womb." *The Washington Post*. 2013. http://www.washingtonpost.com/national/ health-science/newborn-babies-in-study-recognized-songs-played-to-them

-while-in-the-womb/2013/11/02/294fc458-433d-11e3-a624-41d661b0bb78_story
.html. Accessed Dec. 17, 2013.

Kissling, Frances. "Abortion Rights Are under Attack, and Pro-Choice Advocates Are
Caught in a Time Warp." *The Washington Post.* 2011. http://www.washingtonpost
.com/wp-dyn/content/article/2011/02/18/AR2011021802434.html. Accessed
July 3, 2013.

Kliff, Sarah. "The Abortion Ban Texas Is Debating? It Already Exists in 12 Other States."
The Washington Post. 2013. http://www.washingtonpost.com/blogs/wonkblog/
wp/2013/07/01/the-20-week-abortion-ban-texas-is-debating-already-exists-in
-12-states/. Accessed July 1, 2013.

———. "Exclusive: NARAL President Nancy Keenan to Step Down." http://www
.washingtonpost.com/blogs/wonkblog/post/exclusive-naral-president-nancy
-keenan-to-step-down/2012/05/10/gIQAn85PGU_blog.html. Accessed Dec.
3, 2014.

Lang, Joshua. "What Happens to Women Who Are Denied Abortions?" *The New
York Times.* 2013. http://www.nytimes.com/2013/06/16/magazine/study
-women-denied-abortions.html?_r=1&adxnnl=1&smid=fb-share&pagewanted
=5&adxnnlx=1385208844-zEtlwu9V8oxGn+Xz5WxShw. Accessed Nov. 23, 2013.

LaPoint, Terri. "Bill to Protect Women from Being Tricked or Forced into Taking Abortion Pills Called Senseless by Democratic Party Chair." *The Inquisitor News.* http://
www.inquisitor.com/1253139/bill-to-protect-women-from-being-tricked-or
-forced-into-taking-abortion-pills-called-senseless-by-democratic-party-chair/.
Accessed May 17, 2014.

Levitt, Steven D., and Stephen J. Dubner. *Freakanomics Intl.: A Rogue Economist Explores the Hidden Side of Everything.* New York: Harper, 2011.

Lewis, Aaron. "Bill Clinton Responds to Anti-Abortion Rights Activists." *CBS News,*
Feb. 18, 2008.

Little, Margaret Olivia. "Abortion at the Margins of Personhood." *Rutgers Law Journal*
39 (2008): 3331-40.

Mansfield, Caroline, Suellen Hopfer, and Theresa Marteau. "Termination Rates After
Prenatal Diagnosis of Down Syndrome, Spina Bifida, Anencephaly, and Turner
and Klinefelter Syndromes: A Systematic Literature Review." *Prenatal Diagnosis*
9 (1999): 808-12. http://onlinelibrary.wiley.com/doi/10.1002/(SICI)10970223
(199909)19:9<808::AID-PD637>3.0.CO;2-B/abstract. Accessed June 24, 2013.

McComb, Chris. "Teens Lean Conservative on Abortion." http://www.gallup.com/
poll/9715/Teens-Lean-Conservative-Abortion.aspx. Accessed Mar. 29, 2014.

"Medical Symposium: Abortion Is Never Medically Necessary." *Zenit.* 2012. http://
www.zenit.org/en/articles/medical-symposium-abortion-is-never-medically
-necessary. Accessed Sept. 5, 2013.

Moran, Caitlin. "Feminism for a New Generation of Women." *The Cycle.* Recorded July
16, 2012, MSNBC. http://video.msnbc.msn.com/the-cycle/48200177. Accessed
June 20, 2013.

The New York Times and *CBS News.* "Americans on the Catholic Church." http://www

.nytimes.com/interactive/2013/03/05/us/catholics-poll-graphic.html?ref=us &_r=0. Accessed Feb. 24, 2014.

O'Brien, George Dennis. *The Church and Abortion: A Catholic Dissent.* Lanham, MD: Rowman & Littlefield, 2010.

Obama, Barack. "Address to Notre Dame's Class of 2009." Notre Dame, IN, May 17, 2009. National Public Radio. http://www.npr.org/templates/story/story.php?storyId=104226887. Accessed June 24, 2013.

O'Loughlin, Anna. "Boyfriend Challenges 'Forced' Abortion." *Irish Examiner.* 2013. http://www.irishexaminer.com/archives/2013/0718/world/boyfriend-challenges-aposforcedapos-abortion-237188.html. Accessed Nov. 19, 2013.

Online Etymology Dictionary: "innocent." http://www.etymonline.com/index.php?term=innocent&allowed_in_frame=0. Accessed Sept. 5, 2013.

Nathanson, Bernard. *Aborting America.* New York: Doubleday, 1979.

Nixon, J. Peter. "A Pro-Life Victory?" *Commonweal.* 2010. http://www.commonweal magazine.org/blog/?p=7442. Accessed June 30, 2013.

Norcross, Don. "It's About the Bike." *Union-Tribune,* July 16, 2004.

Padawer, Ruth. "The Two-Minus-One Pregnancy." *The New York Times.* 2011. http://www.nytimes.com/2011/08/14/magazine/the-two-minus-one-pregnancy.html?ref=magazine. Accessed June 24, 2014.

Page, Cristina. *How the Pro-Choice Movement Saved America.* New York: Basic Books, 2006. p. 147.

Parens, Erik. *Prenatal Testing and Disability Rights.* Washington, DC: Georgetown University Press, 2000.

Patten, Dominic. "CNN's 'Crossfire' Back In June; Cancelled In 2005." https://tv.yahoo.com/news/cnn-crossfire-back-june-cancelled-2005-224421441.html. Accessed May 9, 2014.

Perinatal Hospice. "Frequently Asked Questions about Perinatal Hospice and Palliative Care." Last modified 2014. http://www.perinatalhospice.org/FAQs.html. Accessed Dec. 10, 2013.

Pew Research Religion and Public Life Project. "Roe v. Wade at 40: Most Oppose Overturning Abortion Decision." Last modified Jan. 16, 2013. http://www.pewforum.org/2013/01/16/roe-v-wade-at-40/. Accessed June 30, 2013.

Preston, Julia. "Settlement for a Shackled Pregnant Woman." *The New York Times,* Oct. 17, 2013.

Princeton UCHV. "Open Hearts, Open Minds, and Fair Minded Words: A Conference on Life and Choice in the Abortion Debate." http://uchv.princeton.edu/Life_Choice/. Accessed June 21, 2013.

Proussalidis, Daniel. "Liberal Candidates Must Be Pro-Choice: Trudeau." http://www.sunnewsnetwork.ca/sunnews/politics/archives/2014/05/20140507-154734.html. Accessed Mar. 17, 2014.

Reid, Sue. "Slaughtered in the Thousands: The British Babies Killed in the Womb Just for Being Girls." http://www.dailymail.co.uk/femail/article-2548349/Slaughtered-thousands-British-babies-killed-womb-just-girls.html. Accessed June 2, 2014.

Republican Majority for Choice. "About RM4C." http://www.gopchoice.org/about/. Accessed Dec. 1, 2012.

Richman, Josh. "Bills Increasing Abortion Access Signed by Gov. Jerry Brown." *Mercury News.* 2013. http://www.mercurynews.com/politics-government/ci _24274908/. Acessed Dec. 1, 2013.

Rovner, Julie. "Restrictions on Abortion Multiply This Year." *Shots: Health News from NPR.* 2011. http://www.npr.org/blogs/health/2011/07/14/137848984/ restrictions-on-abortions-multiply-this-year. Accessed Oct. 4, 2011.

"Rubalcaba: The Reform of Abortion Is an Unacceptable Setback for Women." *El Pais: Sociedad.* 2012. http://translate.google.com/translate?act=url&depth=1&hl=en &ie=UTF8&prev=_t&rurl=translate.google.com&sl=auto&tl=en&u=http:// sociedad.elpais.com/sociedad/2012/01/25/actualidad/1327505385_935304.html. Accessed Nov. 23, 2013.

Rubin, Alissa J. "The Catholic Abortion Paradox." *Beliefnet.* 2001. http://www.belief net.com/Faiths/Catholic/2001/01/The-Catholic-Abortion-Paradox.aspx?p=1. Accessed Dec. 1, 2013.

Rudulph, Heather Wood. "Why I Filmed My Abortion." http://www.cosmopolitan .com/advice/health/why-i-filmed-my-abortion. Accessed June 2, 2014.

Rue, Vincent, Priscilla Coleman, James Rue, and David Reardon. "Induced Abortion and Traumatic Stress: A Preliminary Comparison of American and Russian Women." *Medical Science Monitor* 10, no. 10 (2004): 5-16.

Saad, Lydia. "Americans Still Split along 'Pro-Choice,' 'Pro-Life' Lines." Gallup. 2011. http://www.gallup.com/poll/147734/americans-split-along-pro-choice-pro -life-lines.aspx. Accessed June 21, 2013.

————. "'Conservatives' Are Single-Largest Ideological Group." Gallup. 2009. http:// www.gallup.com/poll/120857/conservatives-single-largest-ideological-group .aspx. Accessed June 30, 2013.

————. "Generational Differences on Abortion Narrow." Gallup. 2010. http://www.gallup .com/poll/126581/generational-differences-abortion-narrow.aspx. Accessed July 3, 2013.

————. "In U.S., Nonreligious, Postgrads Are Highly 'Pro-Choice.'" http://www .gallup.com/poll/154946/non-christians-postgrads-highly-pro-choice.aspx. Accessed Apr. 30, 2014.

————. "Majority of Americans Still Support *Roe v. Wade* Decision." Gallup. 2013. http://www.gallup.com/poll/160058/majority-americans-support-roe-wade -decision.aspx. Accessed June 30, 2013.

————. "Plenty of Common Ground Found in Abortion Debate." Gallup. 2011. http:// www.gallup.com/poll/148880/Plenty-Common-Ground-Found-Abortion -Debate.aspx. Accessed Dec. 12, 2013.

Saletan, William. *Bearing Right: How Conservatives Won the Abortion War.* Berkeley: University of California Press, 2004.

Salt and Light Media. "The Emperor's New Clothes and Other Myths: Cardinal Sean O'Malley at Vigil for Life." http://saltandlighttv.org/blog/general/the-emperors

-new-clothes-and-other-myths-cardinal-sean-omalley-at-vigil-for-life. Accessed Feb. 7, 2014.

Sandler, Lauren. "The Mother Majority." *Slate.* 2011. http://www.slate.com/articles/double_x/doublex/2011/10/most_surprising_abortion_statistic_the_majority_of_women_who_ter.html. Accessed Oct. 29, 2011.

Savulescu, Julian. "Abortion, Infanticide and Allowing Babies to Die, Forty Years On." *Journal of Medical Ethics* 5 (2013). http://jme.bmj.com/content/39/5.toc. Accessed July 21, 2013.

Schwartz, Barry. *The Paradox of Choice.* New York: HarperCollins, 2005. http://books.google.com/books?id=zutxr7rGc_QC&vq=barry+schwartz+paradox+contents. Accessed Nov. 23, 2013.

Sedgh, Gilda. "Induced Abortion: Incidence and Trends Worldwide from 1995 to 2008." *The Lancet* 379 (2012): 625-32.

Sedgh, Gilda, et al. "Legal Abortion Worldwide: Incidence and Recent Trends." *International Family Planning Perspectives* 3 (2007). http://www.guttmacher.org/pubs/journals/3310607.html. Accessed Nov. 30, 2013.

Shettles, Landrum, and David Rorvik. *Rites of Life.* Grand Rapids: Zondervan, 1983.

Silverleib, Alan. "House rejects Abortion Ban Based on Sex of Fetus." *CNN Politics.* 2012. http://www.cnn.com/2012/05/31/politics/house-abortion-gender/index.html. Accessed Dec. 10, 2013.

Simmons, Paul. "Religious Liberty and Abortion Policy: *Casey* as 'Catch 22.'" *Journal of Church and State* 42 (2000): 69-82.

Simonton, Anna. "The Future of the Pro-Choice Movement." *The Nation.* 2013. http://www.thenation.com/article/172713/future-pro-choice. Accessed July 3, 2013.

Simpson, Connor. "McCain Wants to Leave Abortion Alone." *The Atlantic Wire.* 2012. http://news.yahoo.com/mccain-wants-leave-abortion-alone-republicans-move-away-200053520.html. Accessed Dec. 1, 2012.

Skotko, Brian, Susan Levine, and Richard Goldstein. "Self-perceptions from People with Down Syndrome." *American Journal of Medical Genetics* 10 (2011): 2360-69. http://onlinelibrary.wiley.com/doi/10.1002/ajmg.a.34235/full. Accessed June 24, 2013.

Slifer, Stephanie. "NYC Victoria's Secret Shoplifting Suspect Found with Dead Fetus in Bag, Police Say." *Crimesider.* 2013. http://www.cbsnews.com/news/nyc-victorias-secret-shoplifting-suspect-found-with-dead-fetus-in-bag-police-say/. Accessed June 21, 2013.

"Spain Grapples with Abortion Revision." *Euronews.* 2013. http://www.euronews.com/2013/11/15/spain-grapples-with-abortion-revision/. Accessed Nov. 23, 2013.

Stevenson, Betsey, and Justin Wolfers. "The Paradox of Declining Female Happiness." http://www.nber.org/papers/w14969.pdf. Accessed Nov. 23, 2013.

Stulberg, D. B., A. M. Dude, I. Dahlquist, and F. A. Curlin. "Abortion Provision Among Practicing Obstetrician-Gynecologists." *Obstetrics and Gynecology* 3 (2011): 609-14. http://www.ncbi.nlm.nih.gov/pubmed/21860290. Accessed Nov. 23, 2013.

Sulmasy, Daniel P. "Emergency Contraception for Women Who Have Been Raped: Must Catholics Test for Ovulation, or Is Testing for Pregnancy Morally Sufficient?" *Kennedy Institute of Ethics Journal* 4 (2006): 305-51. http://muse.jhu.edu/ login?auth=0&type=summary&url=/journals/kennedy_institute_of_ethics _journal/v016/16.4sulmasy.pdf. Accessed Sept. 22, 2013.

Supreme Court of the United States. *Planned Parenthoods of Southeastern Pa. v. Casey* (91-744), 505 U.S. 833 (1992). http://www.law.cornell.edu/supct/html/91-744 .ZO.html. Accessed June 24, 2013.

"Survey | A Generation in Transition: Religion, Values, and Politics among College-Age Millennials." Public Religion Research Institute. 2012. http://publicreligion .org/research/2012/04/millennial-values-survey-2012/. Accessed June 30, 2014.

"Survey | Committed to Availability, Conflicted about Morality: What the Millennial Generation Tells Us about the Future of the Abortion Debate and the Culture Wars." Public Religion Research Institute. 2011. http://publicreligion.org/ research/2011/06/committed-to-availability-conflicted-about-morality-what -the-millennial-generation-tells-us-about-the-future-of-the-abortion-debate -and-the-culture-wars/. Accessed June 21, 2013.

Swarns, Rachel L. "Placed on Unpaid Leave: A Pregnant Employee Finds Hope in a New Law." *The New York Times,* Feb. 2, 2014.

"Sweden Rules 'Gender-Based' Abortion Legal." *The Local: Sweden's News in English.* 2009. http://www.thelocal.se/20090512/19392. Accessed Dec. 10, 2013.

Terzo, Sarah. "Raped Women Who Had Their Babies Defy Pro-Choice Stereotypes." http://www.lifesitenews.com/news/raped-women-who-had-their-babies-defy -pro-choice-stereotypes. Accessed Apr. 12, 2014.

"Texas Teen Sues Parents to Stop Them from Forcing Her Abortion." *Fox News.* 2013. http://www.foxnews.com/us/2013/02/13/texas-teen-sues-parents-to-stop -them-from-forcing-her-abortion/.

Thomson, Judith Jarvis. "A Defense of Abortion." *Philosophy and Public Affairs* 1, no. 1 (1971). http://spot.colorado.edu/~heathwoo/Phil160,Fall02/thomson.htm. Accessed Sept. 6, 2013.

Tilley, Terrance W. "The Principle of Innocents' Immunity." *Horizons* 15, no. 1 (1988): 43-63.

Toensing, Victoria. "Pro-choice Republicans Go Public." *The Washington Post.* 2012. http://www.washingtonpost.com/opinions/pro-choice-republicans-have-a -place-in-the-party/2012/11/29/4ab72106-332e-11e2-bfd5-e202b6d7b501_story .html?wpisrc=emailtoafriend. Accessed Dec. 1, 2012.

Toobin, Jeffrey. "The Abortion Issue Returns." *The New Yorker.* 2013. http://www .newyorker.com/online/blogs/comment/2013/05/abortion-returns-to-the -supreme-court.html. Accessed July 3, 2013.

United Press International. 2010. "Remains of Fetus Found at Illinois Laundry." http:// www.upi.com/Top_News/US/2010/03/18/Remains-of-fetus-found-at-Illinois -laundry/UPI-26471268928788/. Accessed Dec. 17, 2013.

United States Conference of Catholic Bishops. "Ethical and Religious Directives for Catholic Health Care Services." http://www.usccb.org/issues-and-action/ human-life-and-dignity/health-care/upload/Ethical-Religious-Directives -Catholic-Health-Care-Services-fifth-edition-2009.pdf. Accessed Dec. 17, 2013.

Bibliography

U.S. House of Representatives. "Final Vote Results for Roll Call 884." United States Congress (2009). unhttp://clerk.house.gov/evs/2009/roll884.xml.

U.S. House of Representatives. "Testimony of Anthony Levatino, M.D., before the Subcommittee on the Constitution and Civil Justice." http://judiciary.house.gov/hearings/113th/05232013/Levatino%2005232013.pdf. Accessed Aug. 8, 2013.

"U.S. Stands Apart from Other Nations on Maternity Leave." *USA Today*. 2005. http://usatoday30.usatoday.com/news/health/2005-07-26-maternity-leave_x.htm. Accessed Nov. 26, 2011.

Univision Noticias. "Univision News/LD National LATINO Electorate Poll Results, November 8, 2011." Last modified Nov. 11, 2011. http://faculty.washington.edu/mbarreto/ld/latino_nov11.html. Accessed July 1, 2013.

Voorhees, Josh. "Abortion Provider Kermit Gosnell Found Guilty on Three Counts of First-Degree Murder." *Slate*. 2013. http://www.slate.com/blogs/the_slatest/2013/05/13/kermit_gosnell_jury_reaches_verdict_in_case_of_pa_abortion_doctor_accused.html. Accessed June 24, 2013.

Wade, Lisa. "My Two Cents on Feminism and Miley Cyrus." *Sociological Images; Inspiring Sociological Imaginations Everywhere*. 2013. http://thesocietypages.org/socimages/2013/12/28/my-two-cents-on-feminism-and-miley-cyrus/. Accessed Dec. 29, 2013.

Watt, Holly, and Claire Newell. "Law 'Does Not Prohibit' Sex-Selection Abortions, DPP Warns." *The Telegraph*. 2013. http://www.telegraph.co.uk/health/healthnews/10360386/Law-does-not-prohibit-sex-selection-abortions-DPP-warns.html. Accessed Dec. 12, 2013.

Whiteside, Kelly. "Tatyana McFadden Chases Marathon Grand Slam." *USA Today Sports*. 2013. http://www.usatoday.com/story/sports/olympics/2013/10/31/tatyana-mcfadden-new-york-marathon-grand-slam/3332109/. Accessed Dec. 10, 2013.

Williams, Juan. *Muzzled: The Assault on Honest Debate*. New York: Crown Publishing, 2011.

Wilson, Nancy A. "War on Woman." *Christian Bioethics* 2 (2013): 242-45. http://cb.oxfordjournals.org/content/19/2/242.full.pdf+html. Accessed Nov. 23, 2013.

World Health Organization: Europe. "Highlights on Health in Poland." http://www.euro.who.int/__data/assets/pdf_file/0020/103565/E88745.pdf. Accessed Oct. 27, 2011.

Index

Abortion: in developing countries, 46, 65; direct vs. indirect, 63-65, 80-81, 106-7; in Ireland, 34, 99-101, 108, 154, 156; media and, 2, 3-4, 6, 11, 15, 19, 22, 27, 112, 132-33, 155, 159-63, 167; methods of, 61-62, 81-82; physicians and, 105-6, 133; in Poland, 99-101, 108, 154, 156; rates of, 18, 94-97, 127, 143, 166-67; reasons for, 4-6, 18-19, 43, 55, 63, 64, 66-82, 84, 86, 93-94, 106-7, 119, 146-47, 149; religion and, 6-9, 49, 55, 86-91; shifting politics and, 2-3, 24, 90
Affordable Care Act, 136-37
Alvare, Helen, 117
America magazine, 73
American views on abortion, 4, 11-12, 26-29, 31-32, 36; Hispanics, 3-4, 36, 39, 166; Millennials, 3-4, 27, 36-38, 132-33, 161-62, 166; women, 2-3, 4-6, 17-18, 36, 38-39
Analogy, use of, 68-69, 75-77, 79-80, 178n16
Anthony, Susan B., 20-21, 22
Aquinas, Thomas, 91-92, 177n9
Asch, Andrienne, 188n25

Beckwith, Francis, 77
Benedict XVI, 84
Bennett, Jana, 125-26
Bible, 7, 47
Biden, Joe, 25

Binary thinking, 11-12, 27, 132-33, 154-55, 158, 164; conservative/liberal, 12, 27; person/nonperson, 53-55; pro-life/ pro-choice, 11-12, 132-33, 154-55
Borgmann, Caitlin W., 135
Brinkerhoff, Mattie, 21
Bush, George H. W., 25
Bush, George W., 29-30

Cahill, Lisa, 178n16
Calderone, Mary S., 97-98
Callahan, Daniel, 96-97, 112-16
Callahan, Sidney, 110, 112-18, 120, 121, 124, 128
Campbell, David, 7-8
Carter, Jimmy, 23-25
Casey, Robert, 25-26
Casey, Robert, Jr., 30
Catholic social teaching, 53, 60, 69-70, 71, 106, 145; *Evangelium Vitae*, 59, 70; indirect abortion, 64; innocence, 67-68; *Laborem Exercens*, 156-57; moral tradition, 60; Thomson's analogy, 79-80, 82-83
Cavanaugh, Thomas, 69-70
Cavanaugh, William, 122
Child care, 123, 141, 156, 165; Catholic communities and, 131; equality and, 118, 124-25, 136-37, 151; expectations, 84; prenatal, 85, 93
Clinton, Bill, 25-26, 103

204